HMAS SYDNEY

HMAS SYDNEY
1941
THE ANALYSIS

GREG BATHGATE

First published in 2007 by Boolarong Press

National Library of Australia
Cataloguing-in-Publication entry

Bathgate, Greg.
HMAS Sydney : 1941 the analysis.

ISBN 9781921054396 (pbk.).

1. Australia. Royal Australian Navy - History. 2. Sydney (Cruiser : 1934-1941). 3. Kormoran (Ship). 4. World War, 1939-1945 - Naval operations, Australian. 5. World War, 1939-1945 - Naval operations, German. I. Title.

940.545994

BOOLARONG PRESS
1/655 Toohey Road, Salisbury 4107
Typeset by Watson Ferguson & Company
Printed and Bound by Watson Ferguson & Company

CONTENTS

FOREWORD

By Commander O Pelczar RFD RD RANR (Retired)

Australia's most mysterious and controversial wartime naval action continues to remain largely unsolved. Since 1941, the fate of HMAS Sydney has occupied the minds of the public and of the researchers who are intent on finding the true circumstances surrounding the loss of the warship.

Even though more meaningful information has become recently available, we are no closer to solving the mystery. Today, the perplexities and disputations still abound.

Unfortunately, the site of the engagement with the disguised merchant raider, HSK Kormoran has not been positively identified, making the task of finding the wreck sites of both vessels extremely difficult. If HMAS Sydney can be found, a greater understanding of the fateful event can be realized.

The Analysis delivers a practical approach to locating the sunken vessels using conventional methods. However, mindful of the fact that references containing oceanographic data vary considerably, the author sets out to develop the uniform criteria required for the key purpose of drift analysis. With consistent application, a search area, worthy of exploration, has been identified.

These findings have been depicted in the form of detailed diagrams for the benefit of the reader. The quantity of data assembled has been thoroughly presented and it shows the author's preparedness to document the findings, so that others may have the opportunity to share in the search for the vessels and to ultimately locate them.

However, as the former Head of Naval Intelligence (NID) in Western Australia, I do not support the author's criticism of our intelligence agencies. Yet the right to freely ask questions must be preserved. I believe we owe it to those 645 souls lost aboard HMAS Sydney that every lead is investigated in order to finally establish the truth – which will ultimately set us free and let them rest in peace.

I commend *The Analysis* to everyone interested in naval history and especially to all HMAS Sydney enthusiasts as well as my past and future marine navigation students. I consider it well-developed research, constructively presented and compelling reading.

Fremantle, May 2007

GLOSSARY

ACNB	Australian Commonwealth Naval Board
ASIO	Australian Security Intelligence Organisation
C-IN-C	Commander-in Chief
COIC	Combined Operational Intelligence Centre
D/F	Direction Finding
FECB	Far East Combined Bureau
DNI	Director of Naval Intelligence
DNOWA	District Naval Officer Western Australia
EST	Eastern Standard Time
GCCS	Government Code and Cypher School
GMT	Greenwich Mean Time
G	Golf time – GMT plus seven hours
H	Hotel time – GMT plus eight hours
HMAS	His Majesty's Australian Ship
HMAT	His Majesty's Australian Troopship
HMS	His Majesty's Ship
HMT	His Majesty's Troopship
HSK	Handelsstörkreuzer – merchant raider
K	Kilo time – GMT plus ten hours
IJN	Imperial Japanese Navy
NID	Naval Intelligence Division
NNJ	Request for Identification (Signal)
OIC	Operations Intelligence Centre
QQQ	Distress signal – suspicious ship
RAN	Royal Australian Navy
RN	Royal Navy
R/T	Radio Telegraphy
SIS	Signals Intelligence Service
S/L	Squadron Leader
SS	Steamship

SWACH	South West Area Combined Headquarters
T	True course
VAI	Vessels in Area Inventory
WST	Western Standard Time
W/T	Wireless Telegraphy
Z	Zulu time – Greenwich Mean Time

Abbreviations

hrs	hours
kts	knots (speed)
nm	nautical miles
deg	degrees
min	minutes
ss	shaft speed
dev	deviation

Notations

1400/20	1400 hours / November 20 (for November only)
24.35 S	Latitude 24 degrees 35 minutes South
111.30 E	Longitude 111 degrees 30 minutes East
54/115T	54 nautical miles / bearing 115 degrees True

Note: All times refer to 'H' hours (WST) unless otherwise stated

LIST OF ILLUSTRATIONS

Setting the Criteria

Returning from Sunda

Analysing the Action

Positions of Origin

Locating the Site

Sustaining the Evidence

Speculation

Subterfuge

INTRODUCTION

Several books have been published on the subject of the mysterious disappearance of HMAS *Sydney*. Some writers have recorded the events from an historical perspective, based purely on the official documents available, some have based their trust in the evidence given by the German survivors, some have conveyed conspiracy and cover up theories and others have developed indirect and interesting sideline stories. The Australian Government's attitude remains unshaken, preferring to maintain that the findings of over 60 years have stood the test of time. All of the views expressed by the authors, the numerous dedicated researchers and of the Government deserve to be recognized, so that an open-minded assessment can be made on the information available. If we can eliminate the pre-conceived ideas, it is possible to assess all aspects analytically and on a logical basis in order to arrive at justifiable conclusions.

When HMAS *Sydney* was sunk with all hands after engaging the disguised German raider HSK *Kormoran* on the night of November 19, 1941, 645 families were affected by the disaster. Today there are thousands of relatives who have been wondering all these years of the true events and circumstances which caused *Sydney's* demise and of the location of the grave site. More importantly, finding *Sydney* will allow a detailed examination of the vessel and make possible a determination of the cause of the disaster as well as testing the veracity of the German account of the action. Unless HMAS *Sydney* is located, the plethora of opinions and theories that abound, will continue to remain unsubstantiated and her disappearance, an ongoing mystery.

This book constructively examines *Sydney's* final resting place and that of Kormoran in a systematic and analytical approach. It makes independent adjudications on all relevant information and seeks to justify the outcomes and conclusions. Considerable emphasis is placed on ascertaining the navigational, meteorological and oceanographic aspects to obtain the most accurate results. The international politics of the period in conjunction with communications and naval intelligence was required as an adjunct to determine possible concealment of the facts and a reconstruction of timetables was necessary to identify positions and to confirm the sequence of events.

Most previous publications have presented a wide array of subject material on the Sydney / Kormoran affair. However, for the first time, this account concentrates on developing the criteria necessary for locating the elusive grave sites of both vessels. From the known data and from information provided by the *Kormoran* survivors, it has been possible to identify the confines of a search area that has relatively limited search parameters. In consideration of the logical actions and reactions made by the protagonist, Captain Joseph Burnett and his adversary Kapitan Theodor Anton Detmers, this account also portrays a detailed and plausible analysis of the action and establishes the relative positions of the vessels at various times during the interception and engagement phases. These outcomes could not have been achieved without an in- depth study of the prevailing sea conditions and as a consequence, a determination has been made of the drift rates associated with each drifting object. In every case the same method of approach has been adopted and the analyses are consistent with the established criterion.

An established search area per se, should not be presumed to have been finalized without considering all the relevant issues. Once established, there are often other factors that can contribute to, or otherwise support the findings. This study has found that the established location of *Sydney* and *Kormoran* lies within an area which can explain the peculiarities of wind and current drift and indeed, even some of the erstwhile unsubstantiated rumors.

Finally, the method of approach has been an exercise in objectivism and perception, supplemented by numerous confirmatory maps and diagrams. That the following information will contribute to or assist in the endeavors of those seeking to search for HMAS *Sydney* and HSK *Kormoran*, may bring some comfort to those relatives who covet so much, that finding the grave sites may bring closure to sixty -six years of disquiet and uncertainty.

Top: Captain Joseph Burnett
Was it just convenient that he was blamed for *Sydney's* loss, when in fact there is no conclusive evidence that he acted improperly.

Below: HMAS *Sydney* in wartime camouflage

On 19th November 1941, *HMAS Sydney* encountered the disguised German raider *Kormoran* off the Western Australian coast. In a matter of hours after the battle, 725 sailors had perished, including the entire complement of *Sydney*. It has often been surmised that it was the negligence of *Sydney's* Captain, Joseph Burnett that attributed to the greatest loss of life in Australia's worst maritime disaster. But could accusations of this nature in fact be misdirected? In providing a detailed account of the engagement, The Analysis meticulously unveils the maneuvering of the combatants, accounts for the actions necessarily taken by Burnett and reveals the contravention of maritime law.

BASIS OF ANALYSIS

In order to produce the most accurate analysis it has been necessary to ingest an historical and wide- ranging overview of the so called, '*Sydney* Saga'. Although this represents a daunting and often vexing array of information for analysts and researchers and that more forthcoming revelations are sure to surface, this analysis can only be assessed from the knowledge currently available.

Most contemporary publications have adequately canvassed in detail the historic background and the achievements of the respective Captains and of their commands using archival references and interpretations of German texts. Whilst acknowledging the importance of archival information, it is considered that the method of approach herein adopted may not have been influenced by a protracted search for further relevant archival material in the quest to solve the mystery. There can be no simple resolution to *Sydney's* final location unless the relevant archival signals packs can be found, if in fact they do exist. Australian Archives have categorically stated that other than operational signals, no signals either to or from the *Sydney* have been found for the period between 11 and 20 November 1941. Indeed, in view of the magnitude of such a disaster and the extensive research already undertaken by archival staff and others, it is strange that documentation of *Sydney's* final resting place is no where to be found.

In the absence of archival information regarding *Sydney's* final voyage, there is no clear solution to locating the vessel. If the mainstream German story is to be believed, it seems there is a much better chance of finding *Kormoran*. That is not to say complete trust in the accuracy of the story is a precursor to establishing its position, but it is suffice to weigh the overall evidence in conjunction with the typical oceanic and weather conditions of the period to test the logic and veracity of the German story and therefore arrive at the most credible exposition. That is why a comprehensive investigation has been conducted with an emphasis placed on the physical oceanic characteristics in the proximity of the reported action site. Although several references were found to contain conflicting information, it was possible to interpolate on a conceptual basis, the average conditions for any period.

References: Australian and Admiralty Charts, Australia Pilot Vol. V, Australian Bureau of Meteorology, Offshore Resource Mapping Series, *Encyclopaedia Britannica*, *Encyclopeadia of the Oceans* – Stow 2004, *Ocean Forecasting* – Pinardi 2002, *The Indian Ocean* - Pearson 2003, *Climatic Atlas of the Indian Ocean* – Hastenrath & Lamb1979

The above references were also used to establish the relative speed, course and lateral drift of vessels operating in the Sunda shipping lanes. In what may be construed as purely an academic exercise, it is nevertheless foremost that intended courses be accurately defined. Otherwise there can be no accurate correlation of speed and position. It is also recognized that intermediate course corrections and speed adjustments made in accordance with changing oceanic conditions are impossible to forecast. However, it is essential that calculations be made of the lateral drift to ascertain the approximate extent of drift expected during normal sea and weather conditions. After all, there is no evidence to suggest that above average wind conditions which would result in an additional wind driven current component and drift of a vessel, persisted during mid to late November 1941. The drift assessments should therefore be regarded as conservative estimates.

The Parliamentary Inquiry of 1997-1999 convened by the Joint Standing Committee on Foreign Affairs, Defence and Trade investigated the circumstances of the sinking of HMAS *Sydney*. It attracted a plethora of diverse written submissions and oral testimony from the Government and the public. This analysis includes a critique of the findings and takes into consideration the merits of each of the 408 submissions (including supplementary) and the (Hansard) oral evidence.

References: Submissions - 19 volumes plus oral evidence (6) and Final Report. Appendage: *The Sinking of HMAS Sydney – A Guide to Commonwealth Government Records*- Aust. Archives, 1997

That the intelligence services were involved in confiscating many documents, viz. naval and police records, directly relating to and at the time of *Sydney's* demise is beyond dispute. If located, any one of these important items could contribute to solving the mystery. Such terms as unfound, missing or unavailable have been used to describe the whereabouts of the documents, much to the bane of researchers. In addition, the disconcerting link between intelligence and the wartime politics of the allied nations is an historical fact and particularly evident in relation to British foreign policy at the time. It was therefore incumbent to examine the role of these secret organizations surrounding the disappearance of *Sydney.*

References: *British Intelligence in the Second World War* – Hinsley 1979, *GCHQ: The Secret Wireless War 1900-86* – West 1986, *Unreliable Witness* – West 1984, *Days of Infamy* – Costello 1982, *Betrayal at Pearl Harbour* – Rusbridger 1985

It is not beyond dispute that *Sydney's* ultimate fate could have been caused by outside intervention. This controversy has remained in the public arena since it was first reported in the British press soon after the sinking of *Sydney.* The Analysis makes a determination of the whereabouts of the submarines that could have been in the vicinity of the Sydney / Kormoran engagement area.

References: *Stealth at Sea* – van der Vat 1994, *Pacific Islands in World War II* – Steinberg 1978, *Submarines Since 1919* – Preston 1994, *Submarines of the Imperial Japanese Navy* – Polmar 1986, *Twin Ore Islands* – Manuscript Battye Library, circa 1960

It is most difficult to adjudge the character of Detmers when he was under extreme pressure during the confrontation with *Sydney.* In what may have been a rehearsed or planned action if ever the situation arose and if his account of the action is true, he undoubtedly acted impulsively. This contrasts with his reputation, as cautious and certainly not prone to taking risks. That he engaged a far superior enemy warship regardless of what advantage he held, is testament to one who suddenly decides to seek fame with complete disregard for the welfare of the crew. It could therefore be argued that Detmers had surrendered. Alternatively, *Sydney's* commanders were uncharacteristically reckless.

References: *The Raider Kormoran* – Detmers 1959, *German Raiders of World War II* – Muggenthaler 1978

SETTING THE CRITERIA

THE QUEST to determine the location of the grave site of HMAS *Sydney* has always been an intriguing and compelling exercise. Most attempts have, in the past, been hindered by the uncertainties of the prevailing sea and wind conditions of the time and by the conjecture of the whereabouts of *Sydney* when she encountered the raider *Kormoran.* These two requirements are the essential components that require resolution if *Sydney* is to be found. If these accurate assessments are not made, then the only alternative is for the search of a wide area of ocean at great expense for those undertaking such a venture.

Several difficulties arise when making these assessments. Firstly, oceanographic references containing estimates of the associated wind and current velocities for the general area west of Shark Bay vary considerably for the month of November. This makes accurate forecasting and hind-casting troublesome and is not conducive to the application of particular drift values. Secondly, the track taken by *Sydney* for the return passage to Fremantle is indeterminate. Thirdly, due to the individual drift characteristics of the objects recovered, it is not possiblc to apply consistent drift values for each item retrieved by the search vessels. However, it is possible to assess all of these unknowns if criterion is established and it is used consistently in every case.

Crucial to establishing common criteria for locating *Sydney* is to determine the affect of the currents on vessels sailing the Sunda Strait to Fremantle and Cape Leeuwin shipping routes. This can be achieved by reconstructing the sailing schedules of the vessels known to be in the area at the time and responsible for the rescue of *Kormoran* survivors – the troopship *Aquitania* and the tanker *Trocas.* The results can be tested by the application of the known sailing schedule of the troopship *Zealandia* and can be further applied to the troopship *Largs Bay* on passage to Sydney. If the established schedules for each vessel demonstrate common speed fluctuations and lateral drift variations relative to the speed of the particular vessel, then the assigned velocity of the prevailing currents can be substantiated. Once established, the velocity of the currents can be applied to determine *Sydney's* return track from Sunda to Fremantle. More importantly, this exercise makes it possible to identify the key position of Sydney at 1700 hours on November 19, when *Kormoran* was first sighted.

The established criterion becomes invaluable in its application to finding the location of *Sydney* and *Kormoran.* In order to transfix the location, the prerequisite drift analysis of recovered objects can be systematically undertaken for the purpose of finding the positions of origin. In accordance with their drift characteristics, the objects can then be individually assessed by current, by wind or by relevant apportionment. In regard to the wind assessment, a comprehensive investigation has been carried out to determine the average wind speeds and directions affecting the objects for the duration of drift.

The following method of setting the criteria is necessarily intrinsic and in some instances convolute. Nevertheless, a thorough examination, based mainly on navigational calculations and oceanographic data is considered essential to the process of establishing the location of the sunken vessels. Moreover, that such a technical approach is required, has provided for the most accurate and uniform application of the criteria to ascertain the extent of drift of all of the objects and the leeway and speed differentials of vessels operating in the proximity of where *Sydney* disappeared.

NAVIGATING THE SUNDA TRACK

There are differing opinions about *Sydney's* intended return track from Sunda Strait to Fremantle.

In order to gain an appreciation of a likely southern route, a detailed assessment of the prevailing conditions of the time is required, including an analysis of the winds and ocean currents. This analysis is necessary and is a crucial step in the process of finding the engagement site and eventually *Sydney's* final resting place.

In assessing the general sea conditions from November 11 when *Sydney* departed Fremantle to Sunda in company with the troopship *Zealandia* and for the next ten days, it is apparent that slight seas and relatively light winds prevailed. This is corroborated by those aboard the escorted troopship *Zealandia* and to a lesser extent, from the *Kormoran* survivors. Thereafter, to November 27and according to those involved in the search for *Sydney*, a following current with rough seas, persisted. Although the above description only gives an appreciation, it is consistent with the typical and changing conditions along the Sunda route for the month of November.

The main obstacle to accurate navigation from Cape Leeuwin and Fremantle to Sunda and return are the prevailing currents which fluctuate in velocity and direction throughout the year. These currents stem from the Southern Indian Ocean Current, which is set in motion by strong westerly winds and is the primary source of the currents circulating south of the equator. The currents along the Sunda route are directly connected to this source in the form of the Westralian Current, with the resultant northward flow varying in direction before merging with the South Equatorial Current.

The Westralian Current sets to about 340 deg from Cape Leeuwin and generally follows the configuration of the continental shelf to about latitude 25 South and with average wind conditions has an average flow rate of from 0.39 knots in July to 0.68 knots in January (Encyclopaedia Britannica). These figures include the combined effect of wind and current drift and exclude abnormal sea and wind conditions. A seasonal flow of 0.19 to 0.48 knots could be experienced in consistent light wind conditions. The average velocity of the current north to latitude 22 S for mid November during average SSE winds of from 14 to 18 knots is estimated at 0.58 knots. It should be noted that some publications give values of from 0.75 to 1.0 knot, but these figures should not be taken as an average flow because in most cases the frequency and seasonal factors are not specified.

North of latitude 25 S, the Westralian Current gradually turns to an increasingly westerly direction to about latitude 10 S. Near latitude 25 S, the eastern perimeter of the current tends to diverge north- easterly to the west of the Continental Shelf and the north westerly convergence of that flow accentuates the mainstream current along the Sunda route. Due to the dispersion of the Westralian Current over a wider area, the spreading of the current creates a progressive reduction in the northwards velocity. The progressive reduction in the flow north of latitude 22 S can also be ascribed to the light wind conditions of 7 to 12 knots, approximating the direction of the current.

The velocity of the current along the Sunda route north of latitude 22 S can generally be assessed in accordance with the average prevailing November wind velocities, relative to the average flow (0.58 knots) experienced further south in the Westralian Current proper. This can be achieved by estimating the reduced wind driven current component at various latitudes up to latitude 10 S, the northern extremity of influence of the South Equatorial Current.

If the average November wind velocity up to latitude 22 S is 15 knots and the current is 0.58 knots, then there is an average reduction in current to latitude18 S of 0.1 knot if the average wind for the area is 11 knots. Likewise, a further reduction of 0.08 knots applies for the area to latitude 9.30 S if the average wind is 8 knots. North of latitude 9.30 S to Sunda Strait, the South Java Current during the seasonal Monsoon transition period is regarded as weak. This area also experiences extremely light winds in November. Similarly, the westward movement of the currents originating in the Banda and Timor Seas during the transition should not contribute much to the flow across the Sunda route.

At longitude 102 E and between latitudes 10 S and 25 S, the Westralian Current converges due west into the South Equatorial Current and depending on the influence of the South East Monsoon and the adjacent Equatorial Counter Current, it can flow at a rate of between 0.5 and 2.0 knots. This current continues west and then south along the eastern coasts of Africa and Madagascar and then rejoins the Southern Ocean Current to complete the circulatory pattern.

From Latitude 22 S near the coast and extending out to the Continental Shelf is the Leeuwin Current, which flows southwards at an average of about 0.15 knots in November. It sets to approximately 160 degrees and can affect the speed of vessels in some locations along the inshore Sunda route near the Continental Shelf. Closer inshore the current sets south- east towards the coast. Due to the influence of the strong seasonal SSE sea breezes within 15 nautical miles of the coastline, a northerly surface drift is experienced. However, as most mariners would prefer to sail further west to take advantage of the north-flowing Westralian Current, these conditions normally have little impact on Sunda-bound vessels.

As established, all vessels sailing the Sunda track between latitudes 9.30 S and 22 S will encounter a cross current. For vessels sailing north, the current increases the speed of the vessel and for south- bound vessels, the speed is impeded, and in both cases, the current will create significant westerly drift. The extent of drift, more pronounced in the northern latitudes is shown as follows: From latitude 9.30 S to 18 S the average estimated set of the current is 313 degrees; a 326 deg set to latitude 22 S and a 336 deg set to latitude 25 S.

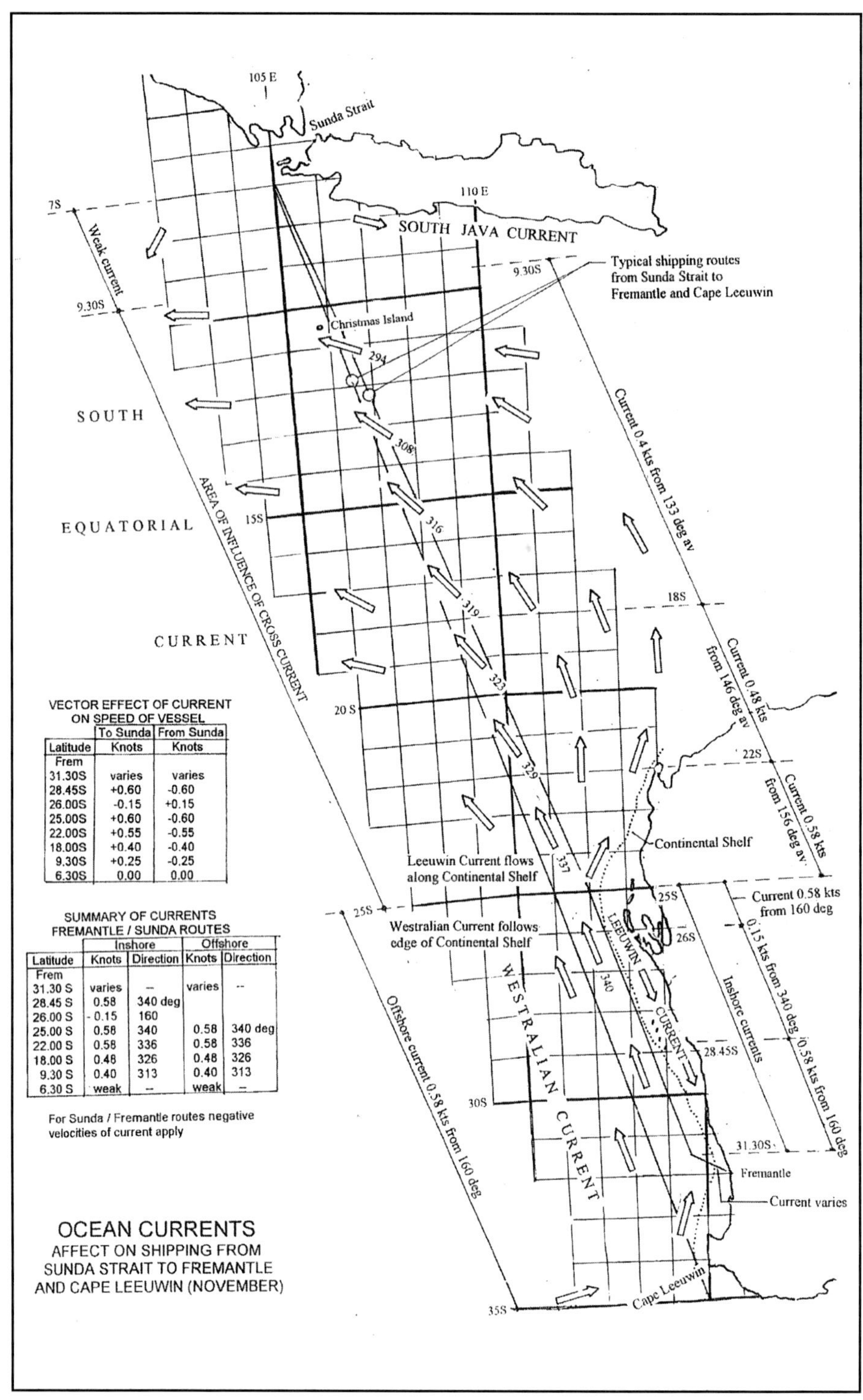

VECTOR EFFECT OF CURRENT ON SPEED OF VESSEL

	To Sunda	From Sunda
Latitude	Knots	Knots
Frem		
31.30S	varies	varies
28.45S	+0.60	-0.60
26.00S	-0.15	+0.15
25.00S	+0.60	-0.60
22.00S	+0.55	-0.55
18.00S	+0.40	-0.40
9.30S	+0.25	-0.25
6.30S	0.00	0.00

SUMMARY OF CURRENTS FREMANTLE / SUNDA ROUTES

	Inshore		Offshore	
Latitude	Knots	Direction	Knots	Direction
Frem				
31.30 S	varies	--	varies	--
28.45 S	0.58	340 deg		
26.00 S	- 0.15	160		
25.00 S	0.58	340	0.58	340 deg
22.00 S	0.58	336	0.58	336
18.00 S	0.48	326	0.48	326
9.30 S	0.40	313	0.40	313
6.30 S	weak	--	weak	--

For Sunda / Fremantle routes negative velocities of current apply

OCEAN CURRENTS
AFFECT ON SHIPPING FROM SUNDA STRAIT TO FREMANTLE AND CAPE LEEUWIN (NOVEMBER)

The extent of westerly drift and its affect on the speed of the vessel can be calculated by applying the average localized current direction and velocity vectors to the actual course and shaft speed of the vessel. This will determine the rate of drift per hour and the reduction or increase in the speed. The total drift is calculated by multiplying the time (hours) of the transit of the vessel by the drift rate per hour for each section of the voyage. The final extent of drift or deviation during the course of the voyage to the point where the vessel is influenced by a head-on or a tail current is the accumulation of all the drift vectors per hour along the route.

Sometimes it is difficult for mariners to predict the behavior of the currents because of the changing seasons and the sudden extreme weather occurrences in the proximity and in remote areas. Nevertheless, the set of the current along the Sunda route does not change much throughout the year, although it must be emphasized that this analysis is applicable only to the Sunda track during average weather and sea conditions as witnessed for about 10 days from 11 November1941 and further sourced from the Bureau of Meteorology. In other instances, the imponderables associated with unseasoned weather are the main obstacles to accurately forecasting the drift and speed fluctuations of a vessel.

Before the introduction of the Global Positioning System, most mariners on the Sunda track would not elect to constantly reassess their position to compensate for current drift. Accordingly, south bound vessels to Cape Leeuwin, sailing a standard 162T course would tend to make the necessary course adjustments near latitudes 25 S and 26 S after the full effect of drift was realized. Vessels sailing to Fremantle on the inner 160T course would need to assess their position if necessary near latitude 26 S, in order to clear the Abrolhos Islands. Alternatively, if the coastal landmark features of Dirk Hartog Island were evident, an immediate and accurate determination of position could be made. Vessels north bound would need to make course adjustments for Sunda Strait when approaching Christmas Island.

In order to obtain some idea of the speed and current deviation experienced by *Sydney* during the return from Sunda, it is considered appropriate to measure the accuracy of the nominated current and drift values against the similarly routed and speed of the south- bound ship *Aquitania*. Further comparisons with the passage and schedules of *Trocas* and *Largs Bay* should also be tested. An examination of the passage of the north- bound *Zealandia* is also considered essential to confirm the departure position of the likely return passage of *Sydney*.

HMT AQUITANIA

The Troopship *Aquitania* departed Singapore en route to Sydney on 19 November and two days later, on arrival at the Sunda departure position at 0315 hours, the Captain set for the standard 162 True (162T) course to Cape Leeuwin. At 0630 hours on November 23 (0630/23), the crew sighted two liferafts on the starboard side and the vessel stopped to rescue *Kormoran* survivors in the position, latitude 24 deg 35 min South, longitude 110 deg 57 min East.

During the voyage from Sunda, *Aquitania* (capable of 25kts max) had sailed 1110 nautical miles (nm) with a constant developed shaft speed of 22 knots. Captain Gibbons was no doubt aware that due to the known currents in the area and despite the gyrocompass setting, the ship was actually many miles west of the original set course. Normally there was no need to make intermediate course adjustments until latitude 25 S because the westerly drift would usually allow for a safe clearance of Cape Leeuwin. After the rescue and having obtained confirmation of his position, Gibbons could therefore resume his normal course of 162 T and unless interim position checks were required, sail about 20 nm west of Cape Leeuwin.

In assessing the westerly drift of *Aquitania* from Sunda to the rescue position, the previously established areas of average cross current can be applied. The greatest variation in drift occurs when the current is at right angles to the course of a vessel, but this did not apply to the south-bound *Aquitania.* The maximum drift occurred between latitudes 9.30 S and 18 S when the average included angle between the current (from 133 deg) and the course of the vessel (162 deg) was 29 degrees. In applying the vectors for the direction and flow of the current, relevant to the course and speed of *Aquitania*, the 0.4 knot current represents a 5.18 nm westerly deviation from the original course in the a period of 24.65 hours sailing and a 0.25 knot reduction in speed.

Similarly, in the current of 0.48 knots (from 146 deg) between latitudes 18 S and 22 S, *Aquitania* drifted west for an additional 1.63 nm for 11.67 hours, after incurring a speed of 21.6 knots and another 0.53 nm (current from 156 deg) over 7.6 hours (speed 21.45 knots) to the rescue position in the 0.58 knot

Westralian Current. The total accumulated westerly current deviation from the original course was therefore 7.34 nm for the 43.92 hours duration of the voyage. (Refer to Diagrams p 26, 28)

The cross current thus progressively affected *Aquitania's* initial speed of 22 knots from Sunda to 21.45 knots at the rescue position. The rest of the 657 nm voyage to Leeuwin was undertaken at 21.4 knots for 30.7 hours against the head-on current with a minimum of drift.

The SSE to SE wind on the tall super-structure of *Aquitania* throughout the journey also undoubtedly contributed to some degree of westerly drift. Even with the moderate conditions experienced, there are instances when wind drift will occur, particularly when full engine thrust is released by the action of the down- swell movement of the vessel. For the period of 43.92 hours it is estimated that a drift factor of no more than 2 nms should be applied.

From the determinations made, it is possible to reconstruct the original course of *Aquitania* relative to the known rescue position. This can be achieved by applying the total current and wind deviation, 9.34 nms east along latitude 24 deg, 35 min south to obtain the longitudinal position. This means that *Aquitania's* original course of 162T set at the Sunda position should theoretically have advanced the ship to a longitude of 111 deg 07 min E (111.07 E). Finally, the Sunda departure position can be identified by reverse plotting along the course of 162 T, and is calculated as 6.58 S / 104.50 E.

It is reasonable to suggest that the westerly drift experienced by *Sydney* south of latitude 9.30 S should be safely within the above drift parameters, provided that the course and speed approximated that of *Aquitania.* This analysis of the track of *Aquitania* therefore, could assist in locating the resting place of Sydney.

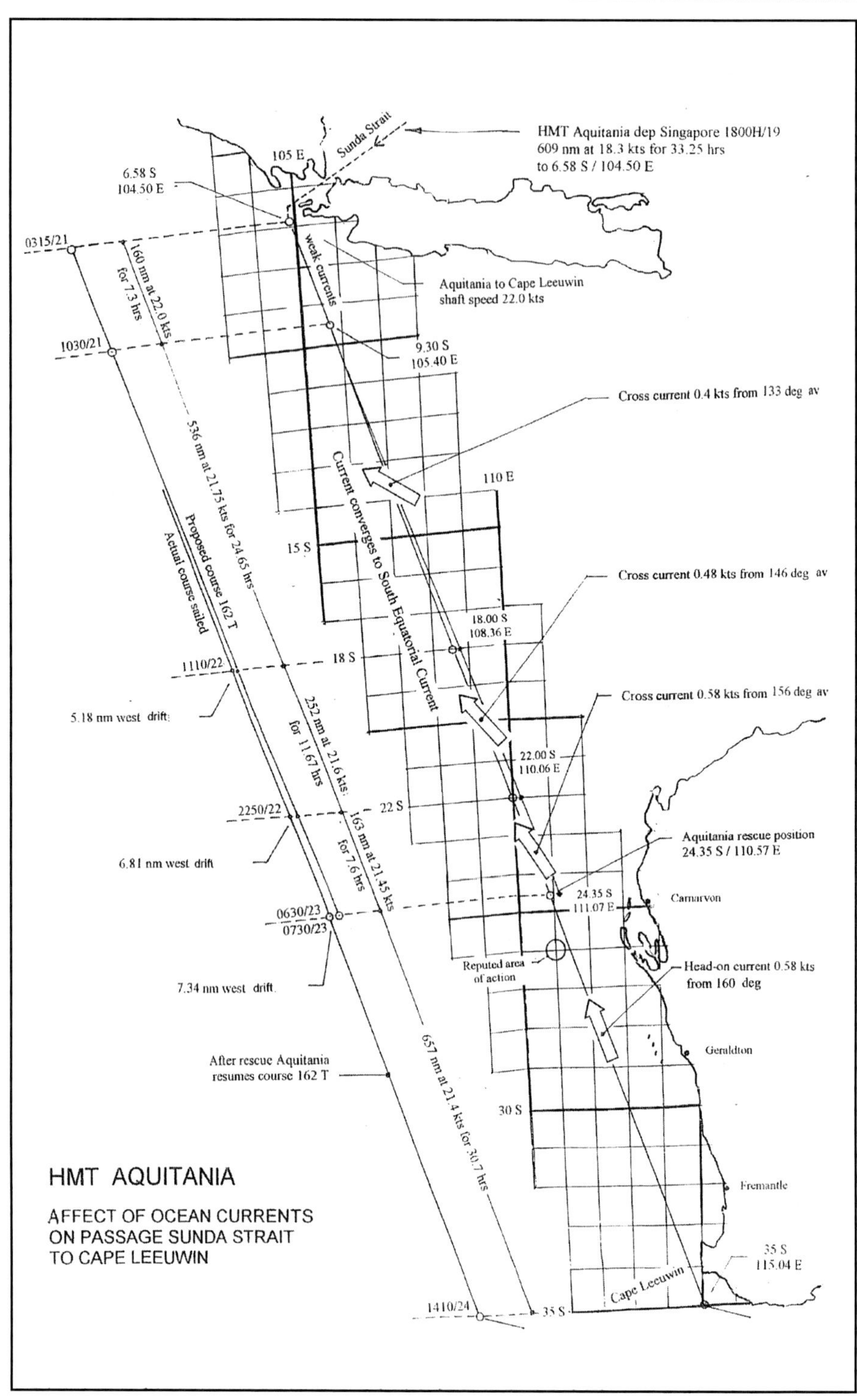
HMT Aquitania dep Singapore 1800H/19
609 nm at 18.3 kts for 33.25 hrs
to 6.58 S / 104.50 E
Sunda Strait
105 E
6.58 S
104.50 E
0315/21
160 nm at 22.0 kts
for 7.3 hrs
weak currents
Aquitania to Cape Leeuwin
shaft speed 22.0 kts
1030/21
9.30 S
105.40 E
Cross current 0.4 kts from 133 deg av
536 nm at 21.75 kts for 24.65 hrs
Current converges to South Equatorial Current
110 E
Proposed course 162 T
Actual course sailed
15 S
Cross current 0.48 kts from 146 deg av
18.00 S
108.36 E
1110/22
18 S
5.18 nm west drift
252 nm at 21.6 kts
for 11.67 hrs
Cross current 0.58 kts from 156 deg av
22.00 S
110.06 E
2250/22
22 S
163 nm at 21.45 kts
for 7.6 hrs
6.81 nm west drift
Aquitania rescue position
24.35 S / 110.57 E
24.35 S
111.07 E
Carnarvon
0630/23
0730/23
Reputed area of action
7.34 nm west drift
Head-on current 0.58 kts
from 160 deg
Geraldton
After rescue Aquitania
resumes course 162 T
657 nm at 21.4 kts for 30.7 hrs
30 S
HMT AQUITANIA
AFFECT OF OCEAN CURRENTS
ON PASSAGE SUNDA STRAIT
TO CAPE LEEUWIN
Fremantle
35 S
115.04 E
Cape Leeuwin
1410/24
35 S

TROCAS

The British oil tanker *Trocas* departed from the Sumatran port of Palembang on 18 November, 1941 en route to Fremantle via Sunda Strait. At 1500 hours on 24 November she stopped to pick up *Kormoran* survivors from a liferaft in position 24.07 S / 111.40 E.

The track to Fremantle was not direct. After the standard 160T course was set at Sunda, *Trocas* would normally attempt to maintain course south to latitude 26 S within sight of Cape Inscription and Dirk Hartog Island, where the identifiable physical land features would confirm the position of the ship. Any necessary course adjustments to Fremantle could then be made.

Although this course diverged east, away from the Leeuwin track, *Trocas* would have experienced similar current and wind conditions as described for *Aquitania*. At a constant developed shaft speed of 10.5 knots, *Trocas* sailed south from latitude 9.30 S and experienced a westerly drift per hour marginally less than for *Aquitania*. However, the total drift was much greater due to the relatively slow speed of the vessel.

If the same vectors used to calculate current drift and velocity for *Aquitania* are applied to *Trocas*, then in consideration of the reduced drift rate per hour, the total westerly current deviation at the rescue position is calculated as 14.57 nm. A smaller nominal wind factor could also be applied due to the low superstructure profile of the tanker. (Refer to Diagram p. 28)

The theoretical longitudinal position of *Trocas* at latitude 24.07 S on the regular 160 T course from Sunda is identified as 111.57 E and the reverse-plotted Sunda departure position is calculated as 6.40 S / 105.00 E. The action of the cross current on *Trocas* resulted in the same reduction in speed experienced by *Aquitania;* from 10.5 to 10.25 knots at latitude 18 S, 10.1 knots at latitude 22 S and 9.95 knots to the rescue position. (Refer to Diagram p 29)

After the rescue of the *Kormoran* survivors, *Trocas* resumed course for a further 19 hours passing 37 nms west of Steep Point and then on to 26.50 S / 112.50 E before she changed course to rendezvous with the search ship, HMAS *Wyrallah*. She arrived in Fremantle at 0530 hours on 27 November.

The significance of the *Trocas* drift results is that even if the slowest vessels maintain the standard course to Fremantle and with average currents prevailing, they should clear the coastline by at least 30 nm at latitude 26 S. However, in mid summer the stronger Westralian Current could increase the drift of a vessel to within 20 nm of the coast and even closer depending on the wind conditions. In the case of *Sydney* sailing from the same position at Sunda, the *Aquitania* drift results reveal that she would have traversed about 40 nm west of the coast.

The westerly drift applicable to *Trocas* is regarded as typical for other vessels of similar speed and is therefore certainly unrelated to the amount of drift applicable to *Sydney*. It does however demonstrate the relatively large current drift experienced by slower vessels along the Sunda route, and further reinforces the general principles employed to determine the extent of the drift of vessels due to the action of ocean currents on vessels from Sunda approaching the Western Australian coast.

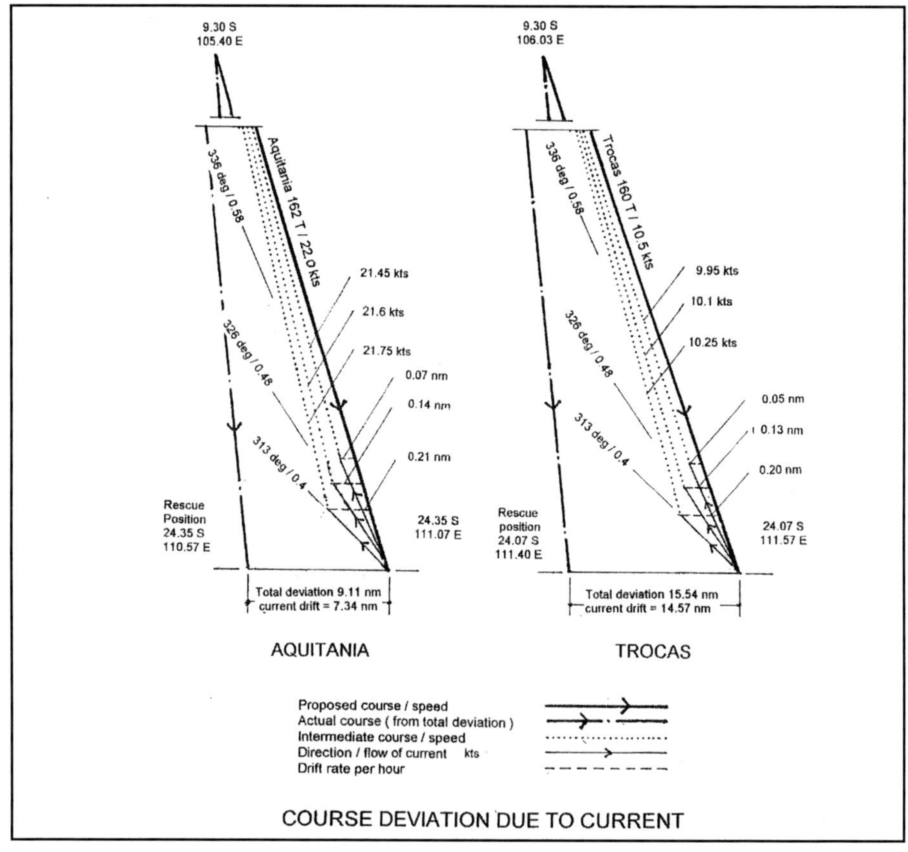

COURSE DEVIATION DUE TO CURRENT

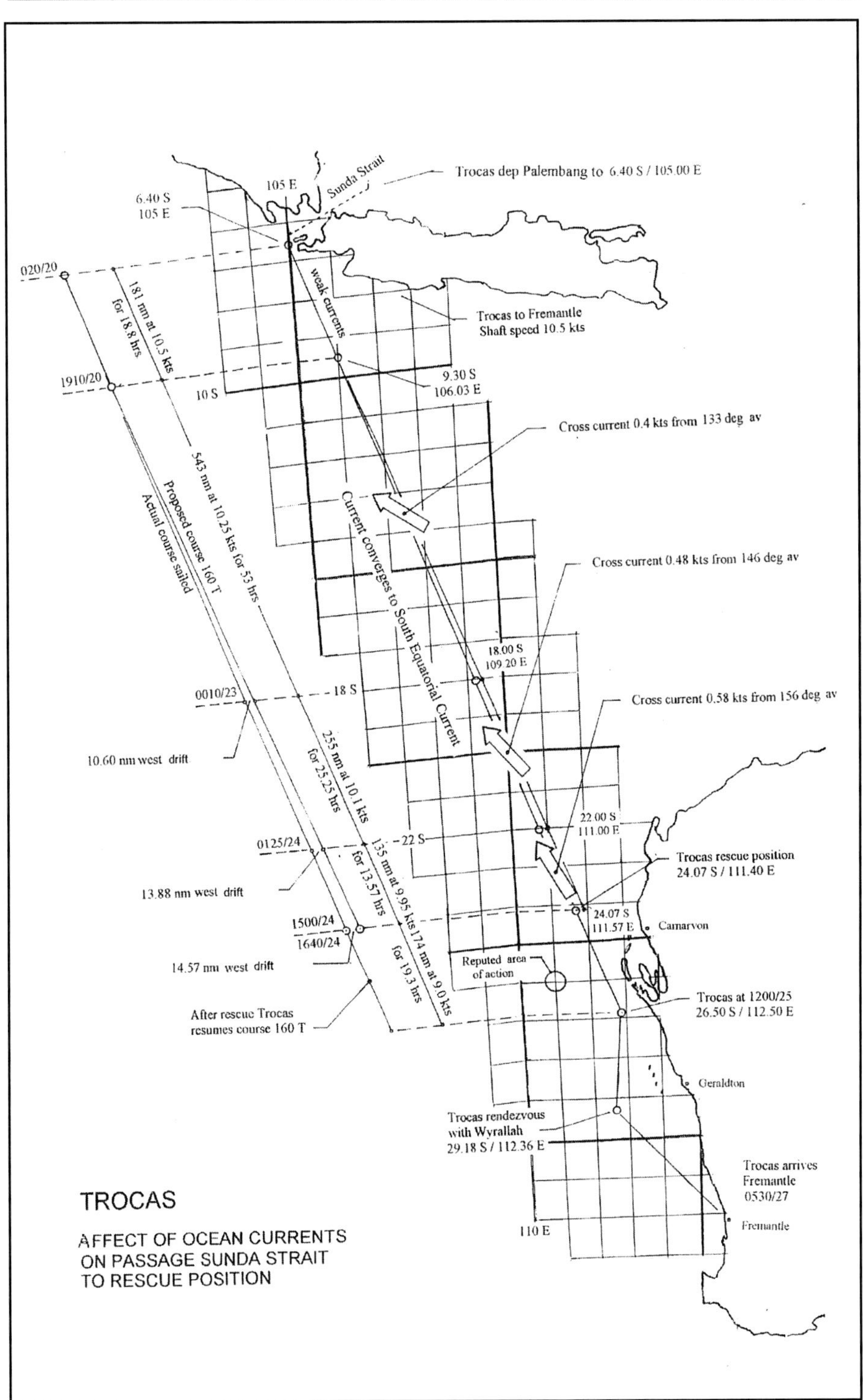
Sunda Strait
105 E
Trocas dep Palembang to 6.40 S / 105.00 E
6.40 S
105 E
020/20
181 nm at 10.5 kts
for 18.8 hrs
weak currents
Trocas to Fremantle
Shaft speed 10.5 kts
1910/20
10 S
9.30 S
106.03 E
Cross current 0.4 kts from 133 deg av
543 nm at 10.25 kts for 53 hrs
Proposed course 160 T
Actual course sailed
Current converges to South Equatorial Current
Cross current 0.48 kts from 146 deg av
18.00 S
109.20 E
0010/23
18 S
Cross current 0.58 kts from 156 deg av
10.60 nm west drift
255 nm at 10.1 kts
for 25.25 hrs
22.00 S
111.00 E
0125/24
22 S
Trocas rescue position
24.07 S / 111.40 E
13.88 nm west drift
135 nm at 9.95 kts
for 13.57 hrs
24.07 S
111.57 E
Carnarvon
1500/24
1640/24
174 nm at 9.0 kts
for 19.3 hrs
14.57 nm west drift
Reputed area of action
After rescue Trocas resumes course 160 T
Trocas at 1200/25
26.50 S / 112.50 E
Geraldton
Trocas rendezvous with Wyrallah
29.18 S / 112.36 E
Trocas arrives Fremantle
0530/27
Fremantle
110 E
TROCAS
AFFECT OF OCEAN CURRENTS
ON PASSAGE SUNDA STRAIT
TO RESCUE POSITION

HMT ZEALANDIA

The Troopship *Zealandia* arrived at Fremantle with HMAS *Sydney* from Melbourne on November 9, 1941 to embark troops for Singapore. On November 11 at 1345 hours she sailed towards Sunda with *Sydney* as escort to the pre-arranged position of 7.15 S / 104.40 E, to rendezvous with HMS *Durban* at 0800H hours on the November 17 and thence to Singapore. *Sydney* had signaled her scheduled return to Fremantle was to be on the afternoon of the November 20.

After clearing Gage Roads there is little doubt that Captain Kerr would have set the most direct and standard 340 T course to Sunda from the point of origin of 31.30 S / 115 E. Fortunately for *Zealandia*, she would be assisted by the current for most of the way, although the cross-current further north always resulted in a significant westerly course deviation. Kerr was also aware that *Zealandia's* engines could sometimes be unreliable and obviously the 1597nm journey would indeed be a tight schedule because an above-average speed of 11.55 knots was required.

The sailing conditions from all reports (and later confirmed) were expected to be perfect, with slight to moderate wind and seas prevailing throughout the journey northwards. Due to the slow speed maintained, *Zealandia* would have been particularly susceptible to westerly drift and maintaining course would have been difficult. As *Zealandia's* engines could produce only 10.7 knots, 0.85 knots less than the speed required, Kerr would have relied on an equivalent average current throughout the journey. In addition, in order to have accomplished the rendezvous within the allocated time, he would no doubt have preferred an earlier departure. [The shaft speed of 10.7 knots for *Zealandia* is calculated using the distance of 1561 nm from Fremantle to the actual rendezvous position, the changing velocities of the current and the intermediate speed differentials applicable to *Aquitania* and *Trocas*]

The initial coastal stage of the journey from latitude 31.30 S in a following 0.58 knot Westralian Current resulted in an increase in *Zealandia's* speed to 11.3 knots until the head-on Leeuwin Current near the edge of the Continental Shelf reduced the 10.7 knot shaft speed to about 10.55 knots at latitude 28.45 S. Thereafter, from latitude 26 S, a following current to latitude 25 S and a cross-current to latitude 9.30 S enabled speeds of up to 11.3 knots, but overall short of the average speed required. *Zealandia* obviously could not have improved on the constant 10.7 knots developed by the engines and it became evident that the rendezvous position could not be reached within the scheduled time.

It was apparent that even if *Zealandia* was able to maintain course she would be short of the 0800H hour rendezvous position at 1200H hours, resulting in a late arrival at 1600H hours and consequently an ill-affordable 8 hour reduction in the time available for *Sydney's* return to Fremantle. Although Sydney's probable delay was not irretrievable, it was considered prudent to notify HMS *Durban* in advance to arrange for the interception south of the intended position.

A position check at latitude 9.30 S would have confirmed that due to the westerly drift, the position of *Zealandia* was nearly 15 nm west of the original set course. [The drift rate per hour and the final deviation due to the current are based on the similar speeds attained by *Trocas*] This was of no real consequence because *Zealandia* could continue to hold course until intersecting longitude 104.40 E Thus the actual hand-over position occurred at latitude 7.56 S, 41 nm south of the intended position. [This position was belatedly confirmed by C in C China at Singapore at the request of the ACNB on November 24] In the end, *Zealandia* had sailed 1561 nm in 142.25 hours at an average speed of 10.97 knots, well short of the 11.55 knots required. Relieved of the escort by HMS *Durban, Sydney* was to return to Fremantle. (Refer to Diagrams pp 32, 33)

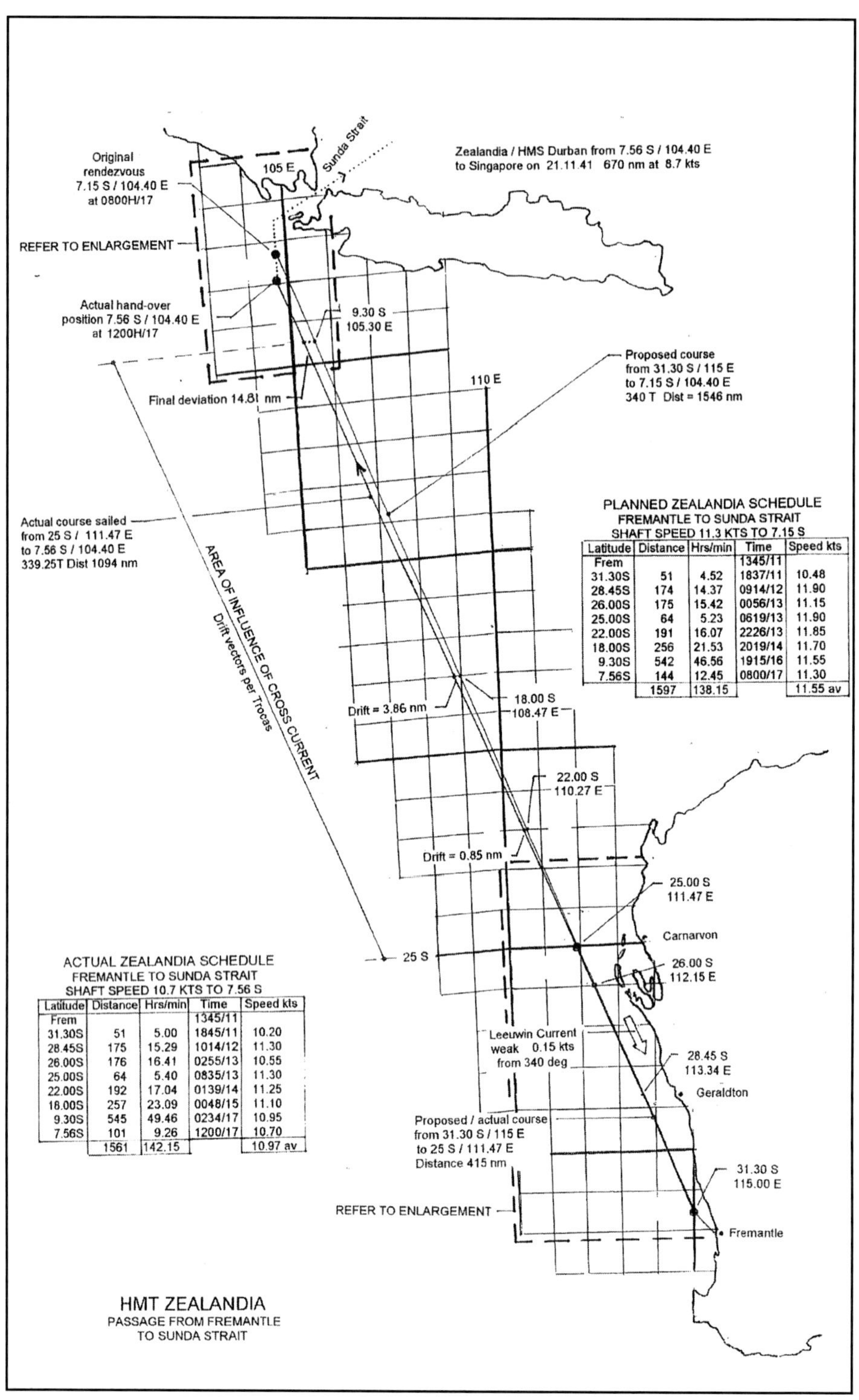

PLANNED ZEALANDIA SCHEDULE
FREMANTLE TO SUNDA STRAIT
SHAFT SPEED 11.3 KTS TO 7.15 S

Latitude	Distance	Hrs/min	Time	Speed kts
Frem			1345/11	
31.30S	51	4.52	1837/11	10.48
28.45S	174	14.37	0914/12	11.90
26.00S	175	15.42	0056/13	11.15
25.00S	64	5.23	0619/13	11.90
22.00S	191	16.07	2226/13	11.85
18.00S	256	21.53	2019/14	11.70
9.30S	542	46.56	1915/16	11.55
7.56S	144	12.45	0800/17	11.30
	1597	138.15		11.55 av

ACTUAL ZEALANDIA SCHEDULE
FREMANTLE TO SUNDA STRAIT
SHAFT SPEED 10.7 KTS TO 7.56 S

Latitude	Distance	Hrs/min	Time	Speed kts
Frem			1345/11	
31.30S	51	5.00	1845/11	10.20
28.45S	175	15.29	1014/12	11.30
26.00S	176	16.41	0255/13	10.55
25.00S	64	5.40	0835/13	11.30
22.00S	192	17.04	0139/14	11.25
18.00S	257	23.09	0048/15	11.10
9.30S	545	49.46	0234/17	10.95
7.56S	101	9.26	1200/17	10.70
	1561	142.15		10.97 av

HMT ZEALANDIA
PASSAGE FROM FREMANTLE
TO SUNDA STRAIT

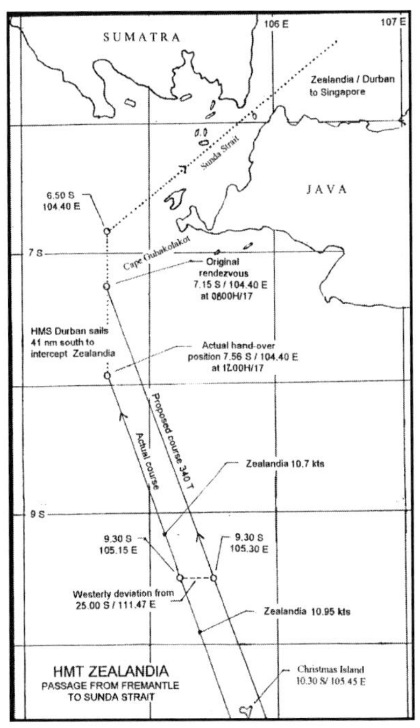

HMT ZEALANDIA
PASSAGE FROM FREMANTLE
TO SUNDA STRAIT

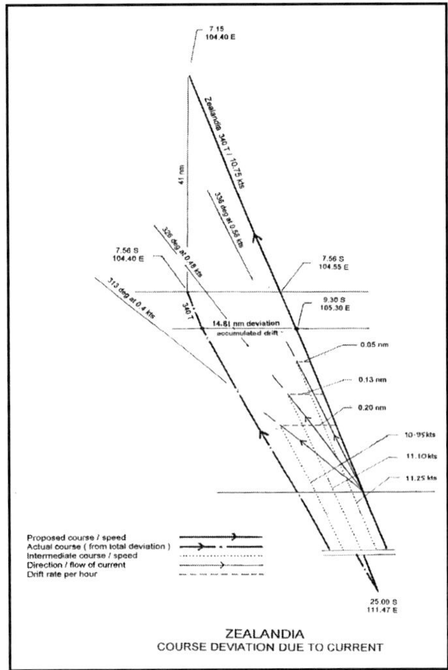

ZEALANDIA
COURSE DEVIATION DUE TO CURRENT

Certain observations can be made of *Zealandia's* track to Sunda. *Sydney* was claimed to have visited the ports of Geraldton and Carnarvon shortly before she was sunk. This may be relevant in the context of *Sydney's* escort duties rather than her return from Sunda, or on an earlier occasion. Interestingly, if a stop- over in these ports was contemplated, for what ever reason, a late night visit and an early morning return to *Zealandia* was possible.

When the course to Sunda of 340T was set at 1845 on November 11 in position 31.30 S / 115 E, the blacked- out *Zealandia* was assured of a slow overnight journey up the coast. At 0810/12 she would be 50 nm from Geraldton, just south of the Abrolhos and later at 1105/12, at latitude 28.36 S. During the intervening period, *Sydney* at 22 kts, could have sailed direct to Geraldton, stay there for up to 5.5 hours and rejoin *Zealandia*. Alternatively, while *Zealandia* was sailing during the night of November 12/13 from latitudes 27.30 S to 24.30 S, *Sydney* could also have made a brief evening visit to Carnarvon of up to 4 hours before rejoining *Zealandia*. (Refer to Diagram p 35)

Although the safety of *Zealandia* when *Sydney* was away could not always be guaranteed, it must be conceded that during darkness there was less risk from attack and considering it was likely to be widely known that *Sydney* had recently departed Fremantle and was therefore still likely to be in the vicinity, this was probably sufficient reason to deter any raider activity near the coast. Moreover, it is inconceivable that Burnett would have left *Zealandia* unescorted unless he was satisfied that the latest intelligence reports on enemy vessels presented no danger.

During the escort to Sunda, *Sydney* most likely used her Walrus seaplane to search for suspicious shipping. On previous voyages, there were instances when *Sydney* would be away for periods, probably investigating such sightings. The Walrus could be deployed to keep visual contact with *Zealandia* when *Sydney* was at a distance, or in the instance of *Sydney* returning from Geraldton or Carnarvon. It could also have been used effectively closer to Sunda to signal or guide HMS *Durban* further south to the rendezvous position if direct communication or wireless telegraphy (W/T) silence was required to be observed.

This synopsis, together with the associated maps and diagrams chronologically outlines the movement of *Zealandia* north to Sunda. It confirms the actual hand-over position based on the expected total westerly drift using the previously established drift rates for *Trocas*. The intermediate speeds are also consistent with the speed reductions established for the south- bound *Aquitania* and *Trocas*. More importantly, it provides the confirmation for the failure of *Zealandia* to reach the designated original rendezvous position.

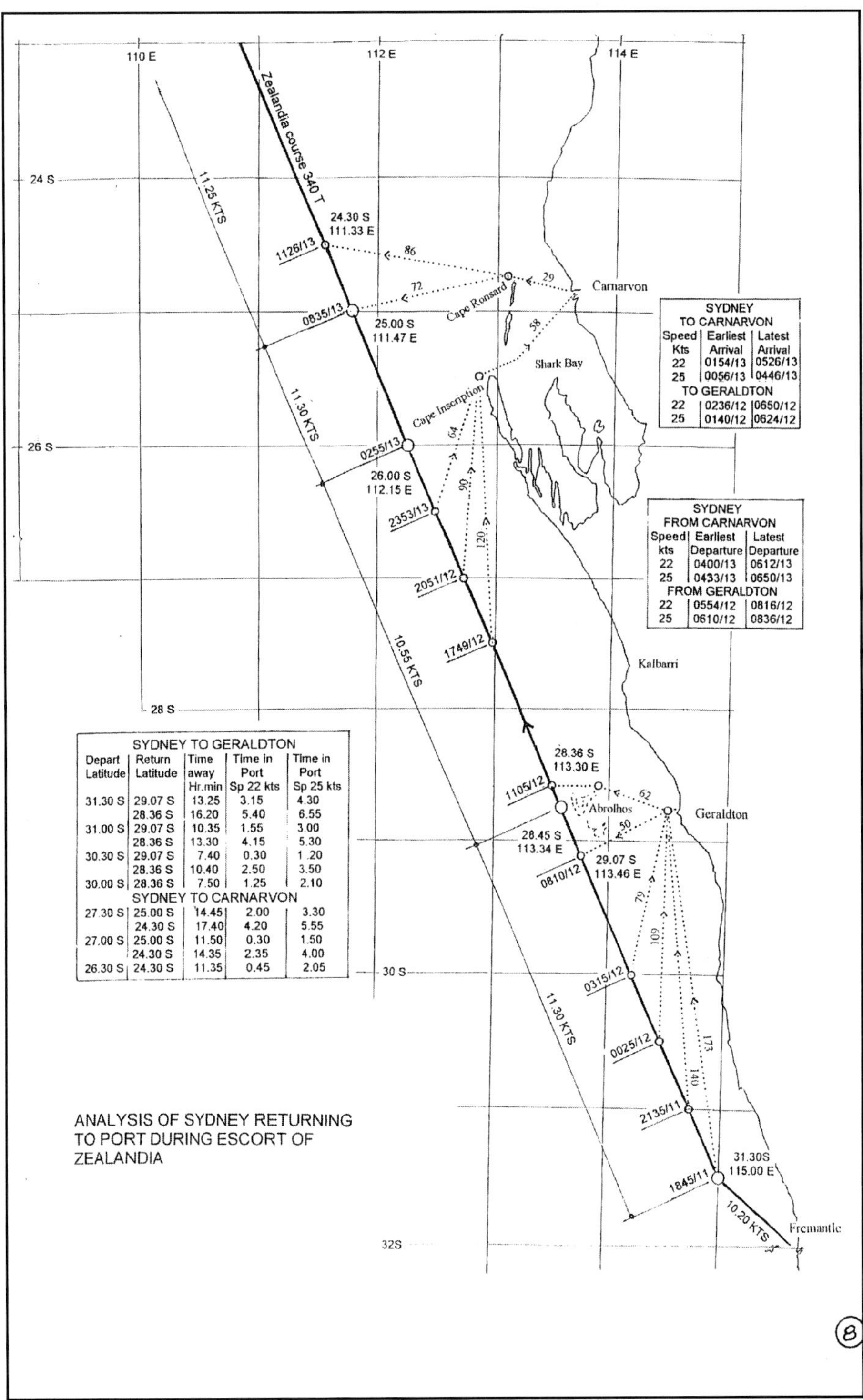

SYDNEY TO CARNARVON		
Speed Kts	Earliest Arrival	Latest Arrival
22	0154/13	0526/13
25	0056/13	0446/13
TO GERALDTON		
22	0236/12	0650/12
25	0140/12	0624/12

SYDNEY FROM CARNARVON		
Speed kts	Earliest Departure	Latest Departure
22	0400/13	0612/13
25	0433/13	0650/13
FROM GERALDTON		
22	0554/12	0816/12
25	0610/12	0836/12

SYDNEY TO GERALDTON				
Depart Latitude	Return Latitude	Time away Hr.min	Time in Port Sp 22 kts	Time in Port Sp 25 kts
31.30 S	29.07 S	13.25	3.15	4.30
	28.36 S	16.20	5.40	6.55
31.00 S	29.07 S	10.35	1.55	3.00
	28.36 S	13.30	4.15	5.30
30.30 S	29.07 S	7.40	0.30	1 .20
	28.36 S	10.40	2.50	3.50
30.00 S	28.36 S	7.50	1.25	2.10
SYDNEY TO CARNARVON				
27.30 S	25.00 S	14.45	2.00	3.30
	24.30 S	17.40	4.20	5.55
27.00 S	25.00 S	11.50	0.30	1.50
	24.30 S	14.35	2.35	4.00
26.30 S	24.30 S	11.35	0.45	2.05

ANALYSIS OF SYDNEY RETURNING TO PORT DURING ESCORT OF ZEALANDIA

LARGS BAY

In some respects the troopship, *Largs Bay* appears to have only a tenuous link with the *Sydney*. On the other hand, establishing the whereabouts of *Largs Bay* in the days before the disappearance of *Sydney* may shed some light on *Sydney's* earlier position and eventual course to destruction.

Largs Bay, a passenger liner of about 14,000 tons, maximum speed 15 knots, was pressed into service as a troopship in 1941 to convey reinforcements to Singapore. It is generally accepted she departed Singapore en route to Sydney via Sunda Strait and Cape Leeuwin in the late afternoon of November 15 and arrived at her destination before noon on November 29. Passengers have claimed that during the voyage, *Largs Bay* was briefly escorted by *Sydney* one afternoon from 1700 hours until about 1900 hours. It has also been claimed that *Largs Bay* was close to the scene of the engagement. If these observations are considered reliable, then they can be tested by the reconstruction of the sailing schedules using the previously established data.

If the influence of the current is taken into account, there are four stages of the voyage to be considered. From Singapore to Sunda and south to latitude 9.30, the speed of the vessel should not have been unduly affected – from latitude 9.30 S to Cape Leeuwin on the standard 162T course, the vessel's shaft speed would have been impeded to the extent shown for *Aquitania*, and from Leeuwin to Cape Howe, *Largs Bay's* speed would be expected to increase under the influence of a following current. The speed of *Largs Bay* would then be impeded from Cape Howe to Sydney by the south- flowing East Australian Current.

The distance by sea from Singapore to Sydney along the shipping route is about 4350 nm and another 40nm if drift is taken into account. If *Largs Bay* left Singapore at approximately 1700H/15 and arrived outside Sydney at 0800H/29 (1000 EST) as reported, an average speed of 13.4 knots over 4390 nm was required. This appears to be consistent with the speed expectations between Sunda and Sydney, but it seems in excess of the limited speeds required in the confined and busy waterway from Singapore to Sunda. In 1941, vessels (without radar) sailing these waters amongst the numerous sailing craft and myriad of islands, should have been restricted to 2/3 of the available speed as evidenced by *Aquitania* and *Zealandia*. In addition, navigation at night was extremely hazardous. *Largs Bay* therefore should have been expected to sail at approximately 10 knots in this area. Alternatively, the unsafe speed was required in order to attempt a pre-arranged rendezvous with *Sydney*.

In assessing the *Largs Bay* Schedule for the 1700/15 departure from Singapore and to account for an average speed of 13.4 knots, a constant developed shaft speed of 13.5 knots was required from Sunda to Sydney. If this was achieved, the derived intermediate reductions in speed to Leeuwin along the 162T course would have matched those of *Aquitania*. The schedule also indicates a 0.35 knot increase from Leeuwin to Cape Howe and a reduction of 0.3 knots to Sydney in accordance with the affect of the current. Finally, the average speed undertaken for the 591 nm from Singapore to Sunda is assessed at 13.27 knots, giving an arrival time of 1332/17 at Sunda.

In the case of *Aquitania* and *Trocas*, the known data (rescue positions and drift) has been used to determine the respective Sunda departure positions, but no information is available for *Largs Bay* to make such a determination. However, the actual drift position can be estimated by using the track and drift vectors applicable for *Aquitania* to latitude 25 S. The accumulated 12nm drift for *Largs Bay* therefore produces a longitudinal position of 111.17 E, a planned position of 111.30 S and a reverse-plotted calculated Sunda departure position of 6.46 S / 104.59 E. (Refer to Diagram p 38)

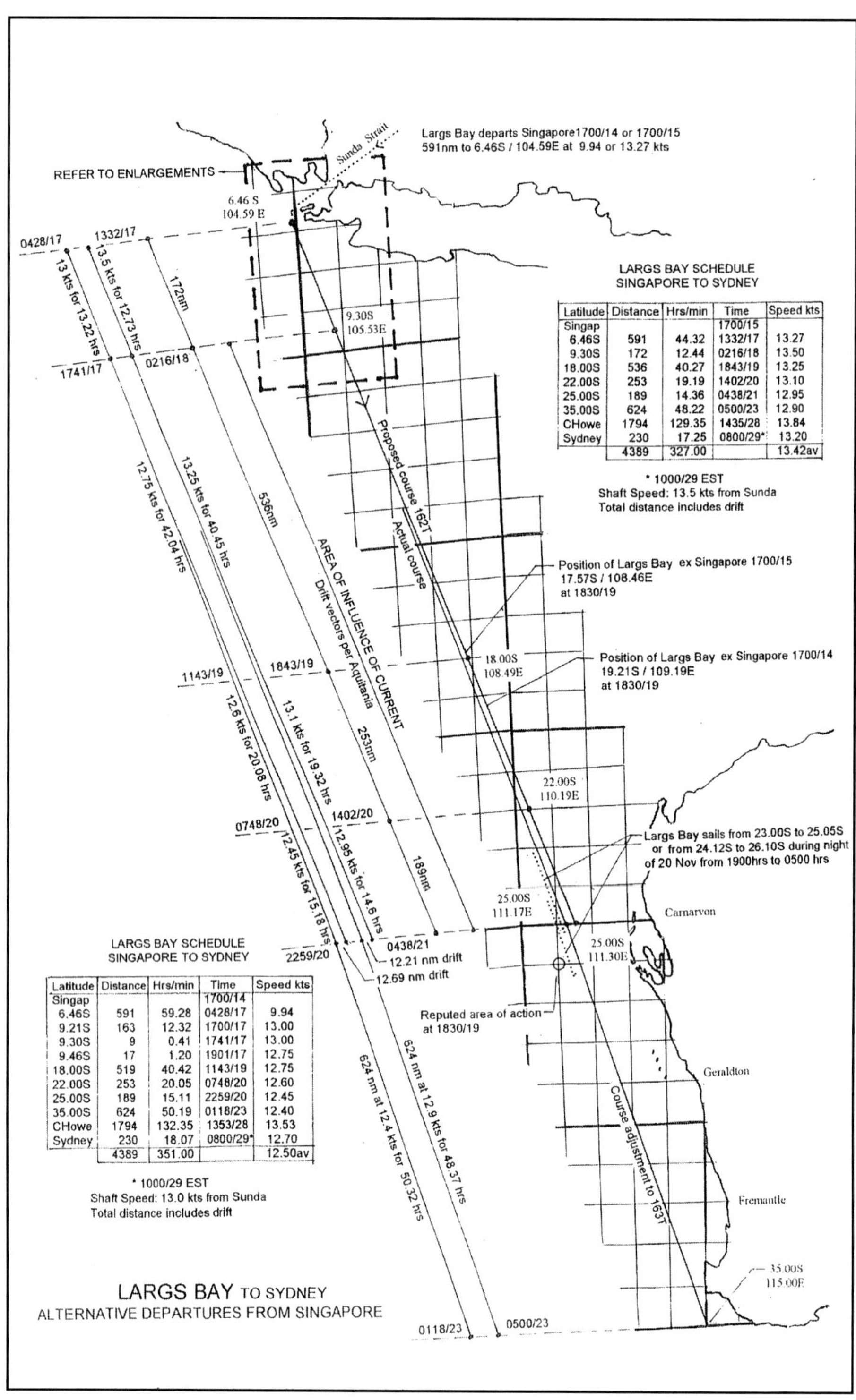

LARGS BAY SCHEDULE
SINGAPORE TO SYDNEY

Latitude	Distance	Hrs/min	Time	Speed kts
Singap			1700/15	
6.46S	591	44.32	1332/17	13.27
9.30S	172	12.44	0216/18	13.50
18.00S	536	40.27	1843/19	13.25
22.00S	253	19.19	1402/20	13.10
25.00S	189	14.36	0438/21	12.95
35.00S	624	48.22	0500/23	12.90
CHowe	1794	129.35	1435/28	13.84
Sydney	230	17.25	0800/29*	13.20
	4389	327.00		13.42av

* 1000/29 EST
Shaft Speed: 13.5 kts from Sunda
Total distance includes drift

LARGS BAY SCHEDULE
SINGAPORE TO SYDNEY

Latitude	Distance	Hrs/min	Time	Speed kts
Singap			1700/14	
6.46S	591	59.28	0428/17	9.94
9.21S	163	12.32	1700/17	13.00
9.30S	9	0.41	1741/17	13.00
9.46S	17	1.20	1901/17	12.75
18.00S	519	40.42	1143/19	12.75
22.00S	253	20.05	0748/20	12.60
25.00S	189	15.11	2259/20	12.45
35.00S	624	50.19	0118/23	12.40
CHowe	1794	132.35	1353/28	13.53
Sydney	230	18.07	0800/29*	12.70
	4389	351.00		12.50av

* 1000/29 EST
Shaft Speed: 13.0 kts from Sunda
Total distance includes drift

LARGS BAY TO SYDNEY
ALTERNATIVE DEPARTURES FROM SINGAPORE

According to the *Largs Bay* Schedule, the distance between *Sydney* at various times can be determined as follows: At 1200/17 when *Sydney* had delivered *Zealandia* to HMS *Durban* at latitude 7.56 S, *Largs Bay* should have been situated 93 nm north, bearing 16T. At 1332 hours, *Sydney,* further south en route direct to Fremantle at 22 knots, is now 102 nm distant and at 1700 hours, 126 nm from *Largs Bay.* This seems to indicate there was no prospect of a rendezvous between the two vessels. However, if a rendezvous was considered imperative, *Sydney* could have awaited *Largs Bay* for 3 hours, 41 nms away, bearing 54T in position 7.31 S / 105.14 E at 1700 hours, and after two hours at 13.5 knots on course 162T departed *Largs Bay* in position 7.56 S / 105.22 E. (Refer to Diagram below)

This scenario means that at 22 knots developed shaft speed *Sydney's* return to Fremantle would take at least an additional 6 hours and a late arrival at 2030/20. However, with an increase in shaft speed to 24 knots she could still accomplish an earlier mid afternoon arrival time at 1530 hours. It is interesting that those same 6 hours were to be lost if *Sydney* had maintained escort to latitude 7.56 S; notwithstanding, Burnett chose to terminate short of that position to return to Fremantle. If in fact the two hour escort occurred, Burnett certainly had no intention and could not spare the time to accompany *Largs Bay* to Fremantle or beyond, unless he had specific information of enemy raider activity in the area.

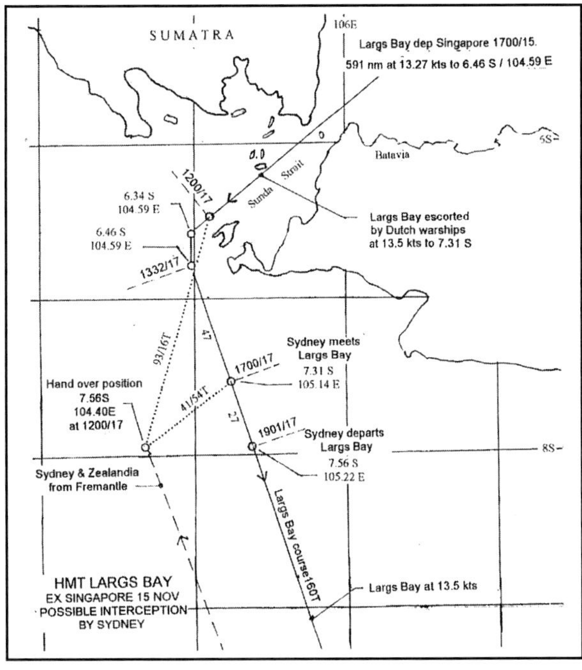

In considering the possibility that *Largs Bay* departed Singapore 24 hours earlier, the schedule for *Largs Bay* to Sydney (in accordance with the same speed fluctuations and drift criteria) shows that from Sunda, a constant shaft speed developing 13 knots was required. At an average speed of 9.94 knots from Singapore, *Largs Bay* would have arrived at the same Sunda position 9 hours earlier at 0428/17, before proceeding south on 162 T to Cape Leeuwin and gaining 0.53 knots to Cape Howe.

At 1200/17, *Largs Bay* would have sailed 98 nm from Sunda to position 8.19 S / 105.29 E, 54 nm from *Sydney*, bearing 115T. With *Sydney* to return to Fremantle at 22 knots developed shaft speed, the rendezvous could now take place at 1700 hours on *Largs Bay's* 162T track in position 9.21 S / 105.50 E and departure made two hours later, in position 9.46 S / 105.59 E. From the departure position, *Sydney* could comfortably sail the 1429 nm to Fremantle at the respective speeds allowed by the current in 67.5 hours and arrive at 1430 hours on November 20. (Refer to Diagram p 41)

Largs Bay's track from Sunda to Cape Leeuwin passes about 30 nm west of the reputed *Sydney / Kormoran* engagement site of 26 S / 111 E. If the departure from Singapore occurred at 1700/15, her location at 1830/19 when the battle started is calculated at 500 nm NNW of the site and 320 nm NNW for the 1700/14 departure. However, it should be noted that for the 1700/15 departure, *Largs Bay* would have sailed to latitude 25.05 S at 0500/21 and during the day approached through the general area where allegedly the *Kormoran* survivors were drifting. This contrasts with the 1700/14 departure as the area was traversed during the night from latitudes 24.12 S to 26.10 S. Regardless of the two schedules, the reason that *Largs Bay* was not sighted by the survivors could have been due to the false location given of the engagement or that a greater separation distance made visual contact impossible. (Refer to Diagram p 38)

The earlier departure from Singapore at 1700H/14 is symptomatic of a pre-arranged and planned rendezvous, whereas it appears that the departure 24 hours later, resulting in the higher speed to Sunda is evidence of a rush to meet a recently arranged rendezvous. In this respect, it is conceivable that Burnett's arrangement to meet *Largs Bay* was rather sudden and decidedly important and therefore every endeavor was made to make the rendezvous.

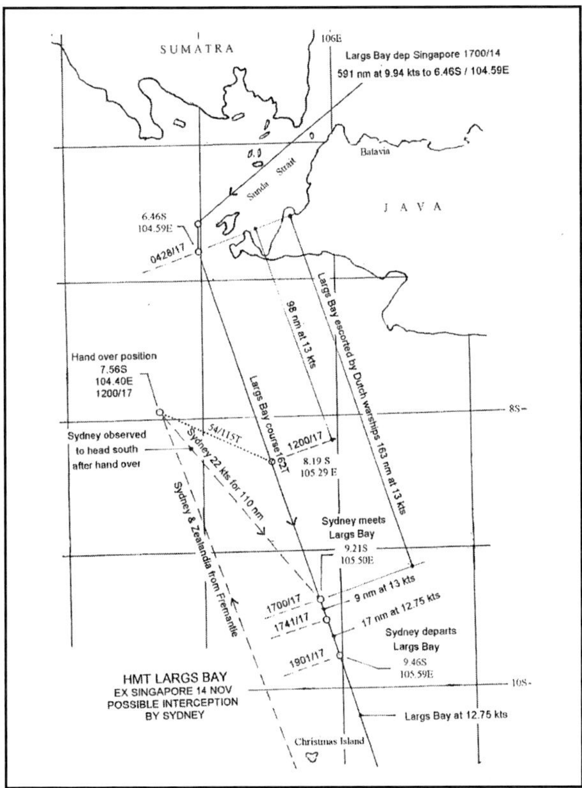

During the voyage from the Sunda, passengers aboard *Largs Bay* noticed that Dutch warships had escorted the vessel throughout the day on November 17 until *Sydney* intercepted at 1700 hours. When available, these warships regularly undertook escort duties for Allied merchant ships from Batavia as far south as Christmas Island. However, there is an alternative view suggesting that because of the similar profiles of the warships, the presence of *Sydney* may have been mistaken. If *Sydney* was escorting as close to Largs Bay as claimed (within 200 metres), the insignia on the superstructure and the ensign should have been easily discernable.

The escort of *Largs Bay* for such a short duration is uncharacteristic, particularly if Burnett considered that the existence of enemy raider(s) in the vicinity was, in fact, a reality. However, in the immediate term, the safety of *Largs Bay* could be guaranteed because *Sydney* was effectively patrolling 'ahead' and at night and the walrus could be used for observation the next day. Although this may have been some comfort for those aboard *Largs Bay* at the time, the remainder of the voyage would be undertaken without escort.

Burnett's suspicion that a raider was in the vicinity may have been signaled, but the assumption there was no danger further south seems curious, unless he had received more accurate information which helped to confirm his belief.

The investigative movements of *Aquitania, Trocas, Zealandia* and *Largs Bay* has been necessary to estimate the likely course and speed of *Sydney's* return from the Sunda Strait. These findings have enabled a detailed examination to be made of the positions and speed of these vessels at any given time, based on the action of the currents. The velocity and direction of the currents is found to be consistent with the extent of the lateral westerly drift of each vessel. In addition, the reconstructed schedule for each vessel is considered an important adjunct to the process of determining *Sydney's* final location.

That the *Aquitania* and *Trocas* rescue positions are accurately recorded has made it possible to ascertain the extent of westerly drift in accordance with the oceanographic conditions of the time and to establish the fluctuations in the speed of the vessels. An examination of the passage of *Zealandia* to Sunda not only confirms the current and drift results, it verifies the actual hand-over position and found that the original destination was not possible within the allowed timeframe. The affect of the current on *Largs Bay's* southward journey proved to be decisive. The results indicate that slower speeds were achieved, casting doubt on the reported date of departure from Singapore and more importantly, it presents a compelling argument that *Largs Bay* was in fact, briefly escorted by *Sydney*.

The developed criterion is invaluable in its application to *Sydney's* last movements and is regarded as the blueprint for subsequent investigations. Moreover, the drift results and the established schedules can be used to determine the likely return path and timetable of *Sydney* and can be likewise applied to the encounter with *Kormoran* and the flotsam found by the search vessels.

RETURNING FROM SUNDA

SOMETIME BEFORE the 11th November, *Sydney's* Captain Burnett was issued with orders to escort *Zealandia* from Fremantle to a destination near the Sunda Straits. Although a copy of this message is unavailable, it is safe to assume this was the same destination included in the message of 0321Z/13, ordering HMS *Durban* to sail from Singapore and relieve *Sydney* in position 7.15 S / 104.40 E. Burnett amended the time of rendezvous to 0800H hours the next day, due to a delay in departure from Fremantle. He also advised that *Sydney* would now return to Fremantle on the afternoon of 20th November. There is no doubt that a planned schedule would have been developed by Burnett in consultation with *Zealandia's* Captain Kerr to determine a departure time and the anticipated speed required to the rendezvous position.

If Kerr was confident that the planned schedule could be met, it appears he may have over- estimated the speed capabilities of *Zealandia*. However, if the rendezvous had been achieved according to plan, a reconstruction of the 1612 nm direct return passage, on course 160T at a comfortable 21.1 knots (moderate despatch speed) against the fluctuations of current (as established), indicates an arrival time of 1330/20 in Fremantle. Even if this average speed of 20.8 kts was reduced to 20 knots *Sydney* should arrive in Fremantle no later than 1630/20. (Refer to Diagram p44)

As established earlier due to *Zealandia's* slower than expected speed, it was not possible to reach the rendezvous position within the prescribed time. The constant shaft speed of 10.7 knots achieved by *Zealandia* was much less than the 11.3 knots required. In reality, the schedule could have only been met if *Zealandia* had sailed from Fremantle 8 hours earlier. However, a more compelling argument for the failure to maintain schedule, was the difficulty in estimating the velocities of the currents. This is not to imply that the entire 0.6 knot deficit was due to an inaccurate forecast of the strength of the current by Kerr, but rather an over-estimation of both current and speed. As evidenced from the reconstructed Schedules and for the reasons given above, it is not surprising that the actual hand-over position at 7.56 S / 104.40 E (confirmed by C in C China at 0451Z/24) was short of the intended position, 41 nm due south.

Throughout the passage to Sunda, *Sydney* was, on occasions, observed to periodically leave *Zealandia*, possibly for the purpose of investigating the bon-a-fides of shipping in the vicinity or for routine exercises. These movements should not have contributed to any delay on the part of *Zealandia*. The notion that *Sydney* permanently departed *Zealandia* prior to the hand-over to HMS *Durban* is difficult to countenance, unless it was approved by C in C China at Singapore.

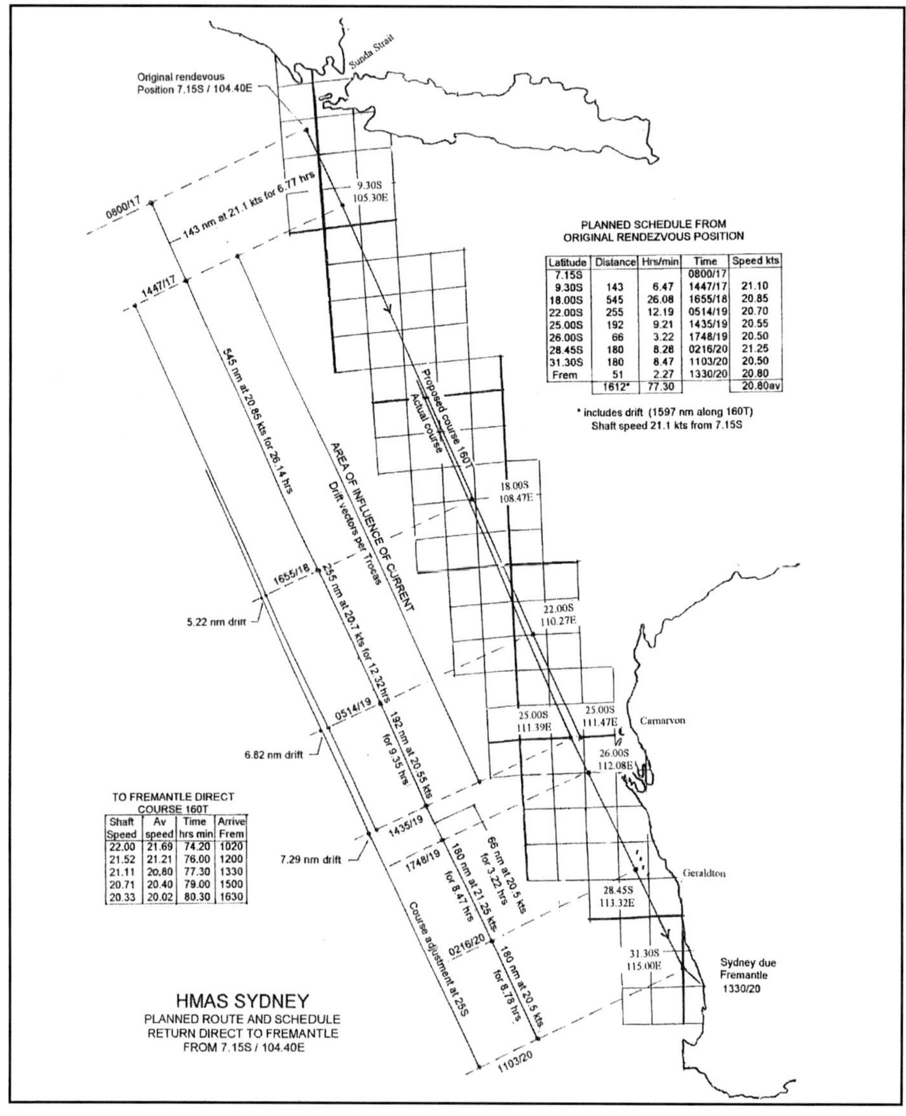

PLANNED SCHEDULE FROM ORIGINAL RENDEZVOUS POSITION

Latitude	Distance	Hrs/min	Time	Speed kts
7.15S			0800/17	
9.30S	143	6.47	1447/17	21.10
18.00S	545	26.08	1655/18	20.85
22.00S	255	12.19	0514/19	20.70
25.00S	192	9.21	1435/19	20.55
26.00S	66	3.22	1748/19	20.50
28.45S	180	8.28	0216/20	21.25
31.30S	180	8.47	1103/20	20.50
Frem	51	2.27	1330/20	20.80
	1612*	77.30		20.80av

* includes drift (1597 nm along 160T)
Shaft speed 21.1 kts from 7.15S

TO FREMANTLE DIRECT COURSE 160T

Shaft Speed	Av speed	Time hrs min	Arrive Frem
22.00	21.69	74.20	1020
21.52	21.21	76.00	1200
21.11	20.80	77.30	1330
20.71	20.40	79.00	1500
20.33	20.02	80.30	1630

Ambit of Return

In assessing the return passage of *Sydney* after handing over *Zealandia* to HMS *Durban* at 1200/17 in position 7.56 S / 104.40 E, consideration must be given to the return speed and course required for an afternoon arrival at Fremantle on 20th November. After all, there is no evidence that *Sydney* had subsequently signaled a revised ETA in Fremantle. As *Sydney* was effectively only 2 hours behind her original schedule, it is difficult to conclude that any increase in the original planned return speed was deemed necessary.

Burnett could have chosen any number of return tracks that would meet his schedule. His suspicion that a raider was operating somewhere in the vicinity, may have resulted in a decision to sail a more easterly or westerly course away from the normal Sunda-Fremantle route. He may also have received a signal from Singapore that the HF/DF network of stations had located a suspect vessel(s) further south and was ordered to investigate. Also, Burnett may have independently decided to sail a different track simply to avoid the Sunda shipping lane, where it was unlikely that raiders or their supply ships would be stationed.

It is rather strange that Burnett had openly made it known to his crew that a raider was active in the area, whereas, there were no reported attacks on allied merchant ships for months and certainly no attacks had occurred anywhere near the Sunda route. In this regard, it is possible that his current views on the proximity of a raider were simply based on assumption or a gut feeling.

In consideration of these uncertainties, the issue of predicting the actual speed and return course of *Sydney* should be put aside. These imponderables can only be logically dealt with by exploring a range of available tracks and speeds, which would accord with *Sydney's* committed afternoon arrival at Fremantle three days later. This is not meant to imply that particular circumstances could not account for an early arrival. Nevertheless, such an exercise should clearly identify the possible routes and eliminate others.

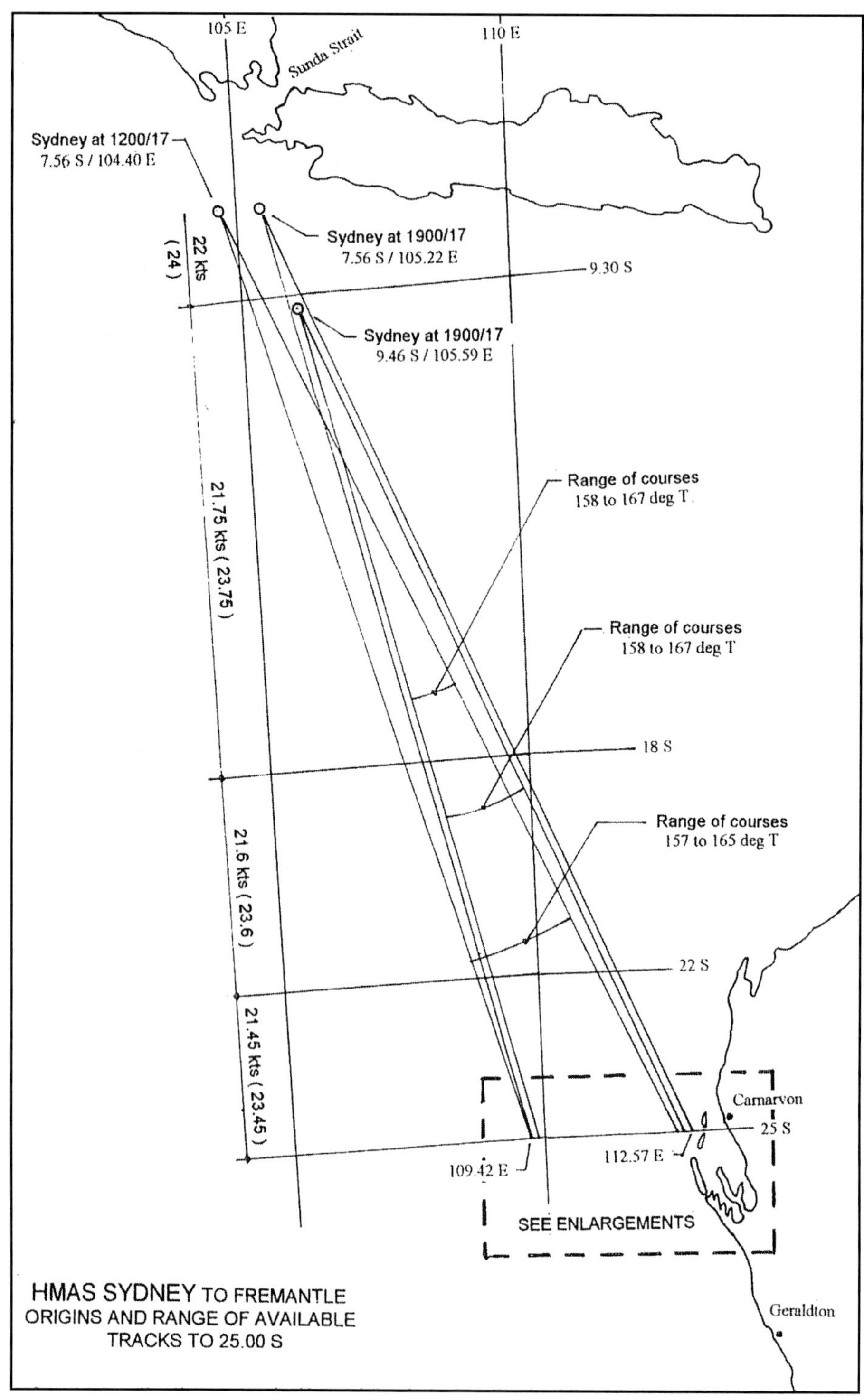
105 E
110 E
Sunda Strait
Sydney at 1200/17
7.56 S / 104.40 E
Sydney at 1900/17
7.56 S / 105.22 E
9.30 S
22 kts
(24)
Sydney at 1900/17
9.46 S / 105.59 E
21.75 kts (23.75)
Range of courses
158 to 167 deg T.
Range of courses
158 to 167 deg T
18 S
21.6 kts (23.6)
Range of courses
157 to 165 deg T
22 S
21.45 kts (23.45)
Carnarvon
25 S
112.57 E
109.42 E
SEE ENLARGEMENTS
Geraldton
HMAS SYDNEY TO FREMANTLE
ORIGINS AND RANGE OF AVAILABLE
TRACKS TO 25.00 S

Return Direct

There are three previously established positions from which *Sydney's* southward course to Fremantle could have originated. In addition to the *Zealandia* hand- over position at 1200/17, the other return tracks which require investigation are those associated with the supposition that *Largs Bay* was escorted by *Sydney* until 1900/17. From one of these positions, Burnett selected a course and speed to Fremantle. Apart from the most direct route, a range of tracks was available to him in order to meet his schedule or for the purpose of investigating areas further south, away from the Sunda track. (Refer to Diagram p 46)

The earlier return passages of *Sydney* in June and October appears to confirm that a direct course of 160T from Sunda was the preferred option. On this occasion however, it was known that Burnett suspected the presence of a German raider and consequently he may have decided to set a more easterly or westerly course. In assessing the options available, it is difficult not to concede that precedence was the motivating factor in Burnett's deliberations.

A direct 160T course to Fremantle from 7.56 S / 104.40 E (the reverse of the outward- bound course) is the shortest route. At a shaft speed (ss) of 22.25 (average 21.85 knots) against the current over the distance of 1573 nm, *Sydney* could be expected to arrive at noon on 20th November. In the context of an 'afternoon' arrival *Sydney* would have sailed at a lower speed. A late arrival at 1730/20 would require an average speed of 20.3 knots (ss 20.7). However, the most efficient speed, based on engine revolutions previously calculated for *Sydney* within these speed ranges and termed 'with moderate despatch', was likely to be employed. In this case, a shaft speed of 21.1 knots (20.7av) could deliver *Sydney* to Fremantle at 1600/20. Further arrivals at 1300, 1400 and 1500 hours can be ascribed to average speeds of 21.55, 21.25 and 20.97 knots respectively. (Refer to Diagram p 48)

Even though these arrival times all fall within the ambit of Burnett's ETA Fremantle, they are irrelevant if Burnett had for some reason decided not to keep to his original schedule. However, in order to assess *Sydney's* course and speed, it is of more relevance to determine the whereabouts of *Sydney* when sighted by *Kormoran* at 1700 hours on November 19. Such an exercise should give broad consideration to the engagement position(s) given by the German survivors and of the sightings made from the coast.

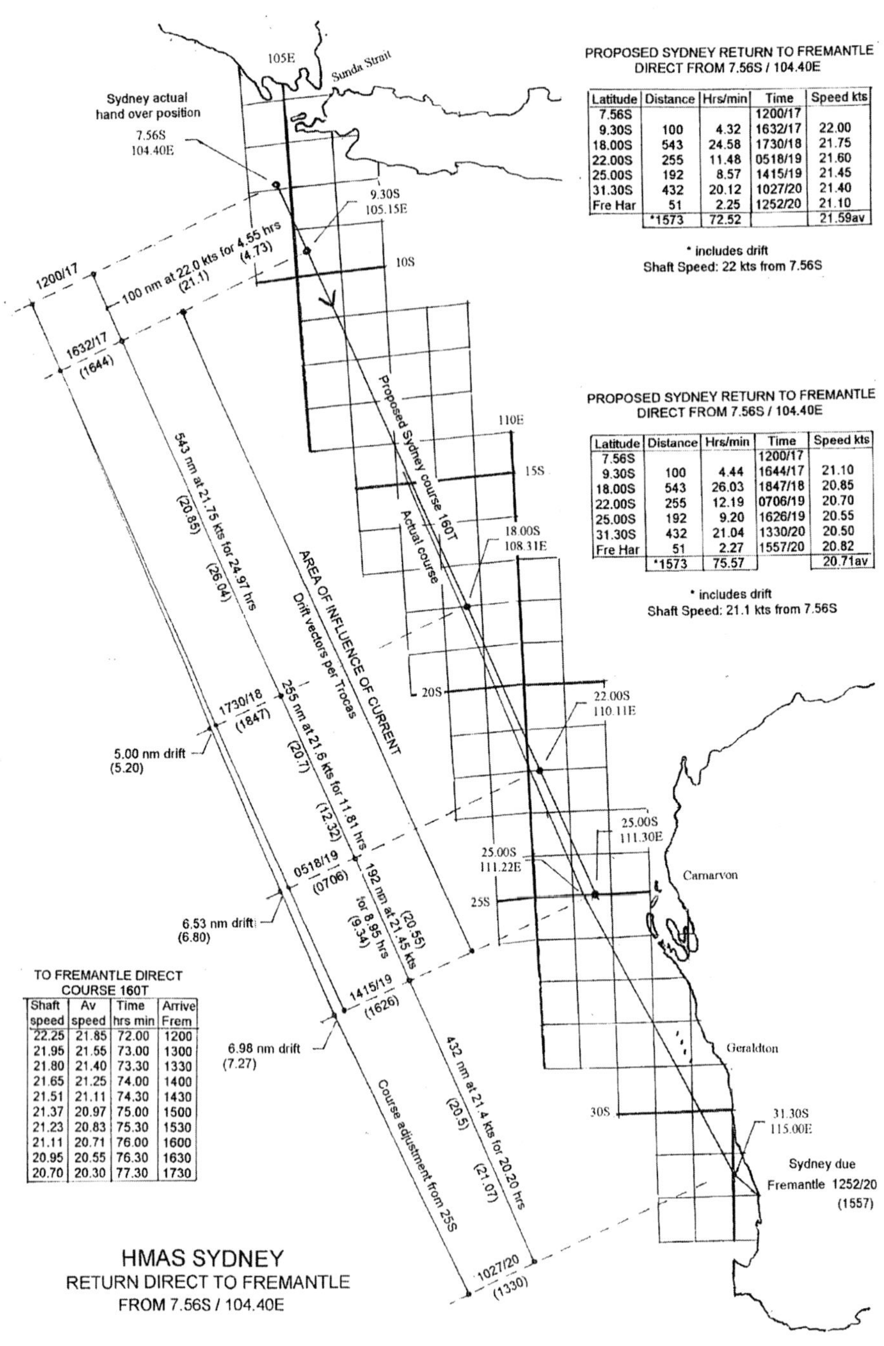

PROPOSED SYDNEY RETURN TO FREMANTLE
DIRECT FROM 7.56S / 104.40E

Latitude	Distance	Hrs/min	Time	Speed kts
7.56S			1200/17	
9.30S	100	4.32	1632/17	22.00
18.00S	543	24.58	1730/18	21.75
22.00S	255	11.48	0518/19	21.60
25.00S	192	8.57	1415/19	21.45
31.30S	432	20.12	1027/20	21.40
Fre Har	51	2.25	1252/20	21.10
	*1573	72.52		21.59av

* includes drift
Shaft Speed: 22 kts from 7.56S

PROPOSED SYDNEY RETURN TO FREMANTLE
DIRECT FROM 7.56S / 104.40E

Latitude	Distance	Hrs/min	Time	Speed kts
7.56S			1200/17	
9.30S	100	4.44	1644/17	21.10
18.00S	543	26.03	1847/18	20.85
22.00S	255	12.19	0706/19	20.70
25.00S	192	9.20	1626/19	20.55
31.30S	432	21.04	1330/20	20.50
Fre Har	51	2.27	1557/20	20.82
	*1573	75.57		20.71av

* includes drift
Shaft Speed: 21.1 kts from 7.56S

TO FREMANTLE DIRECT
COURSE 160T

Shaft speed	Av speed	Time hrs min	Arrive Frem
22.25	21.85	72.00	1200
21.95	21.55	73.00	1300
21.80	21.40	73.30	1330
21.65	21.25	74.00	1400
21.51	21.11	74.30	1430
21.37	20.97	75.00	1500
21.23	20.83	75.30	1530
21.11	20.71	76.00	1600
20.95	20.55	76.30	1630
20.70	20.30	77.30	1730

HMAS SYDNEY
RETURN DIRECT TO FREMANTLE
FROM 7.56S / 104.40E

A Plethora of Battle Locations

From the interrogation of the Germans, there were several battle locations given and these were generally between latitudes 25 and 27 South near longitude111 East, including an auspicious position of 150 nm southwest of Carnarvon. Positions near latitudes 26 and 28 South have also been identified by those near Port Gregory and Steep Point who thought they had witnessed an action off the coast, reminiscent of a naval battle. The RAN's official historian, George Herman Gill placed the position of the engagement at 26.40 South, 110.32 East (hereinafter referred as the Official Position), a similar position given by Detmers. The announcement by Prime Minister Curtin that the battle took place about 300 miles west of Carnarvon should be treated with caution because the prevailing north westerly current and wind drift could not have resulted in an easterly movement of the lifeboats and flotsam found much closer to the coast.

Not surprisingly, such a large search area has in the past made the task of identifying the engagement and wreck sites, most difficult. Nonetheless, it is essential to comprehensively examine the large area within the parameters of latitudes 25 and 28 South. Specifically, this can be accomplished by investigating a range or spread of tracks and speeds originating from the *Zealandia* hand-over position at 1200/17 and from the positions where *Sydney* may have departed *Largs Bay* at 1900/17, hereinafter referred to as positions of origin.

Using the current and speed variations established for *Aquitania* and *Trocas*, the extent of westerly lateral drift of *Sydney* at latitude 25 South can be calculated for a range of courses from the positions of origin. These derived longitudinal positions are significant because they establish the actual course sailed, defining the extended course southwards to where the northerly direction of the current is fairly constant. Although the speed of the vessel is further reduced southwards, the course of the vessel remains largely unaffected by the head- on current. However, vessels sailing inshore south along or near the Continental Shelf would normally experience a small increase in speed, due to the influence of the Leeuwin Current. Moreover, as the (westerly) drift is dependent on the angle between the prevailing current and the course sailed by the vessel from Sunda, the total drift at latitude 25 South becomes progressively larger when sailing further west of the coast.

In the case of *Sydney* sailing at about 20 knots from Sunda, the drift vectors applied for *Aquitania* and *Trocas*, show that the total average westerly drift at latitude 25 S increases from approximately 6nm at longitude 113 E to 9 nm at longitude 109 E in normal sea conditions. As the usual course adjustments to Fremantle were made near latitude 26 S or within sight of the coastline, *Sydney* would progress from latitudes 25 S to 26 S into the head-on current with little additional drift.

The range of courses available to Burnett all relate to the positions of origin. The longitudinal position(s) of *Sydney* at latitude 25 S from the hand-over position and from the *Largs Bay* departure positions, inclusive of drift, on tracks of from 157T to 167T intersect at 109.33E and 112.50E. *Sydney* could thus have been located at any point along this 179 nm wide strip, depending on the chosen course. Similarly, at longitude 26 S, the band extends from 109.51E to 113.00E (170 nm) – at longitude 27 S, from 110.46E to 113.13E (131nm) and at longitude 28 S, from 111.41E to 113.24 E (91nm). Although this defined area to be investigated exceeds 26,000 square nautical miles, positions which are outside these parameters can be largely dismissed, unless of course it is conceded that the positions identified by the German survivors are woefully inaccurate. (Refer to Diagram p 51)

In order to develop guidelines for *Sydney's* position at 1700/19, it is considered fundamental that a diverse range of speeds and courses from the three positions of origin should be assessed to determine whether any of the positions fall within the above parameters. If the designated 'despatch' shaft speeds (ss) of 21.1 knots and 25.9 knots for the range of courses from the positions of origin are applied, the results show that at 1700/19, *Sydney* could have been located in a range of positions across latitudes 25 S or 28 S. The northernmost location generally supports the German positions and the other, although marginally south of latitude 28 S, supports the observed naval action west of Port Gregory. However, the southernmost position requires a more detailed analysis.

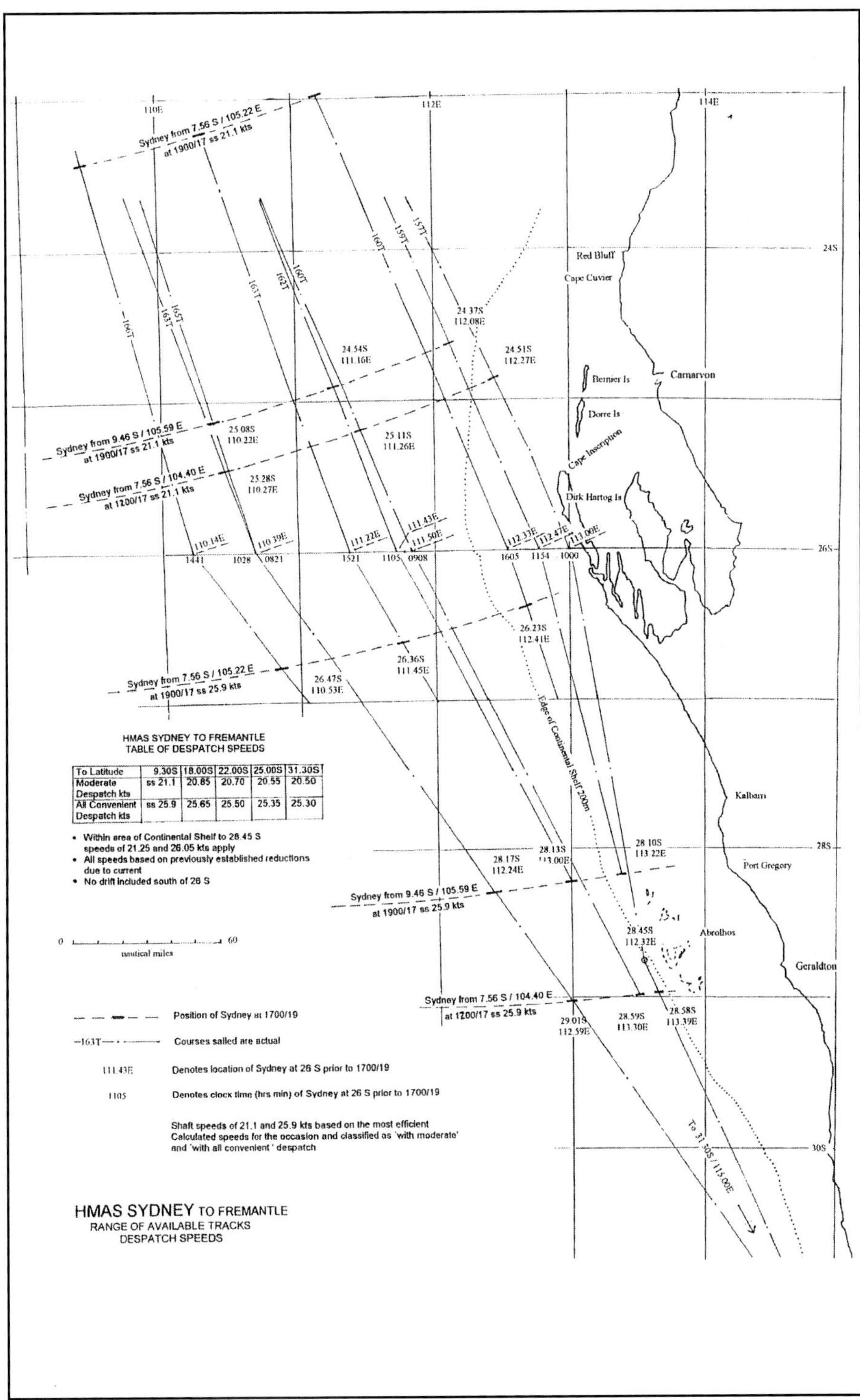

To Latitude	9.30S	18.00S	22.00S	25.00S	31.30S
Moderate Despatch kts	ss 21.1	20.85	20.70	20.55	20.50
All Convenient Despatch kts	ss 25.9	25.65	25.50	25.35	25.30

High Speed Return

On 20th November, a group of visitors, returned from Dirk Hartog Island and reported that a 'destroyer' at high speed was observed about 7nm west of the Island at 1000 hours the previous day. Interestingly, from the hand-over (origin) position at 1200/17, *Sydney* on course 157T to Cape Inscription at ss 25.9 knots, could have conceivably sailed to position 26 S / 113 E near the island at 1000 hours. Although this appears supportive of the reported sighting of the tug *Uco*, en route from Darwin to Fremantle and in the vicinity at that time, the issue has become clouded. [The simple distinction between a warship and a tug ought to be compelling evidence, though not necessarily conclusive] However, even at a reduced speed, *Sydney* could easily have progressed from Dirk Hartog to an area near the Abrolhos by 1700/19. In the case of the 1900/17 *Sydney* departure of *Largs Bay* from 9.46 S / 105.59 E at ss 25.9 knots, a more precise position, which approximates that of the 'observed' action off the coast is identified at 28.10 S / 113.22 E.

It must be conceded that Burnett would have been unlikely to adopt such a high constant speed, (with all convenient despatch) over such a long distance, unless he had received information of a suspicious ship in the area and he undertook to investigate. It is only within this context that consideration should be given to an engagement occurring in the vicinity of latitude 28 S. This possibility should also have regard for the timeframe and distance covered by the drifting lifeboats and other objects found more than 250 nm further north, the analysis of which will be undertaken later. Moreover, Burnett's stated ETA Fremantle is not considered relevant to this argument.

In assessing the possible despatch speeds by *Sydney* from the established points of origin, it is considered prudent to assume that the higher speed option (ss25.9) was not available to Burnett. However, in the case of *Sydney* waiting 3 hours for *Largs Bay* to arrive and after 2 hours escort, departing at 1900/17 in position 7.56 S / 105.22 E, there was no other alternative available if Burnett was to meet his afternoon ETA Fremantle. A reconstructed schedule shows that *Sydney*, already 7 hours behind schedule and at a sedate ss21.1 knots, could only sail to about latitude 23 S by 1700/19, 60nm north of where the survivors were rescued. In order to retrieve the time lost, *Sydney* would need to sail at ss24 knots to be placed south of the northward drifting lifeboats.

That a higher speed was sanctioned or was necessary is difficult to countenance. After all, the evidence suggests that the District Naval Officer in Fremantle was not unduly concerned about *Sydney's* non-arrival the following day, thereby acknowledging that Burnett had considerable discretion to search for and investigate suspicious shipping which could obviously result in a later arrival. In this regard, the 7 hour delay at Sunda would have meant an inconsequential late arrival at 2100 hours with no increase in speed required.

The question of whether *Sydney* increased speed after leaving *Largs Bay* can be logically assessed. If Burnett had no intention of escorting *Largs Bay* all the way to Fremantle and there was no apparent urgency to head south during the elapsed time until 1900/17, it is therefore unlikely Burnett had sought approval for an increase in speed to account for the lost time, or had received a late signal to warrant an urgent dispatch to a destination further south. Accordingly, and in consideration of the doubtful time of departure from Singapore as described earlier, there is only a remote possibility that *Sydney* could have terminated escort with *Largs Bay* at 1900/17 in position 7.56 S / 105.22 E.

At Despatch

The circumstances surrounding the departure of *Sydney* from *Largs Bay* at 1900/17 in position 9.46 S / 105.59 E are completely different. In this instance, that *Largs Bay* was already positioned south of *Sydney* at 1200/17, meant that Burnett would have experienced an insignificant delay in his return schedule. From the departure (origin) point, *Sydney* could sail the 1583 nm direct to Fremantle on course 162T at ss22 .69 knots (av22.25) and arrive early at 1200/20, or at the moderate despatch speed of ss21.1 knots (av20.66) for a later arrival at 1700/20. At latitude 25 S, *Sydney* would have been positioned at longitude 111.18 E, only 3.6 nm west of the 160T return track from the *Zealandia* hand-over position. This shows that from both points of origin, *Sydney* placed at between longitudes 111.18E and 111.22E.

Irrespective of the course sailed, the longitudinal position of *Sydney* at latitude 25 S and the time of arrival are the main factors that will ultimately determine the course and speed undertaken from Sunda. With respect to both of the direct routes from the *Zealandia* (160T) and *Largs Bay* (162T) positions, *Sydney* at ss21.1 knots would have arrived at latitude 25 S at 1626/19 and 1719/19 respectively. Therefore, the calculated positions of *Sydney* at 1700/19 when sighted by *Kormoran* are at 25.11 S / 111.26 E and 24.54 S / 111.16 E. If *Sydney* and *Kormoran* then proceeded in a westerly direction as indicated by the Germans, the location of the engagement at 1830 hours was in the vicinity of position 25 S / 111 E. Alternatively, if Burnett had chosen an easterly inshore course of say 157T, the engagement site was near 25 S / 112 E.

That the engagement occurred near latitude 25 S can be further clarified when the drift analysis of the flotsam is taken into account. However, it must be conceded that *Sydney's* return speed of ss21.1 knots is most appropriate, given this speed from both positions of origin would account for arrival times in Fremantle at between 1600 and 1700 hours. Although these arrival times do not compare favorably with the 1330 arrival at the same speed as originally planned, nevertheless, it is considered that the use of the 'moderate despatch' speed, based on engine (shaft speed) revolutions was likely to be employed on this occasion. For this reason, an engagement site near latitude 25 S should not be dismissed.

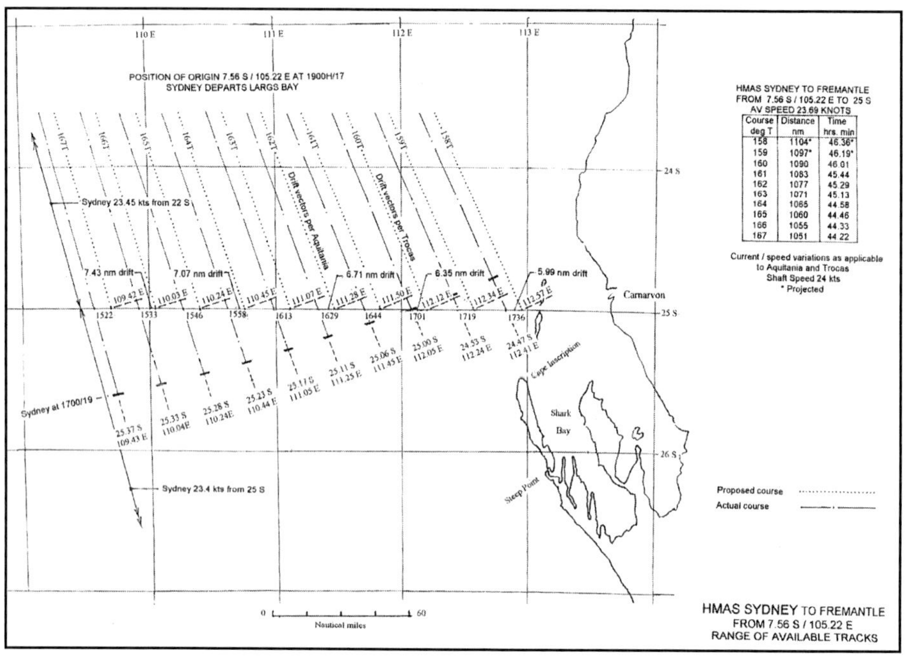

Course deg T	Distance nm	Time hrs. min
158	1104*	46.36*
159	1097*	46.19*
160	1090	46.01
161	1083	45.44
162	1077	45.29
163	1071	45.13
164	1065	44.58
165	1060	44.46
166	1055	44.33
167	1051	44.22

HMAS SYDNEY TO FREMANTLE
FROM 7.56 S / 105.22 E
RANGE OF AVAILABLE TRACKS

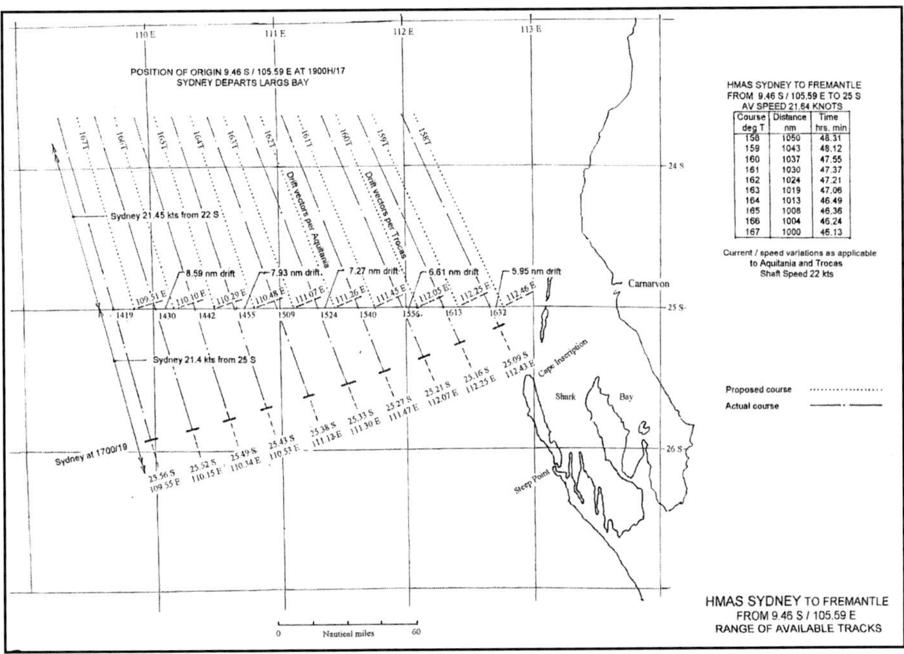

HMAS SYDNEY TO FREMANTLE
FROM 9.46 S / 105.59 E TO 25 S
AV SPEED 21.64 KNOTS

Course deg T	Distance nm	Time hrs. min
158	1050	48.31
159	1043	48.12
160	1037	47.55
161	1030	47.37
162	1024	47.21
163	1019	47.06
164	1013	46.49
165	1008	46.36
166	1004	46.24
167	1000	46.13

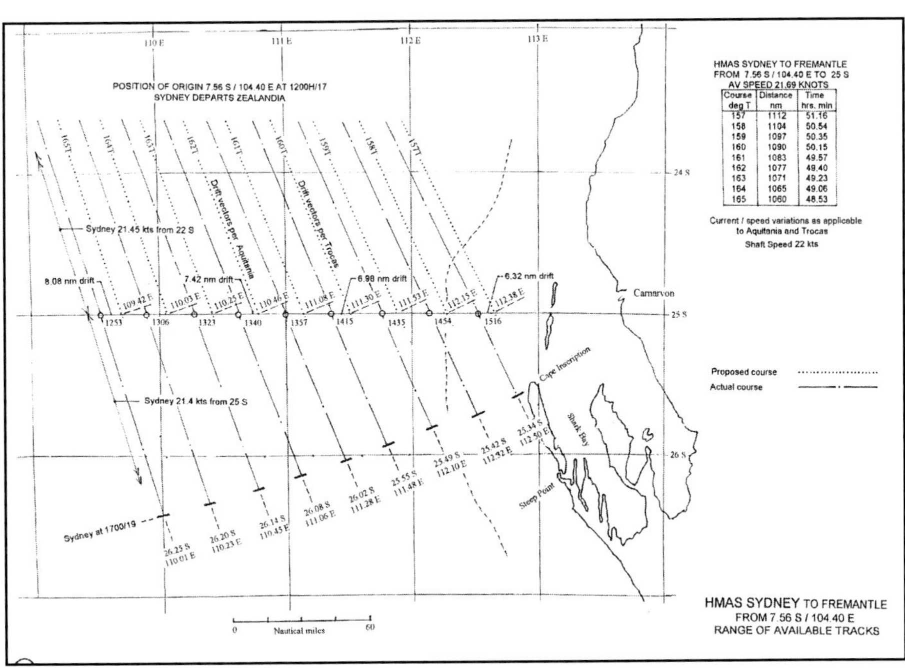

HMAS SYDNEY TO FREMANTLE
FROM 7.56 S / 104.40 E TO 25 S
AV SPEED 21.69 KNOTS

Course deg T	Distance nm	Time hrs. min
157	1112	51.16
158	1104	50.54
159	1097	50.35
160	1090	50.15
161	1083	49.57
162	1077	49.40
163	1071	49.23
164	1065	49.06
165	1060	48.53

Optimum Speed

An engagement site near latitude 26 S is the most commonly identified location. This location is generally attributed to Kormoran's Captain Detmers and Navigator Meyer and should therefore be subjected to thorough examination and assessed in terms of the following data:

The planned direct route to Fremantle from 7.15 S / 104.40 E indicates that an average speed of less than 21.85 knots (ss22.25) was required for an afternoon arrival in Fremantle. At ss21.1 knots, the actual time of arrival in accordance with the prevailing current velocity was 1330/20. However, Burnett's actual arrival time was always going to be later, due (in part) to the over- estimation of the velocity of the current while escorting *Zealandia* to Sunda.

Predictions for the Leeuwin Current vary, although Burnett probably had allowed for about 0.75 knots, thus ensuring a direct return to Fremantle from 7.15 S / 104.40 E (ss21.1) at 1400 hours. That Burnett probably placed little attention to maintaining a strict schedule as evidenced by his general expression of an 'afternoon' arrival, it is also conceivable that his planned arrival time may have been for some reason, significantly important. If a planned arrival at 1400 hours was contemplated, Burnett could select the speed required after allowing for the actual 0.6 knot velocity of the current experienced during the passage north to Sunda.

From the position of origin at 7.56 S / 104.40 E, a shaft speed of 21.65 knots (in accordance with the current and speed variations applicable to *Aquitania* and *Trocas*) was required to meet the same schedule.

At ss21.65 knots on direct course 160T to Fremantle, *Sydney* should have been in position 25.38 S / 111.37 E at 1700/19. Similarly, if a more convenient despatch of ss22.0 knots is applied, *Sydney* would have covered the 1090 nm in 50.25 hours at an average 21.69 knots and arrive at 1700/19 in position 25.55 S / 111.48 E. However, in this case *Sydney* would have arrived at Fremantle earlier at 1252 hours. If these shaft speeds are applied to a range of available tracks, it is evident that at 1700/19 *Sydney* would have been positioned near latitude 26 South.

The notion that *Sydney* intercepted *Largs Bay* provides an interesting comparison. From the position of origin of 9.46 S / 105.59 E when *Sydney* departed at 1900/17, a course selection of 162T would have provided for the most direct route to Fremantle. If Burnett intended to arrive at 1400 hours as shown previously, it is significant that with *Sydney* at ss22.0 knots, this schedule could also be met. In this instance at 1700/19, *Sydney* would be positioned at 25.33 S / 111.30 E. The other available tracks show *Sydney* at 1700/19 positioned equidistant between latitudes 25 S and 26 S. This revelation therefore lends support to the assertion of the incidental involvement of *Largs Bay* just 48 hours before the disappearance of *Sydney*. (Refer to Diagram p 58, 59)

In summary, the investigation into the likely whereabouts of *Sydney* at 1700/19 has only been possible with the application of the movements of *Zealandia, Aquitania and Trocas*. Accordingly, the affect of the current, the resultant speed variations and the impact of the westerly drift on *Sydney* have been applied. The positions of origin from the *Zealandi*a and *Largs Bay* departure points have been established, the range of available courses identified and the optimum speeds for *Sydney* assessed. However, an examination of the events preceding the engagement, the relative position of the action and a drift analysis of the lifeboats and debris is required to be undertaken to further confirm the location of *Sydney* at 1700/19.

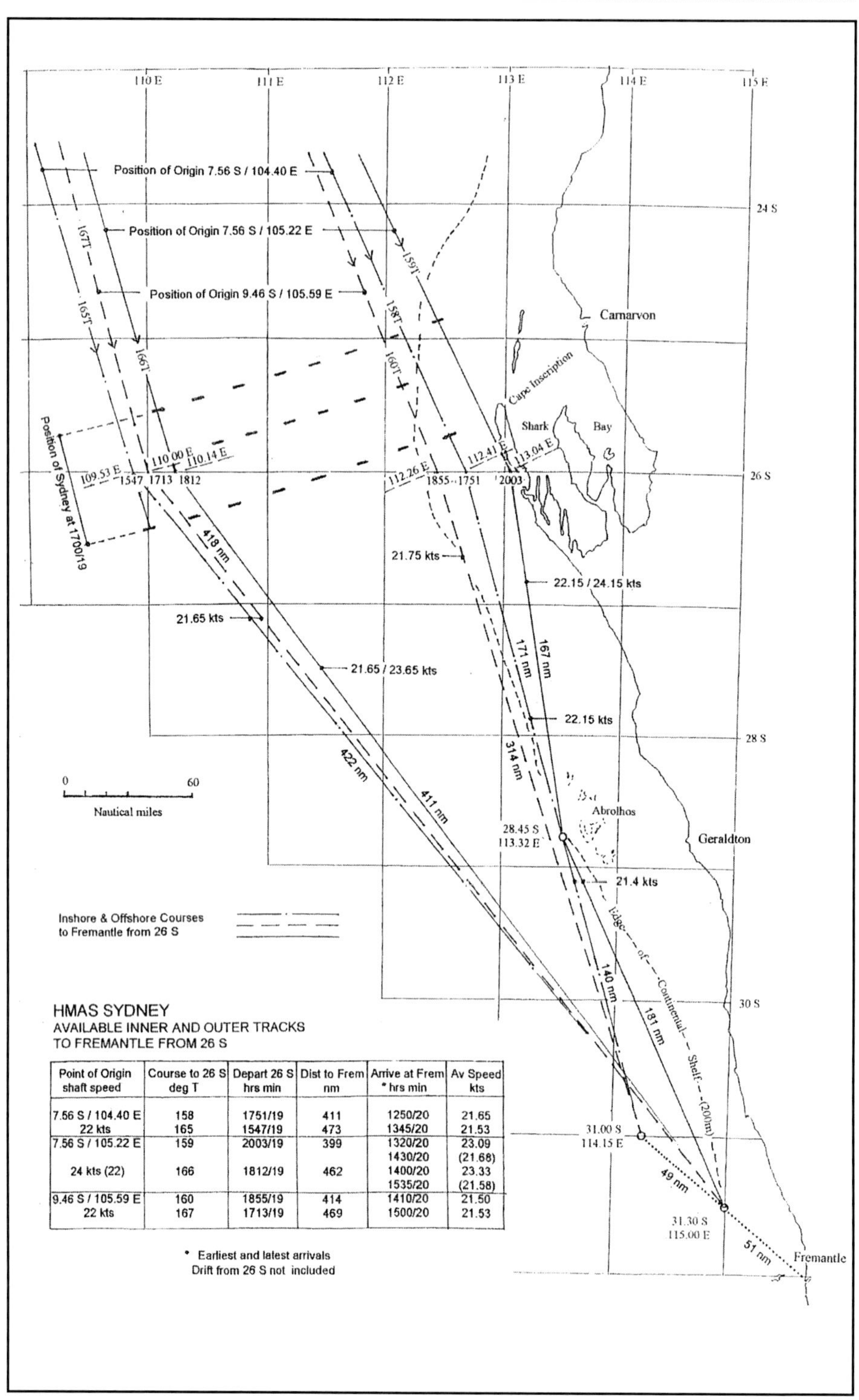

HMAS SYDNEY
AVAILABLE INNER AND OUTER TRACKS
TO FREMANTLE FROM 26 S

Point of Origin shaft speed	Course to 26 S deg T	Depart 26 S hrs min	Dist to Frem nm	Arrive at Frem * hrs min	Av Speed kts
7.56 S / 104.40 E	158	1751/19	411	1250/20	21.65
22 kts	165	1547/19	473	1345/20	21.53
7.56 S / 105.22 E	159	2003/19	399	1320/20	23.09
				1430/20	(21.68)
24 kts (22)	166	1812/19	462	1400/20	23.33
				1535/20	(21.58)
9.46 S / 105.59 E	160	1855/19	414	1410/20	21.50
22 kts	167	1713/19	469	1500/20	21.53

* Earliest and latest arrivals
Drift from 26 S not included

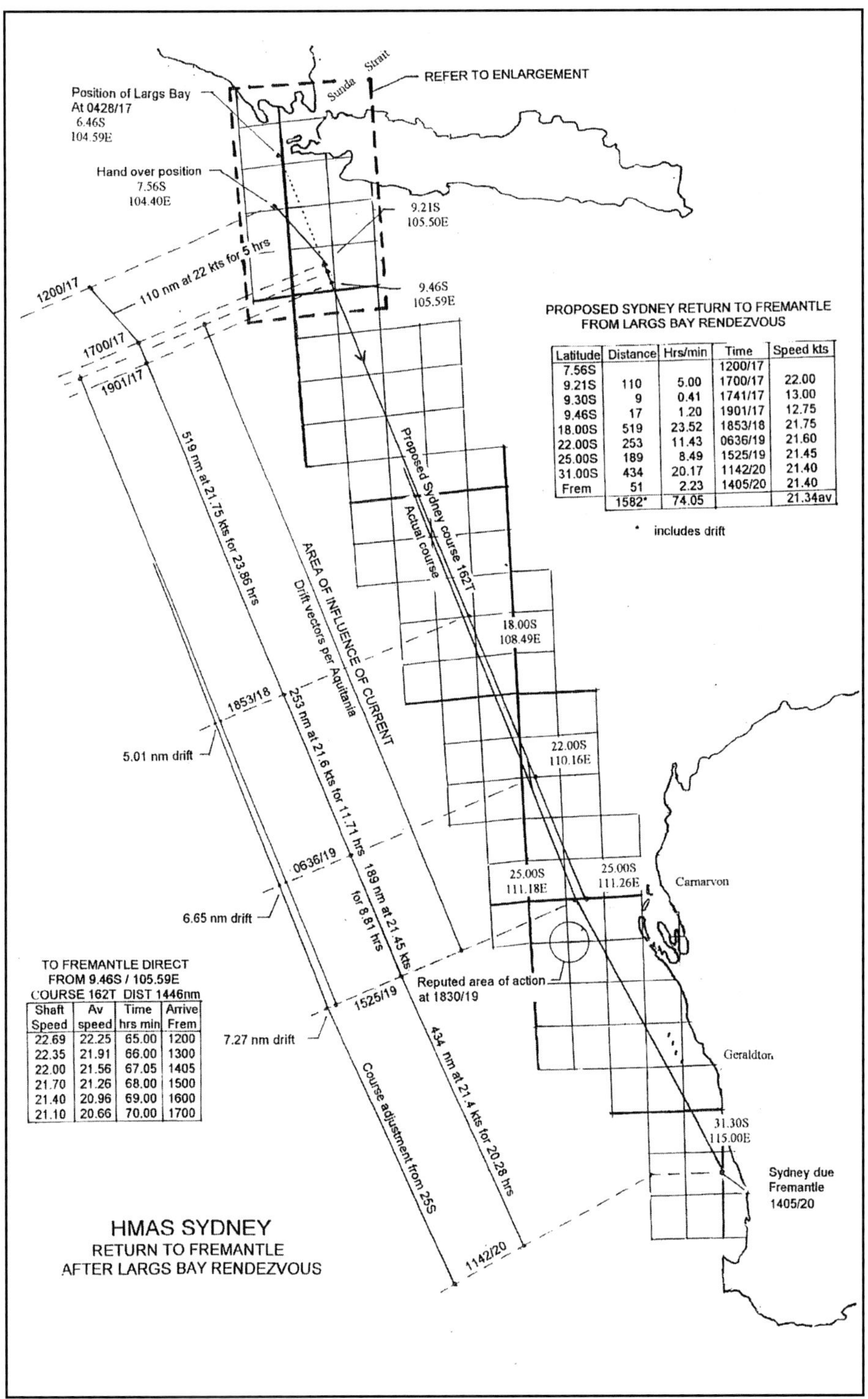

Latitude	Distance	Hrs/min	Time	Speed kts
7.56S			1200/17	
9.21S	110	5.00	1700/17	22.00
9.30S	9	0.41	1741/17	13.00
9.46S	17	1.20	1901/17	12.75
18.00S	519	23.52	1853/18	21.75
22.00S	253	11.43	0636/19	21.60
25.00S	189	8.49	1525/19	21.45
31.00S	434	20.17	1142/20	21.40
Frem	51	2.23	1405/20	21.40
	1582*	74.05		21.34av

Shaft Speed	Av speed	Time hrs min	Arrive Frem
22.69	22.25	65.00	1200
22.35	21.91	66.00	1300
22.00	21.56	67.05	1405
21.70	21.26	68.00	1500
21.40	20.96	69.00	1600
21.10	20.66	70.00	1700

ANALYSING THE ACTION

THE SEQUENCE of events preceding the encounter, the action and the destruction of *Kormoran* and *Sydney* can be largely attributed to the information contained within the Action Report prepared by Captain Detmers. After Detmers's escape from Dhurringile prison camp and his recapture, the Report he was carrying was later decrypted and translated and remains the only documented evidence of the action. In terms of accuracy, it should be noted that the Report is brief and only gives a general idea of the events and timeframes. Consequently, any assessment needs to take into account whether some of the detail may be designed to mislead or is just plainly fabricated. There is also a need to identify any obvious omissions and to assess the logical sequence of the Report. In this respect, it is therefore important to visualize the respective actions that Detmers and Burnett would logically take in the given circumstances. It is also considered that the Report should be interpreted, inclusive of more recent information obtained from other crewmembers of the *Kormoran*. A diagrammatic reconstruction of the timetable of events ultimately depicts a more accurate account of the action.

The Encounter

On 19th November at 1655H hours, the Kormoran lookout, Sub-Lieutenant Jansen sighted a vessel(s) in the distance ahead, bearing approx.020T. Kormoran had been steering 025T across the Sunda shipping lane at 11 knots in ideal sailing conditions with the wind from the SSE at about 15 knots and a moderate swell from the SW. When it was realised there may be more than one vessel involved, Detmers turned Kormoran away to port on course 250T and ordered full speed. Minutes later he identified the image as a Perth Class cruiser and simultaneous engine-failure reduced the speed of Kormoran to 14 knots. At about 1705 hours, the cruiser, more than 8 nm distant, changed course towards Kormoran.

This description of the first phase of the encounter may lack some intrinsic detail, but there is no evidence from other witnesses to suggest it is not an acceptable description of the events. That *Sydney* was the first to be detected is probably true, due to the relative position of the sun and the higher lookout vantage on *Kormoran*. In extremely clear conditions, *Sydney* could have been detected at about 20 nm. However, the late afternoon shimmering haze would have considerably reduced the sighting distance to the point where detection was only possible (with binoculars) when the main features of the vessel could almost be identified.

The use of 'Inman's Tables' used by mariners world- wide provides for an accurate distance to and below the horizon in accordance with the sighted height above sea level. When applied to the structural features of *Sydney* and *Kormoran*, an assessment of the likely distance between the ships, when first sighted, can be obtained. At 35 metres above sea level, *Kormoran's* lookout, Rudolf Jansen's vision to the horizon of 12.8 nm, could in principle include a further 11.9 nm below the horizon to *Sydney's* emerging 33 metre mast- head. At a combined approach speed of about 0.5 nm per minute (30 knots), *Sydney* had emerged 14 minutes later, 7 miles closer (now 17.7 nm apart) and only 5 metres below the horizon, revealing her complete superstructure and bow.

From the reconstruction of the timetable and from Inman's Tables it is calculated that Jansen should have sighted *Sydney* 17.7 nm distant, irrespective of the problems associated with light refraction and glare. In contrast to the 8 nm distance stated in the Report, the separation at 1705 hours would have been about 14.5 nm, with *Sydney* closing at despatch speed of ss28.2 knots until 1745 hours. A minimum sighting distance can be calculated in accordance with the expectation that *Sydney* was moving at a predictable 21 knots when contact was made and approached *Kormoran* at the same speed. Consequently, *Sydney* would have been sighted at 13nm, with 10 nm separating the vessels at 1705 hours. Interestingly, this compares with the lookout distance to the horizon of 12..8 nm when *Sydney's* features had fully emerged. To avoid the risk of subjectively nominating a firm sighting distance in the quest to find the location of *Sydney*, it is considered prudent to allow for an ambit of sighting distances within the range of 13 to 17.7 nautical miles. (Refer to Diagram p 62)

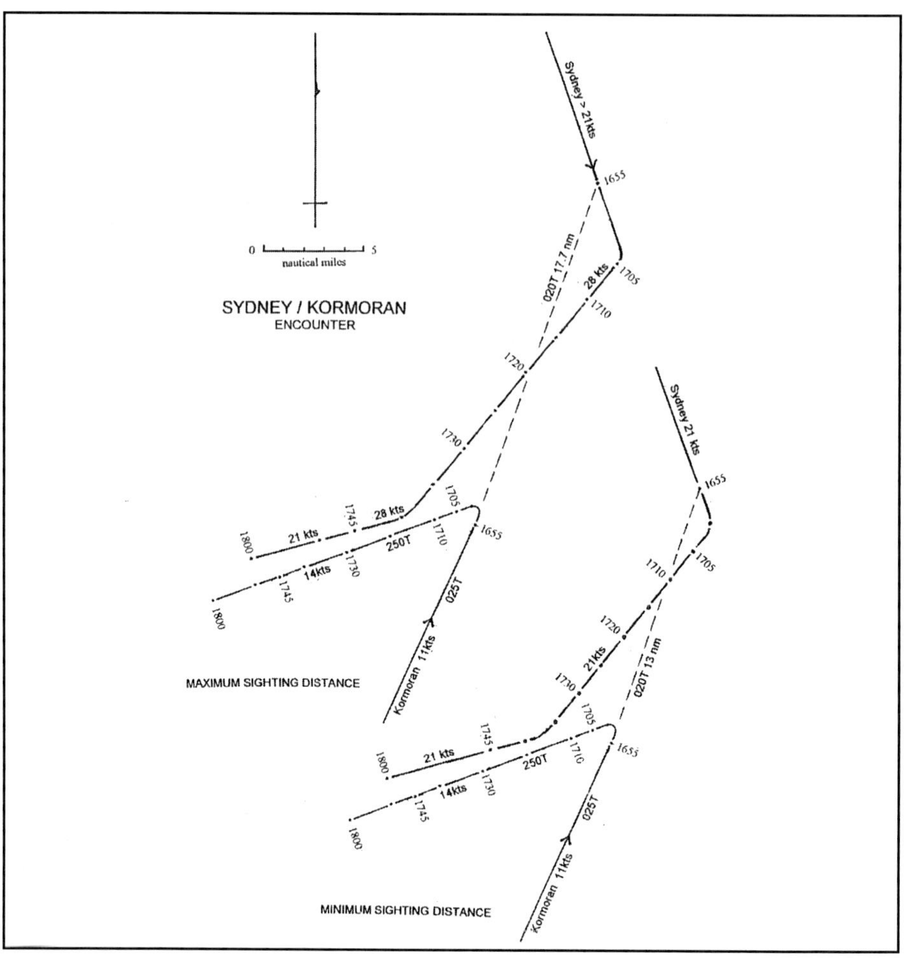

If *Kormoran* was observed by those aboard *Sydney* to suddenly change course, it should have alerted Burnett of the doubtful bona fides of the vessel. His suspicions should have increased if *Kormoran* had been observed sailing an unusual track away from the Sunda route. That *Kormoran* changed course into the sun could also have caused Burnett to construe that the vessel ahead was deliberately trying to avoid contact. Regardless of the circumstances, Burnett, having sighted the vessel, was destined to alter course and investigate, as he had done on previous occasions.

The reason for *Kormoran's* location near the Sunda shipping lane can not be satisfactorily explained. *Kormoran* had recently been replenished by the supply ship *Kulmerland* three weeks prior and had since undertaken some necessary repairs. Detmers's claim that he intended to lay some of the 300 burdensome mines on board near Shark Bay was not corroborated by his mines officer, Heinz Messerschmidt. No other crewmember could offer an adequate reason for *Kormoran's* appearance in this area. The fact that Detmers never even suggested that his presence in the area was to search for and sink allied shipping is indicative that there was some other reason for being there.

In November 1941, the Sunda shipping lane was used by few vessels and regarded as a minor shipping route. Even so, Detmers would have thought it worthwhile to scour for allied merchant ships and he was probably aware that large troopships had recently sailed the Sunda route. If information on the movements of these ships became available from German Intelligence, they would surely have become a prime target. On the 11th November, the troopship *Aquitania* arrived in Singapore en route to Sydney.

Aquitania was to undergo hull maintenance before departure and then sail the Sunda lane unescorted, for a scheduled arrival at Fremantle on the 18th November. The voyage of 110 hours indicates a planned departure from Singapore early on the morning of the 14th November. If this schedule was to be met, *Aquitania*, after 86 hours sailing, would reach latitudes 24 and 25 South late in the afternoon of the 17th November. In order to intercept, Detmers would require confirmation of the departure time of *Aquitania*, so that *Kormoran* could be positioned for action at the required time.

The appearance of *Kormoran* in the same vicinity two days later, could have indicated that Detmers had received information on *Aquitania's* delayed departure and decided to maintain *Kormoran* on station in the general area where *Aquitania* was later expected. In the meantime, Detmers would obviously have avoided any contact or engagement with any vessels along or near the Sunda route. He was obviously aware that any attack on the much faster *Aquitania* would be extremely difficult to arrange, requiring intricate planning, timing and considerable luck.

The Interception

The interception phase of the encounter involves *Sydney's* pursuit of *Kormoran* from 1705 to 1745 hours, during which both ships exchanged signals. Detmers's Action Report describes: ***Sydney* approaches and signals 'NNJ'. *Kormoran* signals by flag her *Straat Malakka* identity.** This period is contentious because of the variety of evidence given on the nature of the signals. Detmers probably would have made an attempt to transmit a distress signal after *Sydney* was identified and had changed course to intercept. If in fact a brief signal was made, it was surely in the enigma raider code and on a frequency undetected by *Sydney*.

During the pursuit, Burnett could be expected to make the necessary signals to quickly establish the identity of the vessel, and if satisfied, resume course to Fremantle. However, at a safe distance, a visual inspection of the vessel would prove difficult if the vessel maintained the westerly course into the glare of the sun. In the event that *Sydney* was not immediately sighted upon signaling, Burnett would need to allow the vessel time to reply.

Kormoran's Yeoman of Signals Erich Ahlbach recounted, that because there was confusion about the meaning of the 'NNJ' signal continuously flashed by *Sydney*, there was an unavoidable delayed response in acknowledging 'PQKI', the signal letters for '*Straat Malakka*'. Having established the identity, it would seem logical for *Sydney* to have then requested the vessels' destination, cargo and last port of call. According to Ahlbach, the given destination was Batavia, whereas Lieutenant von Gosseln nominated Lourenco Marques.

At 1745 hours, Burnett should have had sufficient reason to be suspicious of the bona fides of the vessel he was chasing. The vessel continued to be evasive in maintaining speed (14 knots) and course directly into the sun, had made no attempt to slow and had taken longer than expected to reply to his signals. His suspicions must have heightened when he found that the Dutch registered *Straat Malakka* was not included on the regular VAI (list of ships in the area) and therefore unlikely to have recently sailed from an Australian port. Considering that axis warships were not present in the Indian Ocean at that time, Burnett would have wondered why a Dutch merchant ship would show tardiness in replying to signals and continue an attempt to evade what was obviously a British cruiser.

Burnett must have been perplexed by the destination of the *Straat Malakka*. Although he could accept that merchant ships may instinctively turn away on sighting a warship, most would, after mutual confirmation of identities, signal (in case a sudden move is construed as hostile) a resumption of course. However, this vessel was intent on maintaining a westerly course away from Batavia. Also, if Burnett was cognizant of the original (025T) NNE course of the *Straat Malakka*, the Batavia destination (approx. 340T) could not be substantiated. Moreover, the unusual course (from where) to Lourenco Marques should have confirmed Burnett's suspicions. Burnett therefore had more than enough reasons to maintain Sydney at action stations until the *Straat Malakka* had been positively identified.

From 1745 to 1800 hours, the Action Report continues: ***Sydney* continues signaling, approx. 8000 metres away, approaching slowly on starboard quarter, *Kormoran* maintaining 14 knots.** The reconstruction of the interception shows that because *Sydney* was rapidly closing at 28 knots, Burnett was compelled to reduce speed to 21 knots at 1745 hours to avoid approaching the vulnerable position abeam of the suspicious ship. This speed would provide more time to exchange signals and hopefully confirm the identity of the *Straat Malakka*. As *Sydney* was on a diverging course away from the vessel ahead, Burnett would have been concerned that from his position, the obstruction of the sun would have continued to make visual identification difficult.

If Detmers's Report stating that the separation distance of 4.3 nm (8000 metres) at 1745 hours is accepted, by 1800 hours, *Sydney* was about 2.85 nm (5200 metres) off the starboard quarter of *Straat Malakka*, an exposed position if the vessel ahead was to suddenly change course to starboard. Burnett would therefore not have considered ordering the vessel to stop, unless his suspicions were confirmed and a bows-on approach could be made when there was greater distance between the ships. Consequently, in order to resolve the identification impasse, it was necessary to inspect the vessel from a safer distance and compare the side silhouette features with that contained in the Shipping Register.

The ensuing section of the Action Report requires considerable interpolation. However, it effectively dismantles the previously accepted description and sequence of events, which resulted in the undue criticism of Burnett's tactics and tarnished reputation. The false account provided by Detmers, misled the Australian authorities and researchers into believing that the disaster was caused by Burnett recklessly drawing *Sydney* close and abeam of *Kormoran*. The story portrays both vessels sailing at 14 knots, *Kormoran's* sudden decamouflage and the accurate gunfire and torpedo strike which lead to the demise of *Sydney*. This was seen as a simple, believable and logical explanation. However, this motive was actually designed by Detmers to limit further investigation into the matter and to conceal the truth and the illegality of his actions.

The Reconnaissance

In contrast to the rather predictable events up to 1800 hours, the remainder of the Action Report requires careful interpretation and reasoning. A more accurate perspective of events can be gained by assessing the actions likely to be taken in each circumstance by Detmers and Burnett, together with the more recent evidence available and within the parameters of the Report. ***Kormoran* sends QQQ distress signals by wireless at 1800 hours. At 1815 hours, *Sydney* positioned 9000 metres on *Kormoran's* starboard beam.**

During this 15 minute period, it must be conceded that a lot more happened than is described in the Report. At 1800 hours, Burnett had already decided to conduct a visual examination from a distance, which would hopefully draw a reaction from the *Straat Malakka*. He also signaled in morse for the secret *Straat Malakka* call sign. (Detmers said this occurred at 1825 hours - being unable to reply was the reason given for firing on *Sydney*) *Sydney* was then turned to course 290T so all guns could bear, made ready the walrus seaplane for launching, increased speed to 28 knots and made off in a WNW direction. Detmers would have been alarmed, as this reconnaissance would place *Sydney* in a more favourable position and the *Straat Malakka* disguise was likely to be exposed. At 1803 and 1805 hours, Detmers ordered the transmission of QQQ distress signals in anticipation.

The first message, partly intercepted by the tug Uco south of Shark Bay and the second, by Geraldton Radio, appeared to include the respective positions of 26S / 111E and 27S / 111.15E. In consideration of his predicament, Detmers's priority was to signal his approximate position to Germany. That he subsequently decided to send a false message, signifying that a merchant ship was in trouble further to the south, he was hoping that *Sydney* would be distracted from its immediate task and subsequently investigate.

The first signal sent, probably at low frequency, should have made reference to the '*Straat Malakka*,' and would not necessarily have been detected within close proximity, whereas, the second signal directed at *Sydney* with intent, would obviously not have included the name of the vessel. If *Sydney* somehow picked up the first signal, Burnett would have the confirmation that he was currently dealing with an enemy merchant raider or supply ship. [supply ships would normally be confined to isolated areas and kept clear of recognised shipping lanes] The false signal can only be described as a futile attempt to avoid the inevitable, but it was worth a try.

It must be emphasized that even though *Kormoran* wireless operators Hans Linke and Ernst Pachmann attested that the first signal contained the position of 26S / 111E, it should only be regarded as an approximate location. In this circumstance, an approximate position given was sufficient. After all, Detmers knew there was no possibility of intervention or rescue in this area by an Axis ship that may have intercepted his distress call and in this regard, a more precise position was superfluous.

After the transmission of the signals, the subsequent actions taken by Burnett can be logically predicated. On the other hand, the sequence of events and the actions taken by Detmers as outlined in the Action Report are found to be demonstrably inaccurate. This becomes evident when comparing the relative movements of *Sydney* and *Kormoran* within the designated timeframes shown in the Report and further – substantiated by scaled diagram. (Refer to Diagram p 68)

Shortly after Burnett was made aware of the signal(s) emanating from the *Straat Malakka*, he had no other option than to order the vessel to maintain heading and stop while he completed his observations. At 1807 hours, *Sydney*, at 28 knots and positioned about 6500 metres away, was now in a position for Burnett to observe the emerging silhouette of the vessel. With his crew at action stations, Detmers did not immediately issue an order to stop when the sudden but not unexpected demand was made. However, he knew he would have to comply, and if the opportunity arose, he would contemplate unleashing *Kormoran's* considerable starboard firepower, consisting of 4 x 150mm guns. In hindsight, Detmers would have conceded that he was foolish to create further suspicion to order that the distress signals be sent.

At 1809 hours, Burnett and his officers were satisfied that the physical characteristics of the stern, super-structure and the estimated tonnage of the vessel now 7300 metres away did not match those shown for *Straat Malakka* in the VAI. There was also no response from the demand for the secret call sign. Burnett was now convinced he was dealing with an enemy ship and with caution, it was possible to capture it. In order to provoke some response from the vessel now 7800 metres distant and slowed to 12 knots, Burnett would have had no option other than to order *Sydney's* Gunnery officer Michael Singer, to range the guns and fire at, or near the vessel. [Several of the *Kormoran* crew rescued by *Aquitania* insisted *Sydney* fired first, from a distance]

Detmers was not prone to suicidal tendencies - he had the welfare of his crew to consider. His ship carried no armor protection, had 300 mines on board, hundreds of 150 mm shells with cordite, torpedoes, thousands of smaller munitions and 2000 tons of fuel, a recipe for disaster. As there was no alternative, at 1812 hours, with the ships nearly 9000 metres apart, the surrender is formalised. [The mode of surrender may have consisted of lowering the ships' ensign, hoisting a white flag, or signaling by flag or lamp - *Sydney* may have also issued a warning advising against attempts to scuttle]

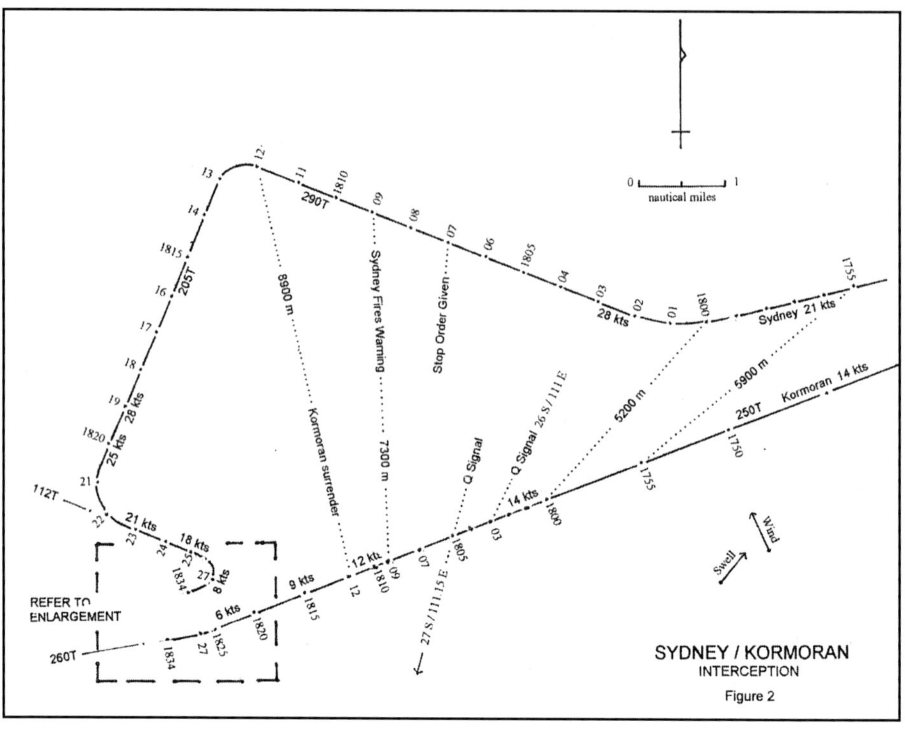

Figure 2

The Final Approach

The Action Report from 1815 to 1830 hours, during the approach of *Sydney* is bereft of any significant detail, such as the relative positions and movement of the vessels and merely refers to: **1825 hours – *Sydney* requests secret call sign. *Sydney* stops, completely unaware of *Kormoran's* disguise.**

It is obvious here that Detmers was seeking the credit for his surprise tactics. The brevity of the description would allow him to insert his personal thoughts and opinions, should he be later requested to provide further information. That the call sign was requested at this late stage when the vessels were only about 1700 metres apart and with Burnett oblivious to any danger, is incredulous.

After the surrender, the priority for Burnett was to board and capture the *Straat Malakka* as quickly as possible to prevent scuttling. *Sydney* maintained 28 knots and altered course (205T) into the SW swell to close the *Straat Malakka*, which at 1815 hours had reduced speed to 9 knots. At 1820 hours, *Sydney*, less than 5000 metres to the NW, reduced speed to 25 knots and made another turn to approach from the WNW (approx.112T) and reduced speed to 14 knots, before turning in a tight arc to starboard and rapidly losing speed into the swell. The seaplane's engine was shut down and preparations hurriedly made for boarding. By 1834 hours, *Sydney* was barely maintaining heading into the swell and nearly stopped.

From the moment of surrender, it was not too difficult for Detmers to anticipate the directional approach by *Sydney.* Detmers decided to slow *Kormoran* gradually, rather than to stop immediately as instructed, because this measure would provide more time to assess the situation and plan for a possible assault on *Sydney.* At 1815 hours, *Kormoran* had reduced to 9 knots and at 1820, maintained 6 knots to 1825 when *Sydney* was 1700 metres abeam. Detmers would need to select the speed required to maneuver slowly ahead of *Sydney* in order to deploy the starboard underwater torpedo, angled 35 deg abaft the beam. To achieve this, Detmers ordered a subtle course alteration from 250T to 260T at 1827 hours and by 1834 *Kormoran* was just making headway and suitably positioned about 1000 metres from *Sydney* and ready for action.

In contrast to the official and historical account, the Action Report effectively changes the complexion of the encounter. The movement of *Sydney* out to 9000 metres, indicates that the pattern of approach within the given timeframe, could not have been regular or sustained. At 1815 hours, *Sydney* (28 knots) was abeam of *Kormoran* (9 knots) and thereafter until 1825, *Sydney*, then at 18 knots, could only have been westward of *Kormoran* (6 knots). Further evidence for this approach was obtained from wireless operator, Hans Linke, who stated that the track of *Sydney* was in the form of an arc, before the approach was made from the west.

The time-line diagram confirms the reconnaissance by *Sydney* out to 9000 metres, the respective speeds and reductions by both vessels, the positions of each vessel every minute, the approach from the west and the general locale of the engagement.

The view of *Sydney* from *Kormoran* moments before the action began.
At nearly 1000 metres separation, the respective targets would have appeared about half the size.

The Engagement

At the moment of action, the Report describes: **1830 hours – *Kormoran* de-camouflaged, Kriegsmarine flag hoisted, guns and torpedoes ready in 6 seconds, Speed 14 knots, *Sydney* drops astern, change to 260T, 2 torpedoes inclination 80.** These events are not necessarily in the order of occurrence. Here, Detmers displays self- gratification and the efficiency of his crew. He thought it was advisable to show he had observed the international rules of engagement before battle by declaring his identity.

Some degree of embellishment of the Report is to be expected, but the 6 seconds taken to reach a state of readiness for action is demonstrably impossible. The flag hoist, announcing the start of the engagement is a curious action to have taken while in surrender mode. With *Kormoran* about to undertake a surprise attack, it is inconceivable that the German flag would be raised before action to give the enemy even a hint of a warning. In this circumstance, the element of surprise could only be retained without raising the flag before firing had commenced. Moreover, if Detmers chose to secret the unlawful action and the national identity of his ship, it is conceivable that the battle flag was not raised at all.

Detmers specifically nominates the use of 2 torpedoes, which was obviously meant to indicate that only the starboard deck torpedoes were used and to conceal the fact that *Kormoran* could deploy an underwater torpedo from the starboard beam. He was aware that any mention of the underwater torpedo could have conveyed the impression that it was launched prior to *Kormoran's* declaration. Due to the amount of explosive material on board, *Kormoran* was placed in a vulnerable position should *Sydney* open fire first. He therefore had no alternative than to use all the firepower available to prevent, or at least limit retaliation from *Sydney*. In these circumstances, it is logical to assume that all three torpedoes were used, firstly, the underwater torpedo, (before declaring) followed by the deck torpedoes, the launching of which would likely be observed by the crew of *Sydney*. In a worse case scenario, if Detmers failed to deploy the third torpedo, he may not have ever had the opportunity to use it.

At 1834 hours, *Sydney* was almost stopped and only just maintaining headway into the SW swell while preparations were being made to lower the port-side cutter for boarding. The surrendered *Kormoran*, about 1000 metres to the leeward and making about 2 knots was in position to launch the underwater torpedo and unleash the guns. This scene is completely at odds with Detmer's description of the prelude to the action, in which he describes both vessels steaming at 14 knots. This scenario was of necessity and meant to be a plausible explanation that would not attract any suggestion he had previously surrendered and that his actions may have contravened the protocols of international law. Nevertheless, it is difficult to imagine Burnett or any other commander taking the surrender for granted or submitting to a reduced state of readiness.

Because of the explosiveness of *Kormoran's* 'cargo', the assault on *Sydney* would require complete surprise and delicate timing. Detmers was therefore acutely aware that the fate of *Kormoran* would essentially be determined by the effectiveness of the surprise underwater torpedo, which was to be released before any declaration was made. The torpedo would take just over a minute to cover the 1000 metres to reach *Sydney* and with no certainty of hitting the target. The deck torpedoes, targeting the bow and stern of *Sydney*, were likely to be detected during launch and would be deployed when the full- scale attack began.

The reason given by Detmers for making a slight change of course from 250T to 260T was 'so that the guns were not obstructed'. However, his and torpedo officer, Joachim Greter's main concern ought to have been that the launch and track of the deck torpedoes traveling across the swell would likely be affected. In this respect, the decision to change course was designed to reduce the problem, with a resultant increase in accuracy.

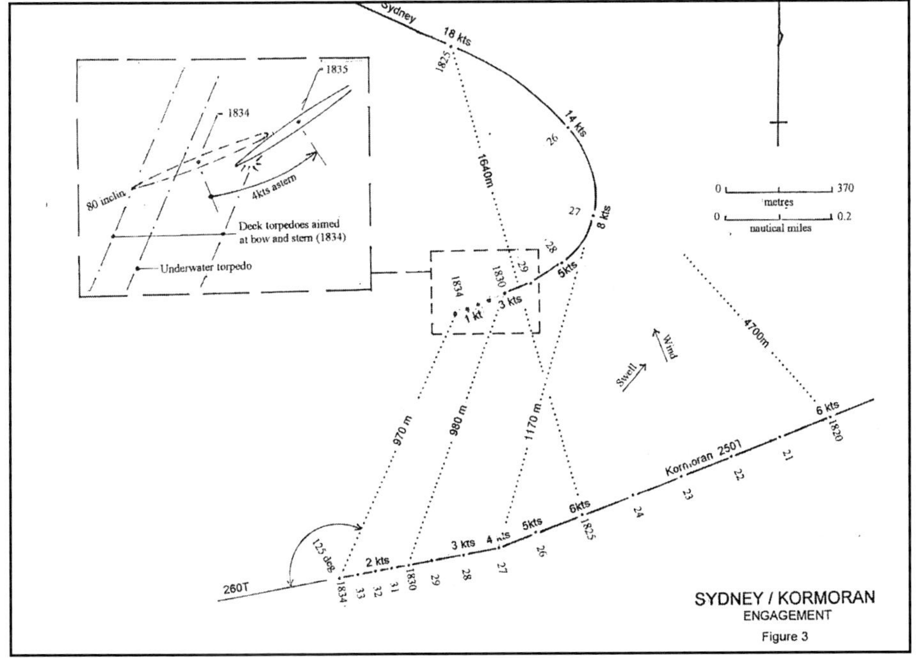

Action Begins

According to Detmers, the bulk of the action takes place over a five minute period, the Action Report describing the artillery duel and then the torpedo strike: ***Kormoran* fires first salvo (1 gun) short - range 1300 metres, second salvo (3 guns) – range 1700 metres, hits on bridge and director control before *Sydney* salvo (8 guns) fires over *Kormoran*. More salvoes hit amidships, seaplane amid firing of anti-aircraft, anti-tank and machine guns - no hits from *Sydney* while *Kormoran* fires 5 salvoes until C turret scores hits in funnel, engine room, turrets A and B silent. After 9th salvo torpedo strikes *Sydney*, top of B turret flies overboard, other torpedo passes ahead.**

These events personify Detmers's moment of glory in an amazing one-sided contest, whose actions after having surrendered can be alternatively seen as infamous. It must be conceded that his actions were instigated by the confidence he placed in the accurate delivery of his concealed underwater torpedo to secure the element of surprise. The Report displays his cool and efficient manner and of his crew and had the occasion allowed, purposely designed to impress his superiors in Germany. Detmers's account therefore merits close scrutiny and interpolation.

Detmers unmistakably describes that *Sydney* was unprepared for the onslaught from *Kormoran*. After all, he had no other option than to convey this impression; otherwise it would have been impossible to explain the sudden demise of the superior British cruiser at the hands of a merchant raider. The notion that Burnett mistook the *Straat Malakka* for an unarmed raider supply ship should not have contributed to a relaxed state of readiness. Moreover, the most perplexing issue in Detmers's version of events is the inability of *Sydney's* guns to find the target at such close range, a scenario which could only indicate that the inaccuracy was due to damage sustained from the torpedo strike made before the salvoes from *Sydney* were fired. Furthermore, in claiming that the survival of *Kormoran* was due to the woeful inaccuracy of *Sydney's* gunnery, Detmers is further concealing the fact that the torpedoes were released and his guns had fired before he had declared identity. Also, that 80 of his crewmen perished, is symptomatic of *Sydney* having incurred much greater damage to *Kormoran*. (According to Detmers, approx. 80 mainly wounded crewmen drowned when their liferaft capsized)

It is ironic that Detmers's account should, in hindsight, unwittingly reveal the reality of the first stage of the engagement wherein he describes the tracks of the torpedoes. In accepting that the torpedoes were accurately targeted (bow and stern) when *Sydney* was almost stopped, he states that one struck near the forward turrets and the other passed ahead of *Sydney*. This obviously means that the stern- targeted torpedo made the contact towards the bow, a distance of some 130 metres from the original point of aim. This demonstrates that *Sydney* had been moving astern in avoidance when torpedoed, thus indicating the torpedoes had been sighted in transit, or observed during launching. If *Sydney* moved 130 metres astern while the torpedo at 27 knots covered the 1000 metres in 72 seconds, then *Sydney's* average speed astern is calculated at 3.5 knots. It also shows that unless in the unlikely event the underwater torpedo was targeted at the stern, it could not have made contact with *Sydney* and was sure to pass ahead. Moreover, in the case of *Sydney* moving forward, the torpedo directed at the bow would have made contact, but the other would pass astern.

When *Sydney* was stopped and holding position into the swell, *Kormoran* would be presented with the simplest target and there would be reason to believe that more than one torpedo could have struck *Sydney*. This situation was actually supported by *Kormoran* laundryman, Shu Ah Fah, who claimed that *Sydney* was struck by three torpedoes. If this had occurred, it would have instantly delivered *Sydney* a mortal blow and as a result, rendered the rest of the Action Report, a complete fabrication. It is inconceivable that three torpedoes launched from an extreme distance of 1000 metres could have been so accurately deployed.

In addition to the torpedo strike, *Sydney* received a severe battering from the heavy guns and smaller caliber weapons. Speculation that *Sydney* exploded as a result of such devastating firepower is supported by gun-layer, Gustav Albers, who claimed that after the cruiser blew up and the smoke cleared, there was only floating wreckage. Although his observation is at odds with Detmers's Report and the views of most other crewmembers, it is accepted that the confines of the *Sydney* search area should also include the locale of the engagement site.

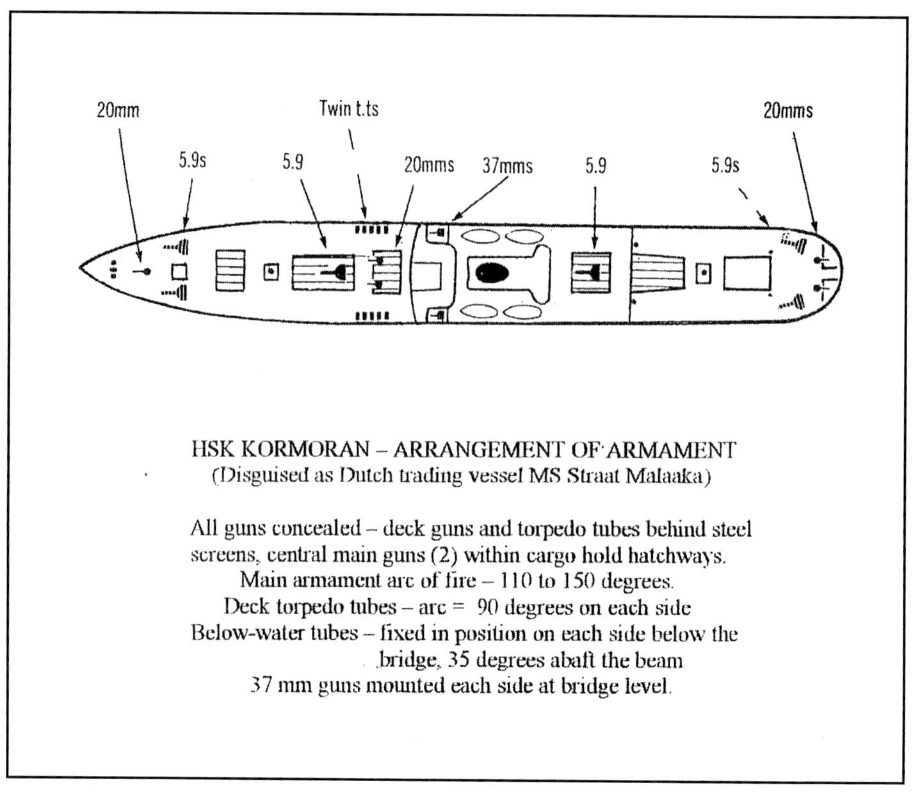

HSK KORMORAN – ARRANGEMENT OF ARMAMENT
(Disguised as Dutch trading vessel MS Straat Malaaka)

All guns concealed – deck guns and torpedo tubes behind steel screens, central main guns (2) within cargo hold hatchways.
Main armament arc of fire – 110 to 150 degrees.
Deck torpedo tubes – arc = 90 degrees on each side
Below-water tubes – fixed in position on each side below the bridge, 35 degrees abaft the beam
37 mm guns mounted each side at bridge level.

Action: 1835 to 1900 Hours

After the initial engagement, the action continues, albeit less intense for another hour, during which *Sydney* moves evasively to minimize exposure to *Kormoran's* gunnery and then belatedly launches an attack. The Action Report outlines: **Approx. 1835 hours – *Kormoran* maintains course 260, heavy smoke from engine-room fire, only stern guns firing. *Sydney* turns to port, crosses stern, range 4000 metres at 1845 hours - *Kormoran* turns to course 240, engines soon disabled, 4 torpedoes from *Sydney* pass astern. 1850 hours - main armament again firing and scoring hits, *Sydney* on fire on southerly course at slow speed. 1900 hours – *Sydney* at 5 knots, *Kormoran* launches torpedo at 7000 metres, inclination 110, misses astern.**

This phase of the action requires little interpretation and, if reconstructed by timeline diagram, it shows the plausibility of the Report. The courses adopted by *Sydney* and *Kormoran* can be traced on a minute by minute basis and appears to accord with the description given by Detmers and the logic of the likely actions taken by the *Sydney* officer(s) now responsible for the survival of the ship. Consequently, it has been possible to determine the relevant speed and separation of the vessels at any given time, as follows:

After the torpedo strike and the devastating gunfire from *Kormoran's* main armament, *Sydney* predictably turned to port to avoid the onslaught and gradually increased speed to 12 knots and by 1840 hours was 2600 metres astern of *Kormoran*, now resumed at 14 knots on course 260T. [During the port maneuver, *Sydney's* starboard side was vulnerable, and if a torpedo had been available from one of the starboard tubes, Detmers could have delivered the coup de grace] Once *Sydney* had gained speed, Detmers could only aim the two stern guns, the other guns being obstructed by the superstructure. Although *Sydney's* main armament was not operational, the starboard torpedo tubes were intact and the only real firepower available. In order to deploy the torpedoes, it was necessary to change course towards *Kormoran* and at 1842 at the extreme range of 3000 metres, a set of four torpedoes was launched. (point of aim - 1200 metres ahead of *Kormoran* at 14 knots, total distance - 4200metres at 35 knots, running time – about 4 minutes)

Instead of steering south easterly after releasing the torpedo, *Sydney* would have been expected to turn to the east to make the narrowest silhouette. If the steering gear was the problem, so too were the engines, because at 1844 hours when *Kormoran* was 4000 metres distant, the speed reduced from 12 to 5 knots. Alternatively, a decision to lower the speed may also have been taken in order to stem the internal flooding. At 1846 hours *Kormoran* changed course to 240Tand soon after the torpedoes from *Sydney* had passed astern, engine trouble developed and within a few minutes *Kormoran* was heaved to. However, Detmers was now able to re-engage his main armament on *Sydney* at 1850 hours at a range of about 6000 metres. From 1850 to 1900 hours *Sydney* received further shellfire in making 5 knots on a course to the south-east, while the disabled *Kormoran*, now drifting with the current, moved to a relative bearing of 170 degrees before launching a single torpedo from the port tube at the long range of 7000 metres. (Refer to Diagram p 77)

There is evidence from other *Kormoran* crewmembers, such as Hans Linke, who suggested that, after recovering from the torpedo strike, Sydney made off in the opposite north- west direction. If this was the case, then *Sydney* would have been exposed to incessant fire from *Kormoran's* main armament for most of the engagement. It would also have suggested that Detmers had reason to conceal the whereabouts of *Sydney* after the action. It seems almost impossible that Linke could have been mistaken, after all, the direction could be readily ascertained by the general course of the vessels to the west into the sun and by the sunset at 1857 hours. However, Linke's assessment may have been confused by a later change in *Kormoran's* heading caused by the current or wind, while drifting. Detmers states that the relative bearing of *Sydney* at approx.1925 hours was 225 degrees (port side / south east), thus indicating *Kormoran's* bows were directed at approx.285T. If *Kormoran's* bows later swung to an easterly direction, then *Sydney* would be positioned to starboard and mistakenly appear to be north- west of *Kormoran's* original heading. Nevertheless, as Linke's evidence was often given candidly and because he was one of the few crewmen willing to discuss the events in detail, the notion that *Sydney* escaped in the opposite direction should be investigated.

From the information contained in the Action Report and in particular the given separation distances and timeframes, it is evident that, in its application, a reconstruction of the reciprocal course by *Sydney* to the north-west, shows surprising similarities. It shows that *Sydney* also initially departed the engagement scene at 12 knots until 1842 hours and thereafter at 7 knots on course 330T, instead of 5 knots (course 150T). Interestingly, although *Sydney* would have been exposed to *Kormoran's* main armament, the diagram demonstrates that *Sydney* could have launched her torpedoes more accurately leaving Kormoran vulnerable, and this could have been the reason why Detmers, on seeing the torpedo tracks, changed course from 260 to 240T. From 1846 to 1850 hours when *Kormoran's* engines failed, only the stern armament would have been available. For the next 10 minutes while drifting, Detmers would have been required to maneuver his ship to effectively apply his main armament and to launch the torpedo at 1900 hours. (Refer to Diagram p77)

The question of whether *Sydney* could have made off on another course to the west of 330T, as suggested by Shu Ah Fah is most unlikely, due to the relatively higher initial speed required of *Sydney*. For example, *Sydney* would need to have achieved a speed of nearly 29 knots by 1842 hours on course 300T and 20 knots on course 315T (north- west). Conversely, if the courses east of 330T are considered, the calculated initial speeds at 1842 hours for courses 340T to 360T, range from 9 to 5 knots. Accordingly, this analysis lends support to the proposition that, after the initial engagement, *Sydney* could have adopted a northerly course of between 330T and 360T. In addition, it could be logically argued that these courses would have narrowed *Sydney's* silhouette and thus reduced the targeted area. It must therefore be recognized that Detmers's Report describing the action timetable, distances and the southerly track of *Sydney* can also be applied to an opposite northerly course, the sector of which should be included in the assessment of the overall search area.

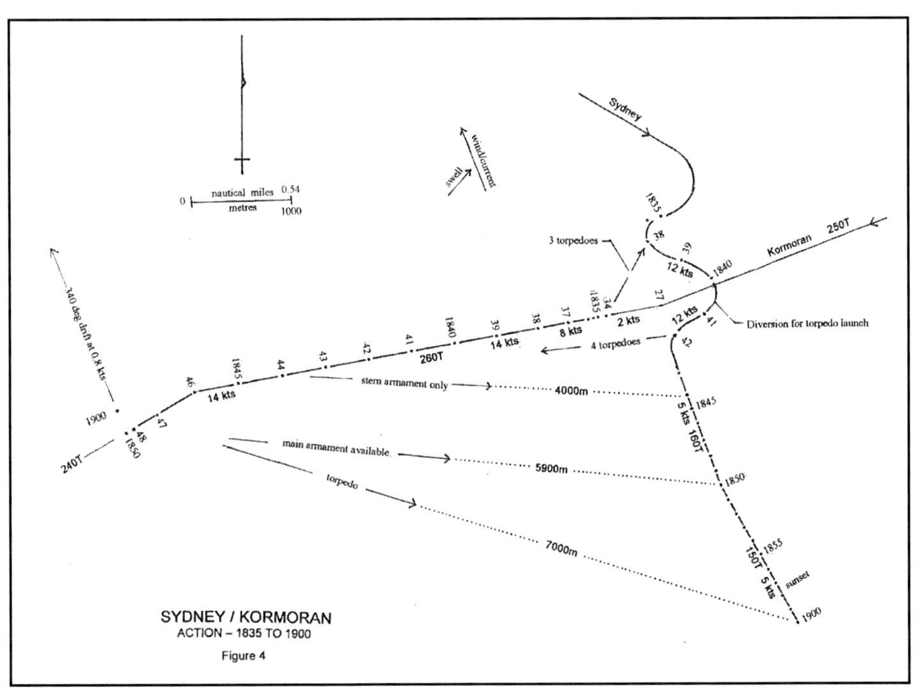

SYDNEY / KORMORAN
ACTION – 1835 TO 1900

Figure 4

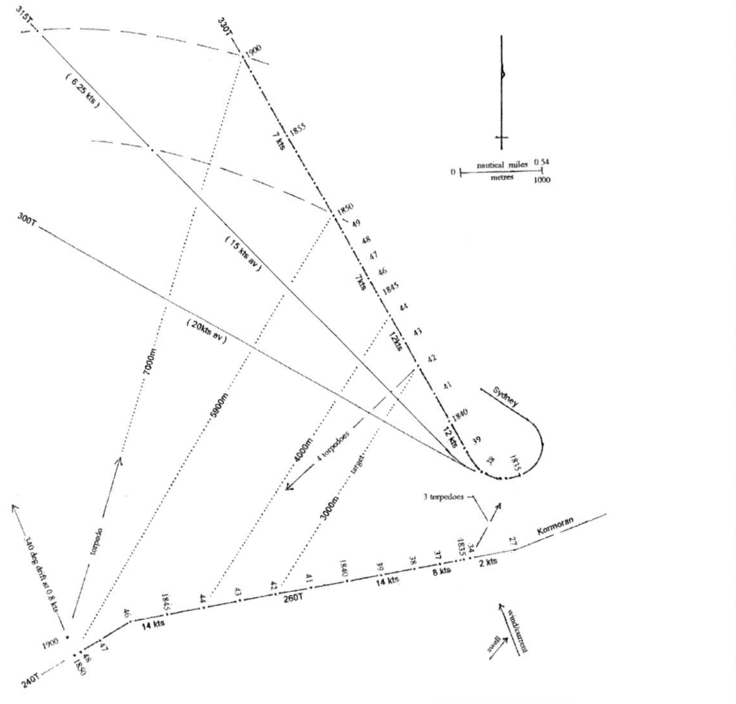

Figure 5

SYDNEY / KORMORAN
ACTION – 1835 TO 1900
ALTERNATIVE

After the Engagement - 1900/19 to 0135/20

During the period 1900 to 1925 hours, *Kormoran's* guns continued to fire at the now distant *Sydney*, until Detmers turned his attention to the uncontrollable fires aboard and the safety of his crew. He had no choice but to abandon the ship. In the Report, he describes: **1925 hours – Ceased fire at 10400 metres, approx. 550 rounds expended, relative bearing of *Sydney* 225, engine-room completely afire, preparations to launch lifeboats and scuttle. *Sydney* 16000 metres, course 150, glow visible until 2300 hours. 2200 hours – crew take to lifeboats and rafts, 120 mainly o⊠ cers remain to man guns, 2 boats to be retrieved from hold. 0030 hours – scuttling charges set, one boat lowered. 0100 hours – last boat away. 0135 hours – ship explodes, sinks by the stern.**

The situation on board *Kormoran* and the actions taken by Detmers to ensure the survival of the crew is self-evident, but the true predicament of *Sydney* is unclear. After all, it is impossible to determine the actual extent of damage to *Sydney* from the Report. The capacity of the crew to remedy the necessary repairs would ultimately decide *Sydney's* duration of time afloat. Nevertheless, the position of *Sydney* relative to *Kormoran* can be assessed at intervals (while drifting) within regular timeframes.

Although this last section of the Report specifically refers to the southward movement of *Sydney*, the stated separation distances can also be applied to a northward course. If the separation of *Sydney* (5 knots) and *Kormoran* (drifting at 0.8 knots) was 10400 metres at 1925 hours, at 2000 hours the distance between the vessels is estimated at 16000 metres in accordance with Detmers's assessment. However, in the case of the northward course, the speed of *Sydney* increased to 6.4 knots, in lieu of 4.7 knots for the southern course. Detmers's Report also states that at 1925, *Kormoran's* aging 5.9 inch guns (max. range 16000m) ceased fire at a range of 10400metres after expending a total of 550 rounds. This suggests that the over-worked guns were no longer capable, but more likely to indicate that the target had become obscure in the twilight during the period of sunset. It therefore may be concluded that the final twilight after sunset occurred at approx. 1915 hours, thus giving a clue as to the longitudinal position of the action.

Another clue regarding the sea conditions is offered in the Report. If the relative bearing of *Sydney* was 225 at the time, then *Kormoran's* bows had swung with the wind from 240 degrees to a heading of 260 degrees between the hours of 1850 and 1925. This small change in heading while drifting is indicative that light winds of no more than 10 knots from the south- east were prevailing at the time.

In consideration of the prevailing south- easterly wind and south- westerly swell, a northerly heading ought to have been adopted by *Sydney* after the engagement. The otherwise southerly course into the wind and swell would likely have increased the internal flooding and intensity of the fires to further affect the stability of the ship. However, it is accepted that, as the sudden attack would have resulted in an uncontrolled and hasty exit from the engagement scene, the situation may not have been favorable for such an expeditious decision.

It is logical to assume that *Sydney*, when out of range of *Kormoran's* guns and after having received the extensive damage described by Detmers, would have stopped to make repairs. The earliest opportunity appears to be at 1925 hours, when the cease- fire was ordered, although it is conceded that it was probably delayed until about 2000 hours when the ships were further apart, 16000metres (8.6 nm) distant. If *Sydney* was ultimately unable to resume speed and with both vessels drifting at the same rate (0.8 kts) and direction (340 degrees), the relative positions would remain unchanged. Similarly, the distances between the vessels would remain constant to the point where *Sydney* stopped at any stage for the period while *Kormoran* was afloat, until 0135 hours. In summary, the minimum distance separating the sunken vessels is about 8 nm and the maximum distance depends on the interim distance sailed by *Sydney* before stopping between the hours of 2000 and 0135.

The issue of whether *Sydney* maintained slow speed and course(s) for a longer period is debatable. There is no doubt that urgent assistance was immediately required and every effort would have been made to transmit distress signals and hopefully attract the attention of any nearby shipping by the firing of flares. It would seem rather incredible to imagine that *Sydney* could have continued on, despite the extensive damage and severe flooding. Moreover, the distress signals intercepted in Geraldton that evening tacitly support the notion that *Sydney* had stopped.

Signals from Sydney

Sydney was equipped with three wireless telegraphy (W/T) rooms, each capable of transmitting and receiving signals (morse) to and from the naval shore stations. Throughout the Sunda and return voyage she would be directed if necessary, by the control station, HMAS Harman in Canberra, or by the C in C China Station in Singapore.

The closest ordinary short wave receiving station was located in Applecross near Perth. Direction finding (D/F) stations located in Singapore and Ceylon to cover the Indian Ocean area could be supplemented by stations at Coonawarra (Darwin), Jandakot (Perth) and Sydney, which gave rudimentary coverage of the Australia Station. That there are no archival records available, that any of these stations received W/T signals or detected D/F intercepts from *Sydney* at any time before or after the engagement, has been the genesis for the controversy and mystery surrounding the whole affair. Fortunately however, the authenticity of a distress signal received at Geraldton has recently been recognized as having originated from *HMAS Sydney*.

The encoded message (in morse), transmitted between the hours of 2140 and 2325 on November 19 and received on a short-wave wireless set at the Esplanade Hostel, was decoded by RAAF Cpl Dawson in the company of others. The message was then relayed by phone to RAAF Perth by Squadron Leader Cooper and passed to the Combined Operational Intelligence Centre (COIC) to ensure the RAN was made aware of *Sydney's* plight. Inexplicably, the Navy took no action and any hope of an early rescue was dispelled.

Presumably, the messages recorded at Geraldton comprised only part of the overall distress signal and therefore it is most likely that signals were transmitted soon after the action and certainly before 2140 hours when the first message was received. The explicit text of the messages which are held in the Archives, appear to indicate the urgency of the situation. The wording of 'all men on board,' suggests that *Sydney* was probably not under way and the crew had not at any stage abandoned the ship. The message also suggests that it had become necessary to abandon the ship, but that was impossible, probably because the lifeboats and other lifesaving apparatus had been destroyed or were unserviceable.

The 'Sydney calling Darwin' portion of the message, gives a similar connotation. It seems that the originator of the W/T message aboard *Sydney*, (probably signalman Lockard) tried unsuccessfully to contact Darwin W/T ('telegraph') operator requesting a 'carrier', (frequency) so that the distress call could be delivered. Also, he could not detect any signal from D/F Darwin, in order that the bearing of the signal emanating from *Sydney* could be determined by D/F. Again, the indications are that *Sydney* had stopped, otherwise there would be no point in seeking a D/F bearing if *Sydney* continued on, albeit at slow speed.

Furthermore, the fact that the messages do not contain coordinates (they are regarded as mandatory for all distress signals, if rescue is paramount), suggests that the surviving officer(s) were uncertain of *Sydney's* position. However, it is possible that an undetected earlier signal may have contained a coordinated position.

The message referring to 'Singapore call Darwin' may signify that C in C China at Singapore were cognizant of *Sydney's* plight and having reverted to Australia Station from 0700/18 near latitude 15 S, *Sydney* was for some reason still under the control of Singapore. Alternatively, *Sydney* had been in previous contact, or a response had been received from Singapore. It could also be argued that the message was just an act of desperation, or an assumption that Singapore would detect the signal and contact Darwin, so that a cross- bearing could be obtained. This may well have been the intention. However, the message speculates that Singapore and hence the Admiralty were more aware of the circumstances of the action and the predicament of *Sydney* than they were prepared to acknowledge at the time. The role of British Intelligence, particularly the role played by the Far East Combined Bureau (FECB) in Singapore is later dealt with in more detail.

The last part of the message, purportedly received at 2255, indicates that *Sydney* may have established contact with an unidentified W/T station and undertook to signal that station in morse at 2310 hours. As no further messages were received, it is indicative that *Sydney* capsized at approximately 2300 hours. The notion that *Sydney* exploded should be not be dismissed, although if *Sydney* had remained afloat until 2300, the flooding of the magazines should have prevented such an explosion. Significantly, the bulk of evidence given by the *Kormoran* survivors does not support this occurrence. (Refer to Messages p82, 83)

Taken over phone by Signals Clerk written as for 5 A.S.U. N.B. from S/L Cooper Geraldton

R.A.A.F. Form A 23 (Revised May, 19..)
(R.A.F. Form 96A.)
(S.575A. General.)

MESSAGE FORM

Office Serial No.

Call and Preface	IN — OUT	24.50 metres:	No. of Groups. GR	Office Date Stamp
		Geraldton Geraldton is under the		

(Above this line is for Signals use only)

TO* in impression came from Aeradio Sydney.

FROM* | Originator's Number. | Date. | In reply to Number and Date.

(Write horizontally.)

R/T & morse | Mr Palmer (Batavia)

2140H 2325H
Calling during 0940 till 1125.
"Calling Darwin or Technical Telegraph Operator" — "Call from Sea Sydney calling send Correct men on board" — "Calling Fraser D/F & Darwin" — "Cannot detect you" — "Singapore call Darwin"
"This HMS Sydney calling (is) message received frequency satisfactory will put through in morse"
(at 2310 1100H) Cal Dawson & Aeradio Ge.
— Four stations transmitting in morse on one wavelength —
— "Sydney calling Darwin Distress sig — Stats

This message must be sent AS WRITTEN and may be sent by W/T. Signature
This message must be sent IN CYPHER and may be sent by W/T. Signature
Originator's Instructions. Degree of Priority.
Sgt Ward
TIME OF ORIGIN. T.O.R. T.H.I.

†Originator to insert "NOT" if message is not to go by W/T over any part of the route. (Below this line is for Signals use only.)

System in.	Time in.	Reader.	Sender.	System out.	Time out.	Reader.	Sender.	System out.	Time out.	Reader.	Sender.

The Signal Department is responsible that those details are transferred to the appropriate portion of the message form and that all possibility of compromising distinguishing signals, &c., by enabling to remove their significance from the address, &c., is avoided. Before delivery of the message these details are to be re-inserted in P/L.

S/L Cooper

Distress call from Sydney - The RAAF message form of notes taken from S/L Cooper's phone call from Grealdton.

11A

2140 (Calling Darwin Telegraph Operator (Repeated several times). Call from C. Sydney calling. Send [illegible] on board all men on board Calling [illegible] D.M. Darwin Cannot detect you. repeated couple times)

2150 R.T. Sydney calling Darwin Distress signal Sturt Leichardt. Send morse after 2050. DSZD.

2240 Singapore Call Darwin. HMAS Sydney calling 2050

2255 Message received frequency satisfactory will put through in morse

Heard by 3 women 2 men Cpl Dawson } at Esplanade Hostel on ordinary short wave Broadcast receiver. Dawson phoned S/L Cooper at [illegible]. S/L Cooper phoned area.

Passed [illegible] Col C [illegible] per phone from F/O Bogue [illegible] 1630 4/[illegible]

This handwritten version clarifies the timetable of events.

Relative Location of Sydney

The key to establishing the position of *Sydney* relative to *Kormoran's* sinking position is contained in the distress signal as described previously. The message 'men on board' transmitted at 2140, implies that *Sydney* was afloat at that time, had stopped and therefore had been drifting in the current at the same rate and in the same direction as *Kormoran.* It must therefore be concluded that *Sydney* had stopped between 1925 hours when the cease- fire occurred and 2140 hours, when the first message was detected.

During this period it was possible for *Sydney* to have sailed an additional 10.5 nm at 4.7 knots to the south east, or 14.4 nm at 6.4 knots to the north- west, both positions being about 17.5 nm distant from *Kormoran.* Interestingly, Detmers states that *Sydney* was visible until about 2300 hours, whereby at this time *Sydney* would be 25 nm away, if still moving at slow speed. This is further evidence that *Sydney* had stopped some time before and shows that it was unlikely that Detmers could have made the sighting over such a distance.

The proposition that *Sydney* escaped to the west on a northerly course has already been canvassed and largely dismissed, due to the relatively high speeds required. Similarly, a westerly course to the south of *Kormoran* would also involve speeds that are inconsistent with the separation distances stated in Detmers's Report. If for example, *Sydney* had escaped on a more westerly course, the speeds required within the hours of 1843 and 1850 for bearings of 170T, 180T and 190Tare 8.3, 13 and 19 knots respectively. These higher speeds attribute to the fact that during this period, *Kormoran* had progressed another 1.15nm further west before engine trouble developed, while *Sydney*, on a more southerly course, would have covered a greater distance within the timeframe and therefore at a higher speed. After 1850 hours and due to the fact that *Kormoran* was stopped, there is no discernible difference in the speed of *Sydney* (about 6 kts), irrespective of the chosen course.

In accordance with the separation distances, it appears that *Sydney* changed course at 1850 hours from 160T to 150T,probably in response to the resumption of *Kormoran's* main armament and to deliberately present a narrower profile. However, for the purpose of defining the search areas, it is assumed that *Sydney* could have continued south on course 160T and the southern search areas therefore, should include the range of available bearings of from 130T to 160T. The equivalent courses which accord with the separation distances in the northern search areas are within the range of 330T and 350T.

The relative position of *Sydney* to *Kormoran* is dependent on the time at which *Sydney* was stopped and drifting. As shown earlier, the earliest time is at approximately 2000 and the latest at about 2300 hours. Although these positions are 13.5 nm apart in the southern search area and 19 nm in the northern area, the relative distances from *Kormoran* remain constant at any stage after *Sydney* has stopped, due to the common drift rate of the vessels. For example, if *Sydney* was stopped at 2000 hours, the relative separation distance of 8.6 nm would remain constant while both vessels were afloat or until one of the vessels had sunk. Detmers states that *Kormoran* exploded and was sunk at 0135/20, but there is no such precise time of *Sydney's* demise. It is therefore considered prudent to extend the search areas on the basis that *Sydney* could have drifted throughout the night until 0600/20. However, that there were no further signals received at Geraldton after 2300 hours is indicative of *Sydney* at that time, having capsized. This approach therefore mitigates any requirement to provide for an even larger search area, based on the notion that *Sydney* continued at slow speed for an indeterminate distance and in a variety of directions.

The scope of the search areas can be assessed within the parameters described above. The search areas comprise separate overlapped areas, which encompass the established southerly and northerly courses and are further derived from the rate of progress of *Sydney* per hour and the extent of drift. The weight of evidence regarding *Sydney's* direction from the engagement site suggests that priority should be given to the search of the southern area. Moreover, in consideration of the likelihood that *Sydney* stopped shortly after the cease-fire, the designated Primary Search Area, which includes the engagement site, should be searched first. If a search of this area proved successful, *Sydney* should be found no more than 10 nm south west of *Kormoran*. (Refer to Diagram p86, 87)

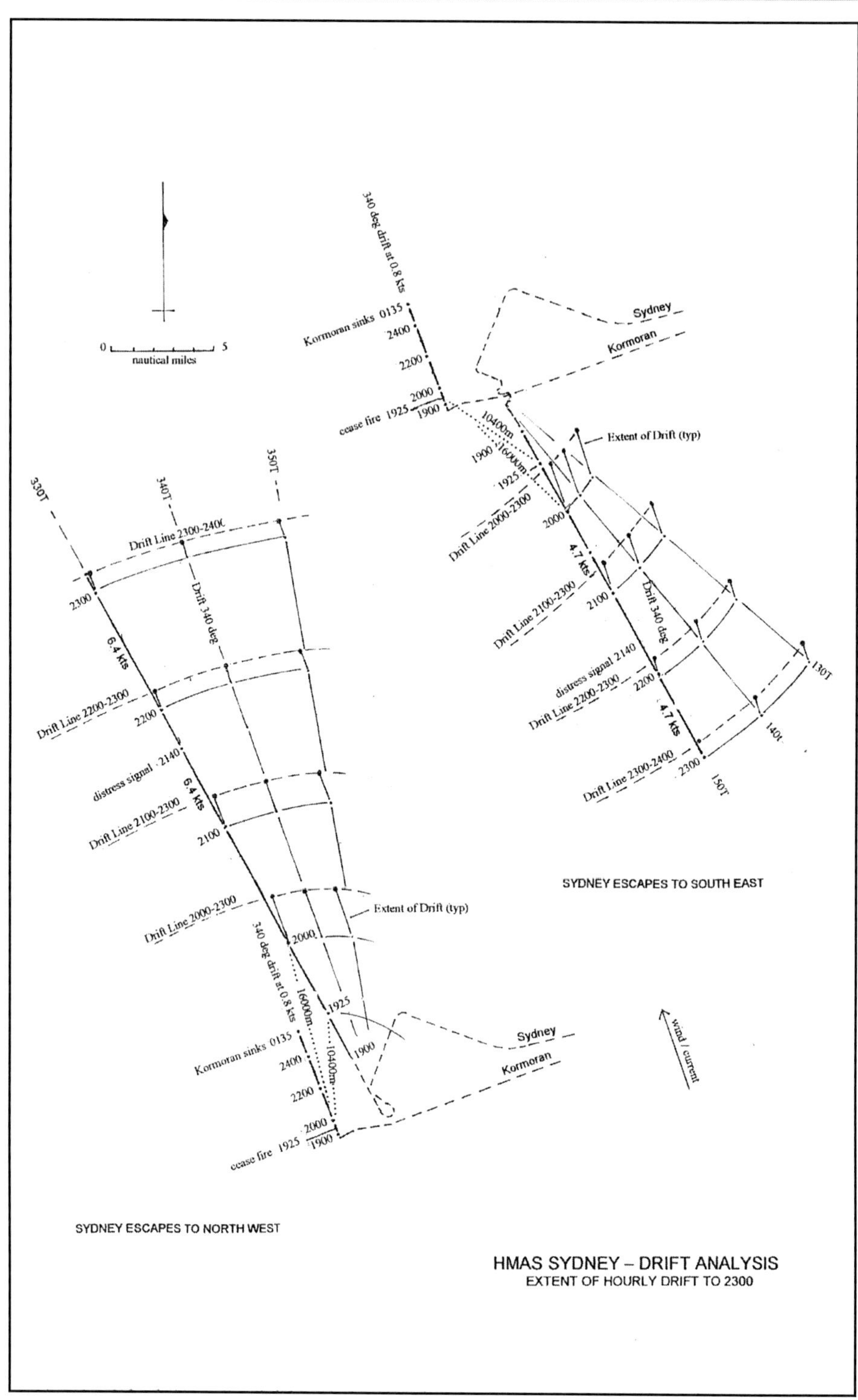
0 nautical miles 5
340 deg drift at 0.8 kts
Kormoran sinks 0135
2400
2200
2000
cease fire 1925
1900
Sydney
Kormoran
10400m
16000m
1900
1925
Extent of Drift (typ)
Drift Line 2000-2300
2000
4.7 kts
Drift Line 2100-2300
2100
Drift 340 deg
distress signal 2140
Drift Line 2200-2300
2200
4.7 kts
Drift Line 2300-2400
2300
130T
140T
150T
SYDNEY ESCAPES TO SOUTH EAST
330T
340T
350T
Drift Line 2300-2400
2300
6.4 kts
Drift 340 deg
Drift Line 2200-2300
2200
distress signal 2140
6.4 kts
Drift Line 2100-2300
2100
Drift Line 2000-2300
Extent of Drift (typ)
2000
340 deg drift at 0.8 kts
16000m
1925
Kormoran sinks 0135
2400
10400m
1900
Sydney
Kormoran
wind / current
2200
2000
cease fire 1925
1900
SYDNEY ESCAPES TO NORTH WEST
HMAS SYDNEY – DRIFT ANALYSIS
EXTENT OF HOURLY DRIFT TO 2300

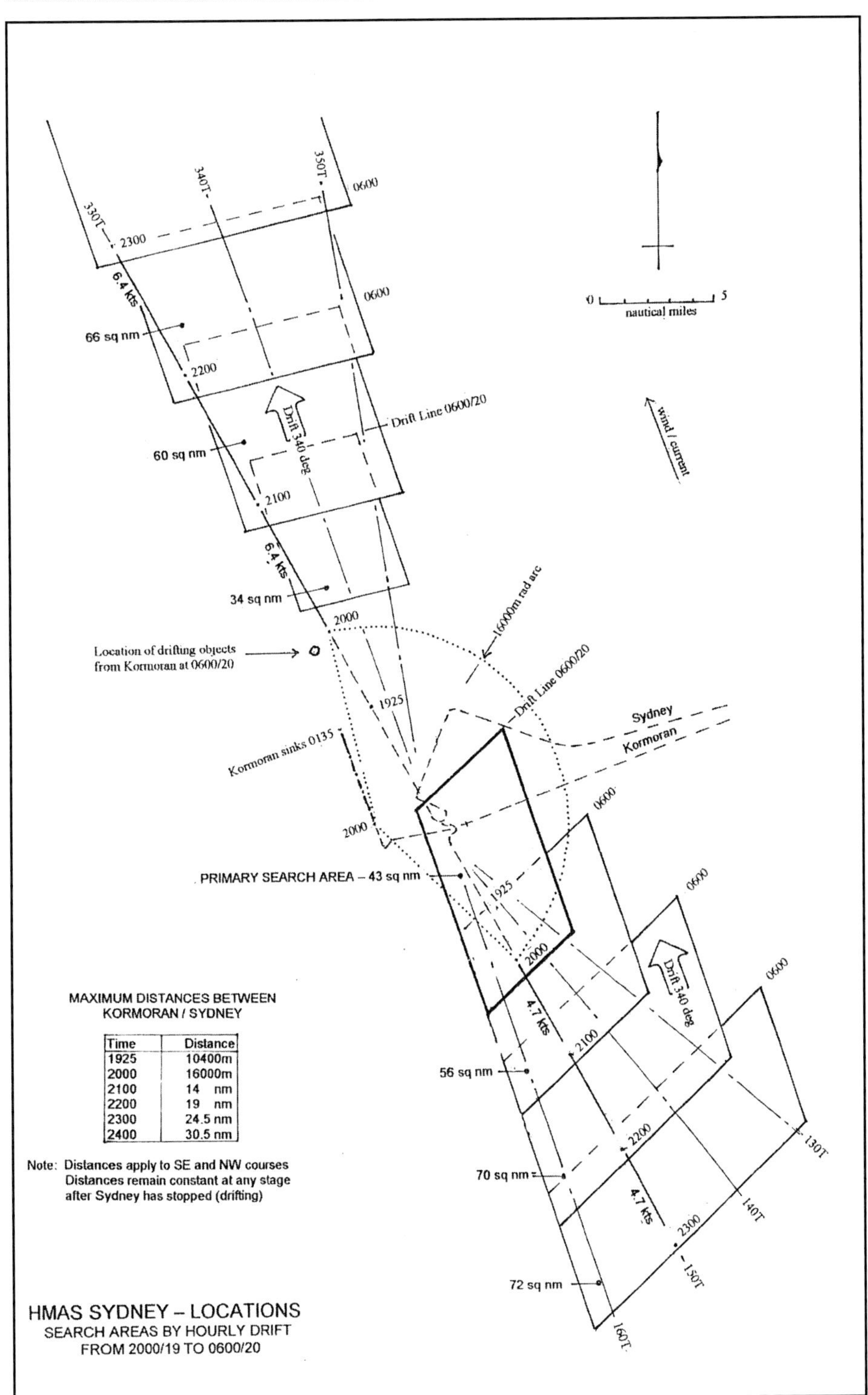

Time	Distance
1925	10400m
2000	16000m
2100	14 nm
2200	19 nm
2300	24.5 nm
2400	30.5 nm

Summary

This detailed study of the Action Report includes an assessment of each event and assesses the logical actions and reactions that would likely be taken by Detmers and Burnett. During the process, it has been necessary to make some interpretations and resultant interpolations in plotting the actual timing and sequence of events in order to produce a plausible account of the engagement. Some changes have also been instigated due to the observations of key witnesses. It is not surprising to learn that Detmers's account, otherwise often surmised as a complete fabrication, is now found to be chronologically acceptable. The investigation has shown that the act of surrender, an event to which there could never be an admission, may be regarded by some as sufficient reason to consider the whole context of the Report as a dubious and unreliable account. Additionally, that *Kormoran* was found to be moving very slowly instead of the purported 14 knots when the action commenced has also been confirmed. However, it is more realistic to contend that the brief Report was presented as a genuine attempt to record the events and that any illegalities by Detmers were for obvious reasons, omitted.

There has been sufficient information contained in the Action Report to readily plot the tracks taken by *Kormoran* and *Sydney*. The final location of *Kormoran* relative to *Sydney's* sighted position(s) at 1700/19 has been identified-average bearing approximately 243T, 30 nm distant. (Refer to Diagram p89) The location of *Sydney* however, can not be determined by relative distance and bearing or within the range of the courses identified, until the drift analysis of the recovered floating objects is undertaken.

During the escort of *Zealandia* and the return to Fremantle, *Sydney* was expected to maintain radio silence, except in cases of emergency. If messages were to be received by *Sydney* from shore stations, they were routinely not to be acknowledged. That *Sydney* like any other vessel in danger of sinking, would have somehow transmitted a distress signal containing coordinates, regardless of the damage sustained, is certainly not contested. It has been reported from various sources that signals from *Sydney* were picked up by Geraldton Radio, in Singapore, Mombassa and possibly HMAS Harman. The failure to locate any of these signals, which should be recorded in the Australian, British or overseas archives, has largely exacerbated the controversy of the whereabouts of *Sydney*.

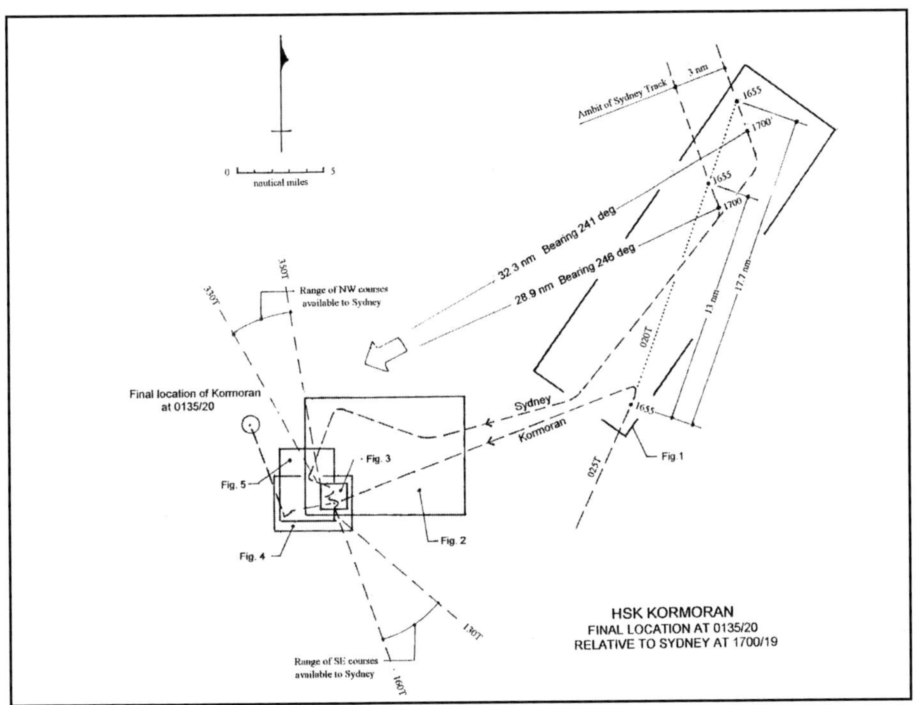

Captain Joseph Burnett on the bridge of HMAS Sydney

Burnett was born in 1899, attended the Royal Australian Naval College and qualified as a midshipman in 1917. He then earned promotion through the ranks and served on various warships in the Australian and British navies, specialising as a gunnery officer. At the age of 33 he was promoted to Commander and in 1938, Captain. The following year he was seconded to the Navy Office in Melbourne and later became Deputy Chief of Naval Staff. In May 1941, Burnett replaced Captain John Collins as captain of HMAS *Sydney*, his first command of an Australian warship.

Kapitan zur See Theodor Anton Detmers displaying his many decorations

Born in 1902, Detmers became a midshipman in 1921. During the inter war years he served on a number of warships and became a proficient torpedo officer. Ironically, in 1933 Lieutenant Detmers visited Australian ports and areas of his future operations in the cruiser, *Köln*. He was promoted to Commander in 1937 and given command of the auxiliary cruiser, HSK *Kormoran* in 1940. As a prisoner of war, he suffered a stroke and was thereafter affected by ill health. Hitler conferred the rank, Kapitan zur See in 1943 and 4 years later Detmers and his crew were repatriated back to Germany. He died in 1976.

HMAS *Sydney* makes a tranquil scene on Port Phillip Bay in 1938

The Modified Leander Class Light Cruiser, originally ordered by the British Navy as HMS *Phaeton* and built in the UK by Swan Hunter at Newcastle was launched in 1934 and commissioned into the RAN in 1935.

Displacement:	6,830 tons
Dimensions (feet):	Length 555 Beam 57 Draught 20
Machinery:	Parsons geared steam turbines, 4 shafts, 72,000 shp.
Performance:	Speed (max) 32.5 knots Range (miles) 7,000 at 16 knots
Armament:	8 x 6 inch guns, 4 x 4 inch guns, 4 x 3 pdr, 12 x 0.5 inch MGs (3 sets)
	8 x 21 inch torpedo tubes, Seagull V (Walrus) amphibian
Complement:	645

This photo of Raider G (*Kormoran*) was issued by British Intelligence in October 1941

HSK *Kormoran* taking on supplies before departing Kiel in December 1941

HSK *Kormoran*, also known as HSK8, Schiff 41 and formerly MS *Steiermark* was built by the Krupp- Germaniawerft yard in Kiel for the Hamburg-Amerika Line and commissioned into the Kriegsmarine in October 1940. In December 1940 she departed Kiel and commenced raider activities, sinking seven ships in the Atlantic Ocean (taking another as prize) and three in the Indian Ocean, a total of 68,274 grt.

Displacement:	8,736 tons
Dimensions (feet):	Length 515 Beam 66 Draught 28
Machinery:	4 x Krupp-Ger diesels, 2 shafts, 16,000 bhp
Performance:	Speed (max) 18 knots Range (miles) 80,000 at 10 knots
Armament:	6 x 5.9 inch guns, 2 x 37 mm guns, 5 x 20 mm MGs,
	4 x 21 inch TT, 2 x 21 inch TT (below water)
	2 x Arado float planes, mine-laying launch, 360 mines
Complement:	400

HMAS *Sydney* departing Fremantle on her fateful voyage on 11 November 1941. The exposed Carley floats positioned on the lower superstructure almost certainly would have been damaged by *Kormoran's* gunfire.

HMAS *Sydney* – 4 inch anti-aircraft gun manned and ready.

Seagull V (Walrus) aboard HMAS *Sydney* at Fremantle in 1941

Rescued - Survivors of the *Kormoran* coming alongside the State Ship *Koolinda*

Left: German survivors aboard *Koolinda* receiving clothing
Right: Sailors disembarking from *Centaur* at Carnarvon.

POSITIONS OF ORIGIN

IN ORDER TO find the wreck sites of *Sydney* and *Kormoran*, a detailed examination of the search and rescue is required. It is essential to trace the movements of the lifeboats and the drifting objects recovered a week after the engagement. Assessments of the extent of drift can be arbitrarily calculated with the application of suitable values for drift (leeway) in accordance with predetermined wind velocities and direction. Alternatively, the drift can be measured using a range of values, relative to the average recorded wind and current conditions for the period. In the absence of a proven scientific method of approach, it is considered that both of these methodologies should be employed after taking into account the physical features of the object. The extent of drift can then undergo reverse plotting, to ascertain the position(s) of origin.

The objects (flotsam) recovered by the search vessels from November 23 to 28 included a variety of lifebelts and liferafts. In accordance with the prevailing wind and current, these items had drifted in a northerly direction away from the scene of the engagement. Inexplicably and except for some oil slicks, no other flotsam was sighted. Considering the vast amount of buoyant material on board *Kormoran* and *Sydney*, it is remarkable that none was found along the drift path of the recovered objects. Curiously, this does not convey the impression that one or both of the vessels exploded, but is rather more synonymous with *Sydney* having capsized, and in difference with Detmers's 'big bang' description, *Kormoran* being sedately scuttled. The wreck sites could therefore reveal *Sydney's* hull largely intact and *Kormoran's* hull separated in two (caused by the scuttling charges), the stern section possibly containing unexploded mines.

The Lifeboats

Between the evacuation hours of 2200/19 and 0100/20, most of the crew abandoned *Kormoran* in five lifeboats, equipped with their own means of propulsion – oars, sails or a combination of both. Those aboard the liferafts had no means of control and were generally at the mercy of the wind and current. The 165 occupants of three lifeboats sighted at sea by aircraft were rescued west of Carnarvon by the ships *Koolinda* (at 2000/26), *Centaur* (2200/26), and *Yandra* (1215/27). Detmers was aboard the boat taken in tow to Carnarvon by *Centaur* and von Gosseln was in charge of the boat found by *Yandra*. At the time of rescue, the searching aircraft observed that these boats had suddenly made a steady and unusual easterly progress toward the coast, across the prevailing wind and current. Meanwhile, the other two lifeboats containing 103 men had earlier landed north of Carnarvon at 17 Mile Well near Cape Cuvier and at Red Bluff, 10 miles to the north at 1600/24 and 0800/25 respectively. Petty officer Paul Kohn and navigator Henri Meyer in charge of the boats had been earnest in making landfall as soon as possible, and in sailing the most direct course, the journey from 2200/19 was accomplished in 114 and 130 hours respectively. (Refer to Diagram p98)

The 3200 ton cargo-passenger ship *Centaur* traded along the West Australian coast to Singapore from 1924 to 1942. After conversion to a hospital ship, she was sunk by the Japanese submarine I-177 near Brisbane in May 1943.

At 4300 tonnes, the State Ship *Koolinda* serviced the West Australian ports from 1927-1958.

This contrast in the rate and direction of movement within the described times highlights the problem of assessing the point of origin, by back-tracking the course and speed of the lifeboats. In considering the positions of where the lifeboats were found by *Centaur* and *Yandra*, it does not suggest that Detmers and von Gosseln were initially intent on heading to the coast. Both men stated that their boats were in the vicinity when *Aquitania* stopped to rescue the 26 survivors aboard the liferafts early on November 23. Detmers also said that he planned to go out to the shipping lane, which could result in rescue by a neutral ship. Notwithstanding his real intentions, the comment 'out to the shipping lane' may have inadvertently exposed that the position of the engagement was in fact much closer to the coast than he had originally suggested. The movements of these two lifeboats shows they were curiously capable at any time of sailing almost due east across a formidable wind and current, similar to being towed by a motorized boat, such as the LS3 minelayer stowed on board *Kormoran*. In view of the foregoing, it is not possible to apply drift or wind values to determine the respective points of origin for these boats. However, the finite journeys made by Meyer and Kohn may be found to be of assistance.

On display at Carnarvon – one of the two 9 metre timber-framed, steel-sheathed lifeboats from *Kormoran* and ostensibly the boat commanded by Meyer. It was previously left derelict at Whiteman Park near Perth.

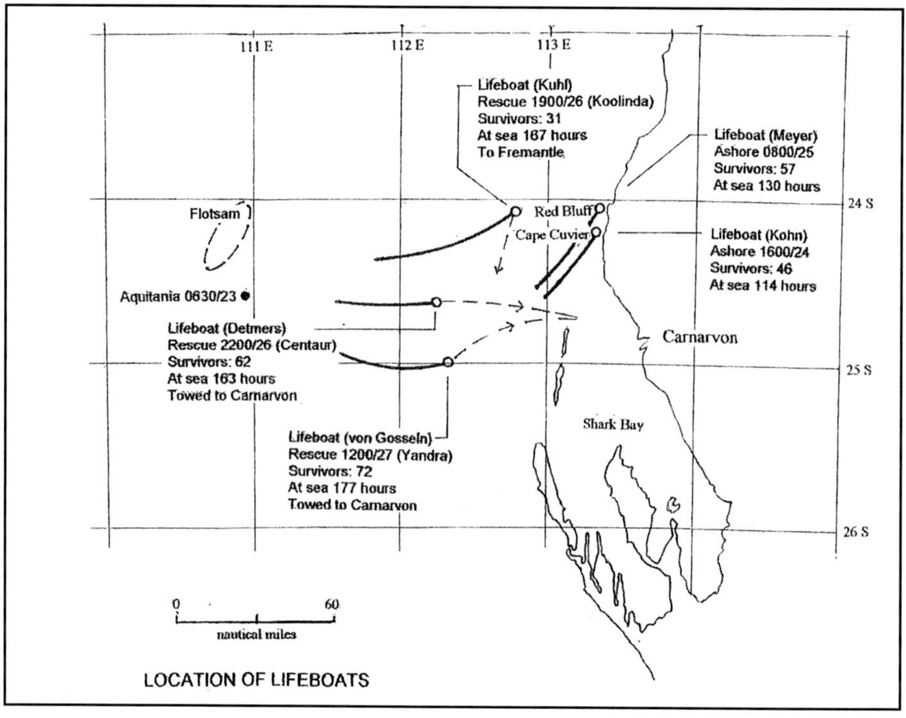

The Drifting Objects

The drifting items from *Kormoran* and found by search vessels were recovered in an area near longitude 111E and between latitudes 24 S and 25 S. These included three rubber rafts containing 51 survivors, another raft containing the body of a German, a German lifebelt and a dog kennel, presumably from the *Kormoran*. The items of British origin recovered included a RAN Carley float and two lifebelts. Each had drifted from the wreck sites at varying speeds for a distance that depended on the characteristics of shape, size, mass and buoyancy of the object, relative to the velocity of wind and current. As the physical features of the objects are individually different, the application of a common set of drift values for each object is therefore not regarded as a satisfactory means of determining comparative drift distances and velocities. It is therefore considered that the rate of movement of the objects should be individually assessed.

The recovered items were found because they had sustained sufficient buoyancy and floated noticeably above the surface. They were significantly influenced by the elements of both wind and current. That the search vessels and aircraft failed to find other debris 8-9 days after the battle is not surprising.

Such items floating at or near the surface would remain largely unaffected by the wind and they would drift at a lesser rate in the direction of the prevailing current. In cases where the wind- driven component velocity on the buoyant objects is greater than the current velocity, the flotsam not influenced by wind could drift in another direction. For example, if the flotsam originated in an area influenced by the weak Leeuwin Current, the more buoyant objects could drift northwards by wind and the less buoyant lower profile objects could drift southwards by current alone. This phenomenon could account for the objects that were reportedly found ashore near Port Gregory.

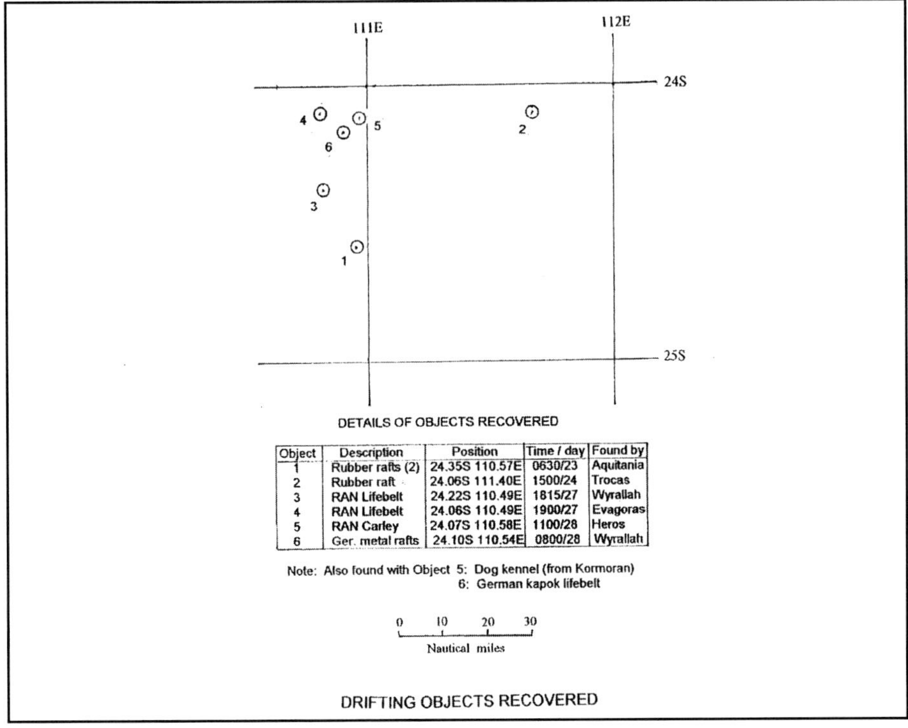

DETAILS OF OBJECTS RECOVERED

Object	Description	Position	Time / day	Found by
1	Rubber rafts (2)	24.35S 110.57E	0630/23	Aquitania
2	Rubber raft	24.06S 111.40E	1500/24	Trocas
3	RAN Lifebelt	24.22S 110.49E	1815/27	Wyrallah
4	RAN Lifebelt	24.06S 110.49E	1900/27	Evagoras
5	RAN Carley	24.07S 110.58E	1100/28	Heros
6	Ger. metal rafts	24.10S 110.54E	0800/28	Wyrallah

Note: Also found with Object 5: Dog kennel (from Kormoran)
6: German kapok lifebelt

DRIFTING OBJECTS RECOVERED

Wind Speed / Direction

The offshore weather observations in the area at the time differ considerably. During the voyage to Red Bluff, *Kormoran's* Radio Officer, Reinhold von Malapert made daily notes of the sea and wind conditions. His diary shows the initial wind at force 2/3 on November 20 and 21, increasing to force 5/6 on November 22 and force 4/6 on November 23. This equates to wind velocities in the order of 8 to 25 knots, with winds varying from the SSE to ESE. When approaching the coast the next day von Malapert would have undoubtedly experienced the usual strong afternoon sea breezes. [It should be noted that the area where the wind conditions were experienced nearer the coast during the latter part of the voyage is remote from the area where the drifting objects were recovered] Some idea of the wind speed for the ensuing period from November 24- 28 can be gained from crewmen on the search vessels, who described the sea as 'rough', a wind likely to be classified as force 5/6 (18 to 25 knots).

In addition to the above observations which are by no means conclusive, information on the average long- term wind speed and direction in the vicinity of the recovery area for the month of November is required for the purpose of comparison and measurement. The'Australia Pilot', a reference for mariners, provides specific information on local seasonal weather and ocean current conditions. It shows the direction, frequency and strength of the wind near the path of the recovered flotsam, from which the relevant values for November can be interpolated. The indicated winds are predominantly from SSW to SSE (categorized south) with a 50% frequency, from SSE to ESE (south east- 23%) and SSW to WSW (south west- 15%). The derived average 24 hour wind velocities are 13.5 knots (south), 14 knots (south- east) and 9.4 knots (south- west). From these figures the average and most frequent wind direction during November is calculated at 355 degrees. These values are relative to position 27 S / 112 E. (Refer to Diagram p101)

The respected publication by Hastenrath and Lamb, the 'Climatic Atlas of the Indian Ocean', provides further evidence and generally supports the above values. Interestingly, the wind speed Chart shows an increase of 4 knots along longitude 112 E, north from latitudes 28 S (11.6 knots) to 24 S (15.6 knots). In the area where most of the flotsam was found, the average wind speed is consistently in the order of 14 to 15 knots. However, the Chart suggests that Kuhl's liferaft, recovered some 40 nm west of the other flotsam could have been affected later by average winds in excess of 15.6 knots. The comparative average velocity of 12.5 knots is applicable to position 27 S / 112 E. Hastenrath generally prescribes a 'southerly' wind in this area throughout November.

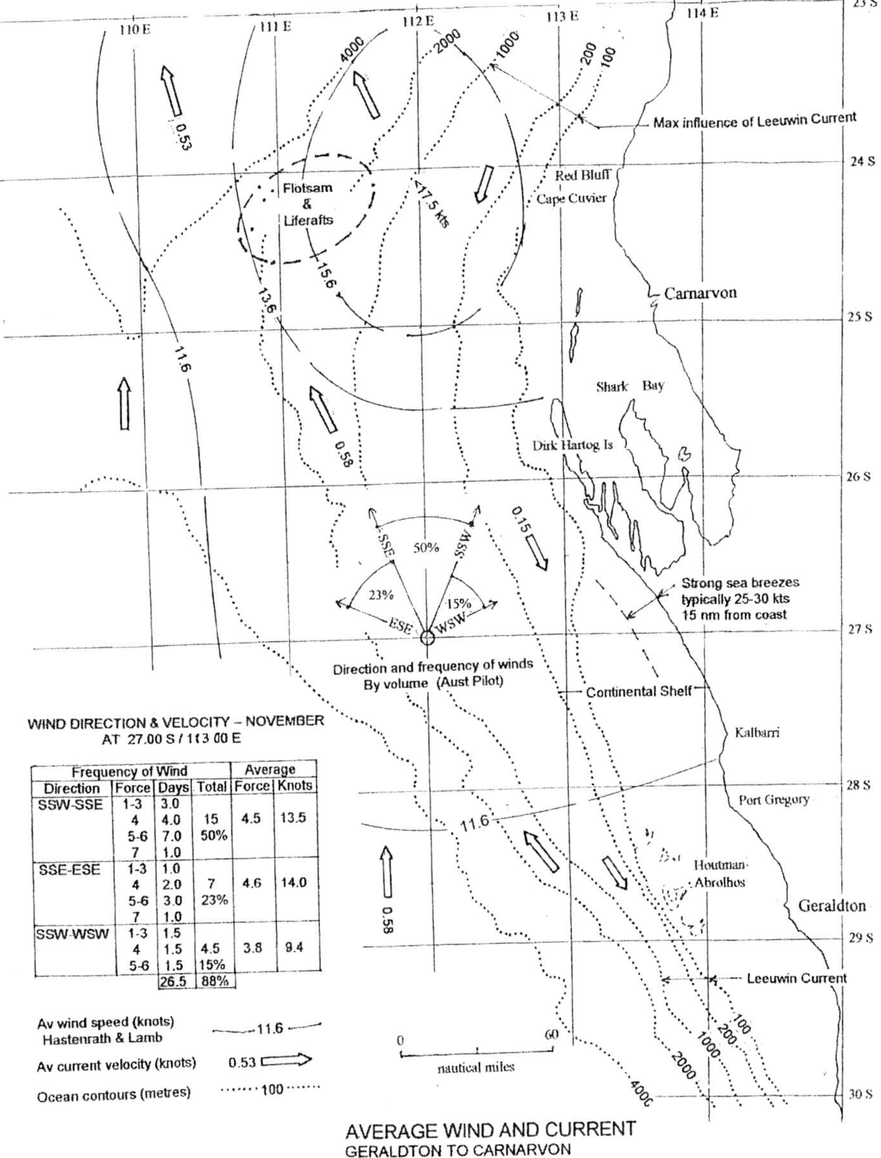

Frequency of Wind				Average	
Direction	Force	Days	Total	Force	Knots
SSW-SSE	1-3	3.0			
	4	4.0	15	4.5	13.5
	5-6	7.0	50%		
	7	1.0			
SSE-ESE	1-3	1.0			
	4	2.0	7	4.6	14.0
	5-6	3.0	23%		
	7	1.0			
SSW-WSW	1-3	1.5			
	4	1.5	4.5	3.8	9.4
	5-6	1.5	15%		
		26.5	88%		

AVERAGE WIND AND CURRENT
GERALDTON TO CARNARVON
NOVEMBER

The comparative data demonstrates that during November, an average wind of Force 4 (11- 16 knots) could be expected to prevail over a 24- hour period. Although these wind speeds appear to be less than some observations, the velocities in fact, account for the period at night when the daytime winds abate considerably, due to the cooling of the atmosphere. It is therefore recognized that constant above average wind conditions should not be regarded as applicable to each day of the period November 20 to 28. A range of arbitrary wind values should be applied to the average daily velocities to determine the median drift distance of the recovered objects. Overall, the average 24 hour wind speed during the period of drift should be assessed at at no greater than 15 knots. The observations made by von Malapert (light winds from the SE and increasing) and others should also be taken into account.

The November Bureau of Meteorology forecasts (1999-2004) of the direction of the offshore winds in the Central West and Gascoyne Regions also lends support to the fact that south easterly winds (av 159 degrees) prevailed from November 19- 22 as recorded by von Malapert. These forecasts, applicable to normal weather conditions and in the absence of low pressure cyclonic systems show that southerly or SSW winds were likely to persist thereafter from November 24 until November28. The general trend of the southerly winds shows a progressive average wind shift at latitude 28 S from SSE to SSW at latitude 23 S. This wind direction generally concurs with the Australia Pilot diagram, wherein it shows a constancy of wind from a southerly direction. Nevertheless, and according to the forecasts, it is important that the direction of the drifting objects should be assessed on a daily basis and specifically that a SE wind component prevailed until November 25, and thereafter a southerly wind component until November28. (Refer to Diagram p103)

Actual forecast wind directions vary markedly from the average southerly wind given by Hastenrath and the Australia Pilot references. In fact, the sample five - year forecast show a regular change in wind direction and are rarely concentrated from a particular direction for periods exceeding a few days. The average maximum wind speed experienced from November 19– 28 during the day at 27 S / 113 E is 18 knots and rarely exceeds 25 knots from any direction.

OFFSHORE WINDS AT 25 S / 113 E
0900 Hours

Nov	1999	2000	2001	2002	2003	2004
17	SE	SW	SW	---	WNW	SW
18	SSE	S	----	SSE	SW	S
19	S	----	S	S	SSW	SSW
20	SE	SE	SW	SSE	SSE	SSE
21	---	ESE	SW	WSW	ESE	----
22	SE	S	SW	SW	ESE	ENE
23	SSW	SW	SE	SSW	----	N
24	WSW	SW	S	----	SW	WNW
25	SW	S	----	S	SW	WNW
26	SW	----	SW	S SE	SSE	WNW
27	SE	S	WSW	SSE	SE	SSW
28	S	SSE	SW	S	SE	----
29	S	SSE	SW	SSW	SE	SSW
30	S	SSE	WSW	SW	----	SSW

OFFSHORE WINDS AT 27 S / 113 E
0900 Hours

Nov	1999	2000	2001	2002	2003	2004
17	SSW	W	SE	---	SW	SW
18	SSE	SSE	----	S	WSW	SE
19	SSE	----	SW	SE	SSE	SE
20	SE	SE	SW	S	SSE	SSE
21	----	ESE	SSW	NE	E	---
22	SE	ENE	SSW	SW	WNW	NE
23	SSW	SW	SE	S	----	N
24	NE	SW	SSE	----	SW	WSW
25	W	SE	----	S	SW	NNW
26	W	----	E	SE	SSE	WNW
27	S	SW	NE	S	SE	W
28	SE	S	SE	S	SE	---
29	S	S	SE	SE	S	S
30	S	SSE	SE	SW	----	S

Source: Bureau of Meteorology

OFFSHORE WIND VELOCITY AT 25 S / 113 E
0900 Hours

Nov	1999	2000	2001	2002	2003	2004	Av Velocity
17	15	15	18	--	18	20	
18	18	15	---	20	18	23	
19	23	--	18	20	18	20	18.7 kts
20	20	18	22	15	20	22	
21	---	18	20	15	20	---	
22	18	15	20	15	18	18	
23	18	15	28	20	--	13	
24	15	15	30	--	15	10	17.2 kts
25	18	18	--	20	15	15	
26	12	--	22	15	20	15	
27	15	25	15	13	15	15	
28	15	22	18	20	20	--	
29	15	20	15	20	15	20	
30	18	18	15	18	--	17	

Source: Bureau of Meteorology

WIND VELOCITY – PROGRESSIVE
24 Hour Average

Hours	November	Velocity	Average
04	19	10 kts	10.0 kts
28	20	10	10.0
52	21	14	12.0
76	22	18	14.0
100	23	18	15.0
124	24	do	15.6
148	25	do	16.0
172	26	do	16.3
196	27	do	16.5
220	28	do	16.7

Average for period = 15.5 knots

TYPICAL WIND MOTION AND ASSESSMENT

Ocean Currents

The flow of the Westralian Current throughout the seasons generally follows the configuration and western slope of the Continental Shelf. In November, the northerly current gradually changes from about latitude 28 S to flow increasingly north westerly at latitude 20 S where a north- easterly component is also evident. The transition of the diverging flows occurs near latitude 24 S in the proximity of where the flotsam was recovered. A drifting object at latitude 26 S, longitude 111.30 E would thus most likely move (without wind) from a NNW direction (340 deg) paralleling the Continental Shelf to a northerly direction and then drift within the ambit of NW to NE at latitude 20 S. Further west, where the current is not influenced by the Continental Shelf, a pronounced north- west current, which forms part of the Southern Indian Ocean circulatory system, would ultimately cause an object to drift in a westerly direction. The perennial Leeuwin Current, which flows south and south easterly is at its weakest in November and its area of influence is generally between the 100 and 1000 metre sea contours.

Various values have been assigned to the strength of the Westralian Current for November. The 'Australia Pilot' assigns a velocity of 0.75 to 1.0 knot, but qualifies the value by indicating that the constancy is less than 50%. In a 1994 Report prepared by Professor of Oceanography, M. Tomczak concerning the drift analysis of the Christmas Island Carley float, an average current speed of 0.6 knots was attributed to the float. This velocity is similar to the interpolated 0.58 knots (nominally 0.6 knots) previously applied to the drift vectors for vessels sailing the Sunda route north to latitude 25 S. Thereafter and due to the dispersion of the current northwards, a 0.53 knot (nom 0.55) current applies up to latitude 22 S, which progressively slows further north.

It is illogical to assume that each of the drifting objects moved directly from the point of origin to the point of recovery. This applies particularly to the liferafts, which are more susceptible to lateral movement by wind. Drifting objects, even if unassisted by the current, do not always follow the direction of the wind. The wind effect may cause such objects to drift up to 20 degrees off wind, thus affecting the actual drift direction and velocity. In this regard, the results from the1994 experimental drift card release near 27 S / 111E by Dr John Bye, reveals that after about 200 hours adrift, the spread of the flotsam was estimated at about 10 kilometres wide. Other factors affecting the drift of the liferafts include the number of occupants, whether the flooring (drogue) is lowered, or whether improvised sails, paddles or sea anchors could have been employed to assist or control the propulsion.

Extent of Drift

A number of methods can be used to determine the extent of drift of objects within a certain timeframe. This can be achieved by applying the average velocity of the current, or by the application of a leeway factor to the average wind speed, or by using vectors displaying the average speed and direction of both wind and current components to determine the resultant direction and velocity.

After assessing the physical features and shape of the object, a typical range of leeway values to determine wind drift can be applied. For liferafts and lifeboats, a range of 3% to 7% of average wind speed is considered appropriate and for the leeway of other flotsam, 2% to 3%. In order to determine the point(s) of origin, the standard procedure of reverse plotting the calculated distances of the drifting objects is normally adopted. In the case of the objects recovered from *Kormoran*, the calculated distances should close the line(s) showing the possible sinking position previously determined in relation to

Sydney's position(s) at 1700/19. The objects associated with *Sydney* can be similarly tracked and a position of origin obtained using the appropriate drift value for the object.

As previously described, the flotsam and liferafts have differing buoyancy characteristics and are thus likely to be unduly influenced by either the wind or current driven components. The velocity of the more buoyant objects, such as the liferafts and inflated lifebelts should be considered to be of wind driven origin and largely unaffected by the prevailing current. In the case of the drift of objects with low- profile buoyancy, the wind effect is regarded as minimal and thus the object is mainly current driven. It should also be noted, that due to the water resistance, wave action and drag on some irregularly shaped objects floating near the surface a 'rotating' effect is often produced, so that the object may be impeded to a velocity of less than the current. In all these instances the drifting pattern from the point of origin to the position of rescue or retrieval is quite indirect. This extra distance covered by the object should therefore be included when ascertaining the final velocity. The wind driven objects move faster and hence normally drift with less deviation than the irregular shaped objects reliant on current alone. In order to determine the final velocity by wind, a deviation (dev) factor in the order of 5% ought to be applied. Other objects driven primarily by current could easily deviate at twice this amount.

Assessment of Wind

The offshore wind direction between latitudes 25 S and 27 S varies markedly during November as evidenced by the sample of forecast winds for the consecutive years of 1999 to 2004. The sample shows that there is constancy of wind from a particular direction for a few days only. However, in most cases there is a general trend in direction from the south east to the south or south west.

If the observations made by Detmers and von Malapert from November 19 to 24 are accurate, it appears to confirm that an initial south easterly wind pattern existed prior to a southerly change from November 24. Unfortunately, the specific wind direction for the 21st was not included in von Malapert's Diary. The Diary describes: Wind - SSE on the 19th and 20th, SSW to SSE (otherwise south) on the 22nd, ESE on the 23rd and SE on the 24th.

In consideration of the forecast trend, the wind direction options therefore available for November 21 are from the SE, SSE or South. In order to minimize any error in the process of plotting wind drift, all of these options should be considered. Similarly, allowance for wind variation should be made for the predicted southerly wind change on November 24. In both cases the error of wind prediction can be minimized by allowing for an accumulated and nominal wind variation of about 15 degrees to be applied to the 'known' and predicted wind directions. After all, the wind directions given by von Malapert must be regarded as approximate. This variation allows for a wider spread of drift area and compensates for errors that could arise when nominating a specific wind direction. Although the alternative wind direction plot options used for November 21 show a similar pattern of drift, it is also evident that from November 24, the southerly accumulated drift vectors encompass the ambit of possible short term winds from the SW, SSW or SSE.

When the wind direction options for November 21 and November 24 to 28 are plotted using the wind variation (15 deg) vectors, the direct distance and bearing from the position of origin to the rescue or retrieval positions remains the same. Although this process unavoidably widens the east- west (longitudinal) search parameters, this method confines and more accurately identifies the latitudinal position of origin. For the purpose of presentation of wind drift, the allocated wind direction for November 21 has been shown from the south- east.

The extent of wind drift is dependent upon an accurate estimation of wind speed. A sample of forecast offshore wind velocities typical for the latter part of November in the vicinity of latitude 25 S reveals an inconsistent range of wind speeds. These velocities average about 18 knots and are by no means considered the maximum speed during the day. In fact, a typical velocity cycle relative to the speeds shown at 0900 hours should show an increase during the day to 1500 hours and thereafter a reduced velocity during the night until 0600 hours the next day. However, as the average 24 hour velocity is the important determinant for the purpose of calculating wind drift along the wind direction vectors, it is considered prudent to apply a daily average rather than an average over the whole period. In this regard, the von Malapert Diary is the most useful guidance for the initial conditions and period of drift.

The wind velocity as described by von Malapert from November 19 to 25 depicts initial light winds (force 2- 3) increasing to force 4- 6; thereafter and according to observations made during the search and rescue period to November 28, fresh to strong winds persisted. Considering that the records for November show that wind speeds below 10 knots in the area are extremely rare, it is considered appropriate, and indifference to von Malapert's estimate, to assign an average wind speed of 10 knots for November 19 and 20. The

Diary shows that the wind had increased to approximately 22 knots for a period on November 22, which is suggestive of an 18 knot average 24 hour velocity and a reduction to a minimum of 14 knots during evening. Von Malapert estimates that on November 21 the wind had moderately increased from the previous day. This assessment falls within the average wind speeds of 10 and 18 knots, resulting in an interpolated intervening wind speed of 14 knots. From November 23 to 28, there is no evidence of sudden or intermittent wind abatement, which is otherwise regarded as a normal cyclic characteristic for wind velocities in the area; and it is certainly not an uncommon event (as shown in the forecasts) for fresh to strong winds to persist for up to 7 successive days.

There is sufficient evidence to conclude that the initial wind velocity significantly increased from November 23 and maintained strength until November 28. Moreover, the average velocity of 15.5 knots over the period compares favorably with the November average as determined by Hastenrath and Lamb (15.6 knots) for position 25 S / 112 E. In order to assimilate the wind drift results, the 24 hour average wind speed is assessed at 2000 hours on each day.

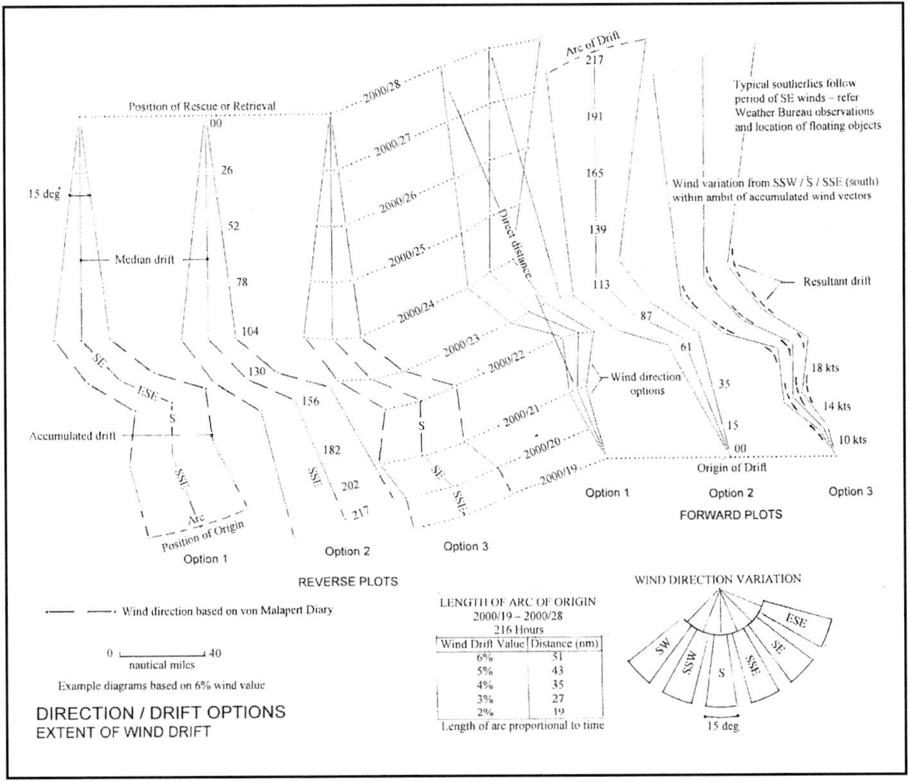

LENGTH OF ARC OF ORIGIN
2000/19 – 2000/28
216 Hours

Wind Drift Value	Distance (nm)
6%	51
5%	43
4%	35
3%	27
2%	19

Length of arc proportional to time

DIRECTION / DRIFT OPTIONS
EXTENT OF WIND DRIFT

Analysis of Drifting Objects

The positions in which the various drifting objects were found occupied a relatively large area. If these objects were of similar buoyancy and shape, it would be expected that the lateral spread of material would have been confined to a much smaller area as evidenced by the aforesaid drift card experiment. Even a cursory glance would conclude that the objects drifted at vastly different rates that are difficult to correlate. The obvious conclusion to be drawn is that each object drifted in accordance with its individual peculiarities.

In assessing the mode of motion for applying either wind or current components, a determination is firstly required of the physical features of the object. In the case of the wind driven objects, a suitable wind drift value (factor) can then be applied, provided that the final velocity is not less than that of the current. For objects mainly driven by current, the velocity should not overtly exceed the speed of the current (0.6 knots).

Liferaft(s) Found by Aquitania

The first object(s) found was recovered by *Aquitania* in position 24.35 S/110.57 E at 0600 on November 23 and consisted of two rubber rafts tied together containing 26 German survivors. That this raft was discovered by *Aquitania* in the Sunda- Leeuwin shipping lane probably occasioned Detmers to later declare that he was hoping to be rescued by a neutral ship. After all, his and von Gosseln's lifeboats were also in the vicinity and both men had recognized the presence of *Aquitania.* This suggests that the raft and lifeboats had maintained a similar rate of drift, although it is conceded that propulsion of both craft could be supplemented by the improvisation of sails. In the case of the lifeboats, steerage by rudder could enable a maneuver to a predetermined position. However, without steerage the destination and path of the liferafts (tied together) could only be reliant on the direction of the wind and compared to an unhindered freely- floating single raft, the speed of the tied raft, due to the effect of the separation, could be expected to be reduced. The rate of drift therefore must be considered indeterminate and should be assessed by using a range of leeway values.

If by using a total leeway value of 5- 7% applied to the reconstructed wind speeds and vectors, the craft should have drifted for a distance of 58 to 82 nautical miles from the position of origin in 80 hours to the rescue position. This equates to a velocity of from 0.76 to 1.08 knots and a median drift of 0.93 knots, inclusive of deviation. In consideration of the mean wind speed over the period (14.6 knots), this velocity can be otherwise comprised of current (0.58 knots) and a 2.4% factor (0.35 knots) for velocity by wind or wind driven current. The reverse- plotted direct distance of 53 to 74 nm from the position of rescue on a bearing of 153 degrees gives an area of origin of 336 sq nm, an area too large to accurately determine a firm origin of the raft. The centre of the area of origin on the central drift line (6% of wind), position 25.32 S / 111.29 E should be regarded as the position of most interest and a focus point for the assessment of other drifting objects from *Kormoran*.

A confirmatory exercise can also be undertaken using separate current and wind components. Utilizing a current vector of 0.58 knots, a 2.5% wind factor and a larger 22.5 deg wind variation for the reconstructed wind speeds, the raft would have drifted for a total distance of 78 nautical miles at a velocity of 0.98 knots. The reverse plot gives a central bearing of 155 degrees from the rescue position, a direct distance of 71 nm to position 25.39 S / 111.33 E. The arc of origin is 10 nm in length compared to the previous example of 18.5 nm.

In summary, both of these drift results of the liferaft per se can not be used to specifically ascertain the origin of drift. However, the enclosed area of origin shown should define the parameters of the points of origin of the other objects which had originated from *Kormoran*.

The path taken by the liferaft demonstrates that the occupants were intent on drifting to an area along the Sunda route where rescue was possible. Conceivably, Detmers even suggested a position based on the likely drift from the prevailing south easterly wind and current at the time of departure from *Kormoran*. Due to the maneuverability of the two lifeboats, it should have been a relatively easy task to navigate to a nominated position. That the raft managed to successfully reach the area of the lifeboats can only be regarded as fortuitous. The consequences of a delayed rescue meant that even though it was possible to limit the drift by the use of a sea anchor, the raft was destined to drift away from the shipping lane, thus reducing the prospect of rescue. The raft survivors were also acutely aware that there was no hope of being taken aboard the already overcrowded lifeboats, a fortunate rescue, indeed.

The fact that *Aquitania's* Captain Gibbons failed to notify Australian authorities immediately after the rescue, was instrumental in a concerted search of the area not taking place for another 33 hours when *Trocas* signaled the rescue of further survivors. The *Aquitania* survivors interrogated in Sydney by Captain Farncombe were ostensibly the only group bereft of any further direction and coercion by Detmers and his officers prior to the interview process. It is significant that some of the survivors volunteered information concerning the engagement, which supports the proposition that *Sydney* opened fire first, at a distance.

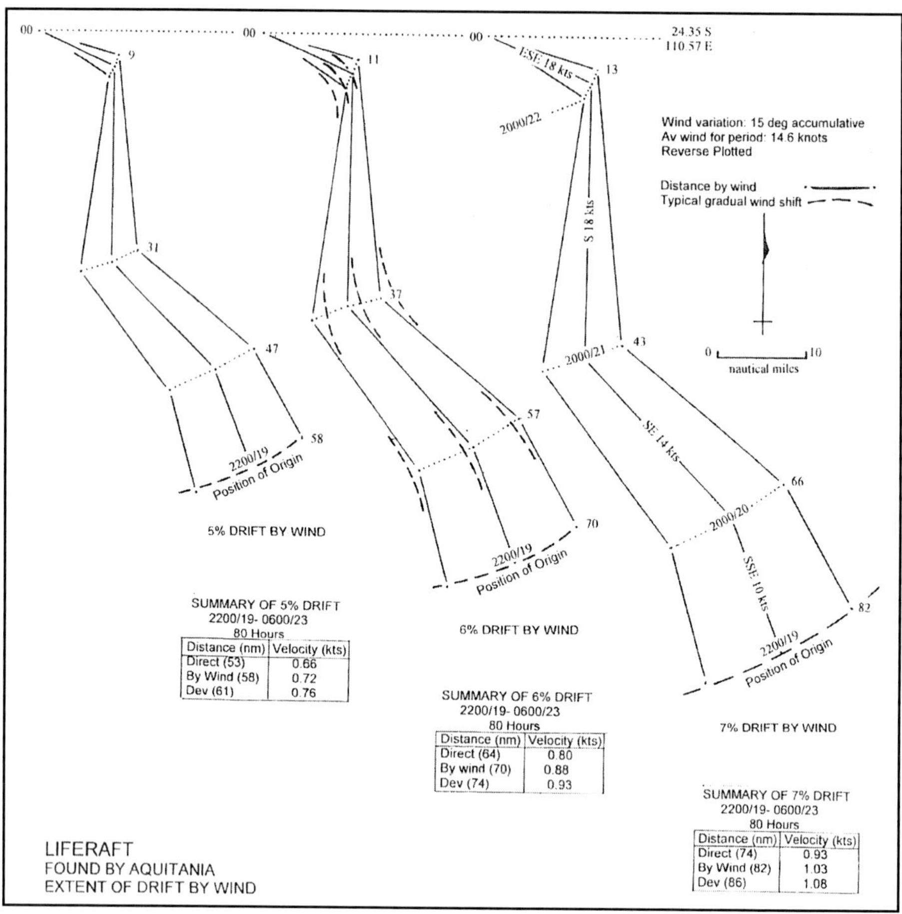

SUMMARY OF 5% DRIFT
2200/19- 0600/23
80 Hours

Distance (nm)	Velocity (kts)
Direct (53)	0.66
By Wind (58)	0.72
Dev (61)	0.76

SUMMARY OF 6% DRIFT
2200/19- 0600/23
80 Hours

Distance (nm)	Velocity (kts)
Direct (64)	0.80
By wind (70)	0.88
Dev (74)	0.93

SUMMARY OF 7% DRIFT
2200/19- 0600/23
80 Hours

Distance (nm)	Velocity (kts)
Direct (74)	0.93
By Wind (82)	1.03
Dev (86)	1.08

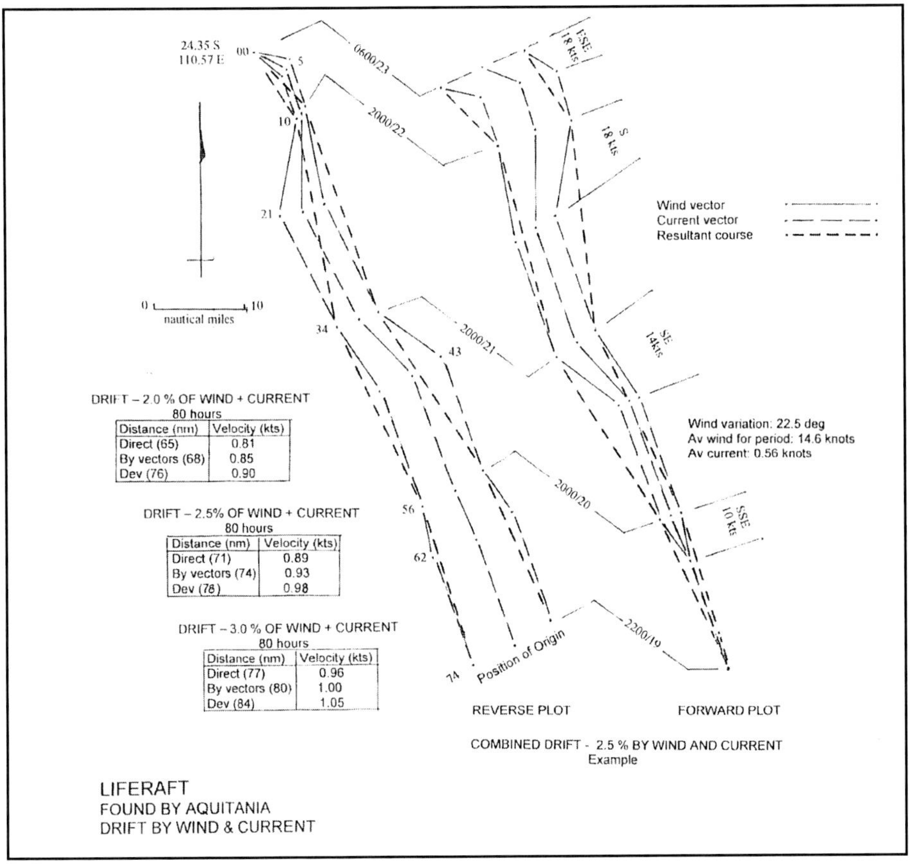

24.35 S
110.57 E
00
5
10
21
34
43
56
62
74
0 10
nautical miles
0600/23
2000/22
2000/21
2000/20
2200/19
ESE 18 kts
S 18 kts
SE 14kts
SSE 10 kts
Wind vector
Current vector
Resultant course
Wind variation: 22.5 deg
Av wind for period: 14.6 knots
Av current: 0.56 knots
DRIFT – 2.0 % OF WIND + CURRENT
80 hours
Distance (nm) | Velocity (kts)
Direct (65) | 0.81
By vectors (68) | 0.85
Dev (76) | 0.90
DRIFT – 2.5% OF WIND + CURRENT
80 hours
Distance (nm) | Velocity (kts)
Direct (71) | 0.89
By vectors (74) | 0.93
Dev (78) | 0.98
DRIFT – 3.0 % OF WIND + CURRENT
80 hours
Distance (nm) | Velocity (kts)
Direct (77) | 0.96
By vectors (80) | 1.00
Dev (84) | 1.05
Position of Origin
REVERSE PLOT
FORWARD PLOT
COMBINED DRIFT - 2.5 % BY WIND AND CURRENT
Example
LIFERAFT
FOUND BY AQUITANIA
DRIFT BY WIND & CURRENT

111 E
112 E
24 S
25 S
26 S
Aquitania 0600/23
25.35 S
110.57 E
00
15 deg wind variation
Bearing 153 deg
25.22 S
111.24 E
AREA OF ORIGIN
25.32 S
111.29 E
5%
Position by current
and wind components
25.41 S
111.34 E
53
6%
25.39 S
111.33 E
64
7%
71
74
Arc = 18.5 nm
LIFERAFT FOUND BY AQUITANIA
0 30
nautical miles

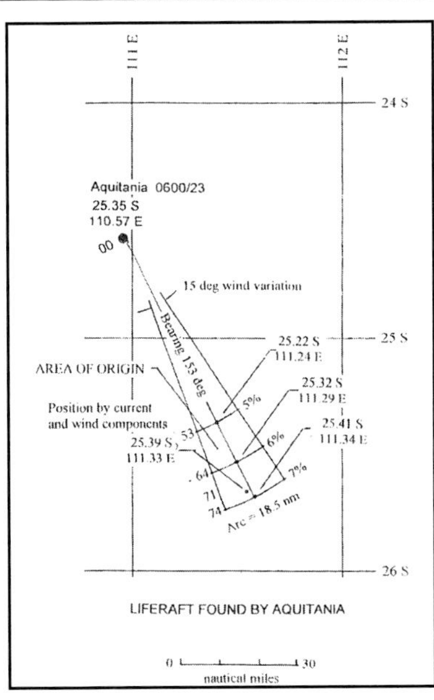

Liferaft Found By Trocas

On November 24 at 1500 hours, the British tanker *Trocas* rescued 25 German survivors from a rubber liferaft in position 24.06 S / 111.40 E. This raft would have been expected to display similar drift characteristics to the *Aquitania* raft and follow a similar drift pattern. That this single raft was found about 40 nm east of the Sunda shipping route and main area of flotsam has confounded most observers. Given that the *Aquitania* and *Trocas* rafts departed *Kormoran* at about the same time (nominally at 2200/19) and therefore at the same position, it is not possible to establish a credible drift path based on either wind or current. The northerly, almost direct path taken is clearly unrepresentative of the drift of the *Aquitania* liferafts.

The occupants, like those rescued by the *Aquitania* had slim prospects of rescue and little chance of making landfall without the means of propulsion required to counter the wind and current. Nevertheless, it is evident that a decision was made to reach the coast, instead of drifting to the location advised by Detmers. Unfortunately, the men on the raft had only a few paddles at their disposal to risk an attempt at the unlikely feat of reaching land. The average daily progress of the raft can be determined from the projected drift in accordance with the established drift criteria used for the *Aquitania* raft.

The rate of drift of this single raft should have exceeded that of the combined rafts, allowing for the application of a maximum drift of 7% by wind. The projected drift by wind, including deviation is estimated at 129 nm, some 72 nm west of the rescue position at 1500/24. The projected average velocity is therefore 1.14 knots over 113 hours to a theoretical position of 24.11 S / 110.22 E Using a 6% wind drift factor, the raft should have drifted to a projected position about 67 nm west of the rescue position on a bearing of 151 degrees at 1500/24. A projected position of origin at 25.41 S / 111.34 E (7% wind), 74 nm from the *Aquitania* rescue position is considered to define the southern extremity of drift for the raft originating from *Kormoran*.

The easterly progress made by the *Trocas* raft toward the coast and across the wind and current can be calculated using the projected drift position and the rescue position at 1500/24. Initially, when light winds prevailed some easterly progress was made, but when the south easterly wind increased it was not possible to make any headway to the coast. In order to maintain an easterly position during the 113 hour ordeal, the raft is calculated to have moved due east at an average rate of approximately 0.6 knots. However, the speed of the raft was not sufficient to prevent the lateral movement created by the wind to overcome the considerable northward drift. This resultant total drift of 87 to

97 nm for the period, on a final bearing of 003 degrees, indicates that the raft actually moved northwards at an average velocity of 0.8 knots.

In hindsight, the men on board the raft were extremely lucky to have been rescued. They were fortunate that the raft had drifted along the Sunda- Fremantle shipping route and saved by the Fremantle-bound *Trocas.* Otherwise, and without constant westerly winds, the raft was destined to drift further north and away from the coastline and possible rescue. Similarly, a decision to follow the *Aquitania* raft may also have not resulted in rescue. At 0600/23, the projected position of the *Trocas* raft lies nearly 10 nm north-west of the *Aquitania* rescue position, a distance probably too far for detection by *Aquitania.* The drift pattern also casts doubt on whether the small raft could have been located by the search aircraft or ships, north of and remote from the main area of flotsam.

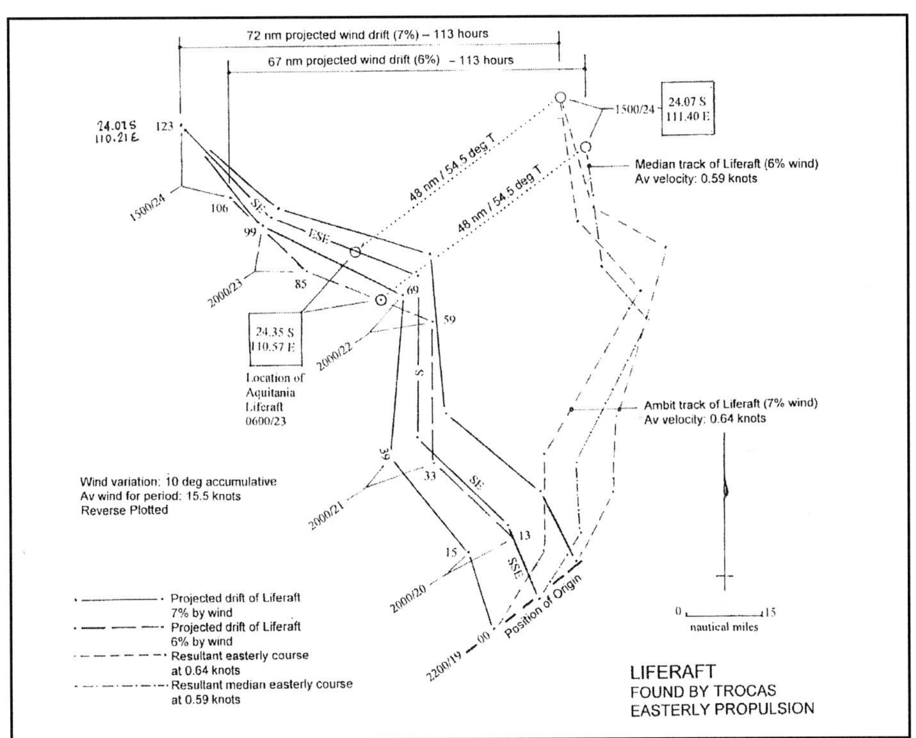

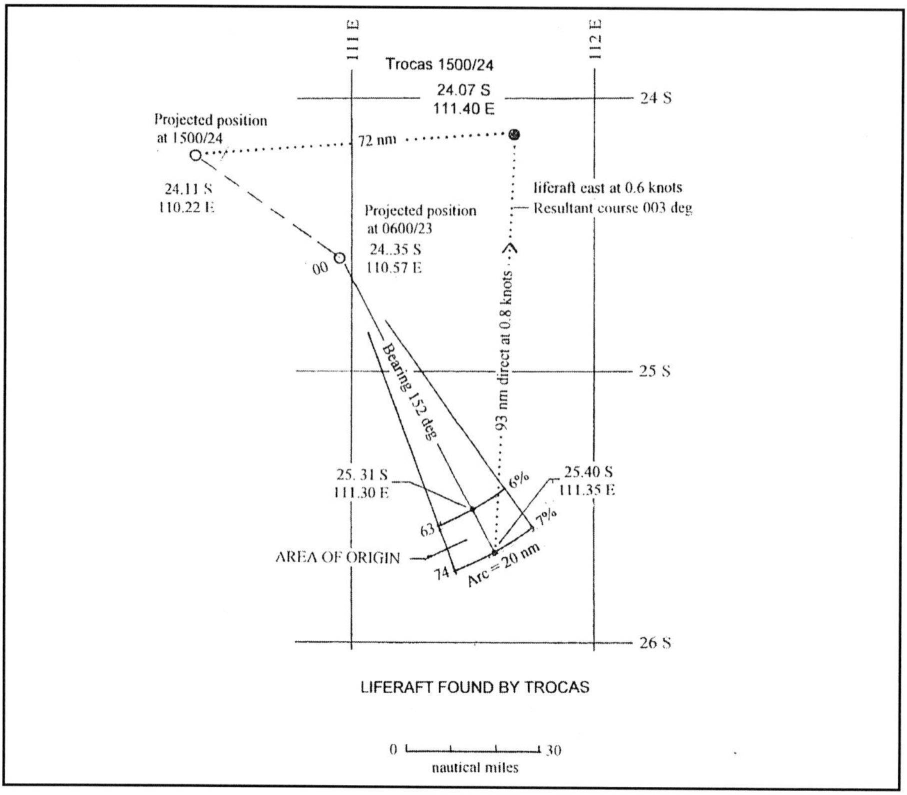

111 E
112 E
Trocas 1500/24
24.07 S
111.40 E
24 S
Projected position
at 1500/24
72 nm
24.11 S
110.22 E
liferaft cast at 0.6 knots
Resultant course 003 deg
Projected position
at 0600/23
24..35 S
110.57 E
00
93 nm direct at 0.8 knots
Bearing 152 deg
25 S
25. 31 S
111.30 E
6%
25.40 S
111.35 E
7%
63
AREA OF ORIGIN
74
Arc = 20 nm
26 S
LIFERAFT FOUND BY TROCAS
0 30
nautical miles

Raft / Lifebelt Found By Wyrallah

The 1000 ton ex coastal steamer *Wyrallah,* shown here designated as HMAS *Wilcannia* in 1943

On November 28 at 0800 hours, a small German metal raft containing a body and a German lifebelt were found by the search vessel HMAS *Wyrallah* in position 24.10 S / 110.54 E. The raft is described as consisting of two conventional oblong steel floats with a platform capable of supporting 4 persons and the lifebelt is presumed to be of the standard issue kapok type. It appears unusual that these contrasting objects, which are considered to have vastly different drift characteristics, were recovered in the same position.

Alternatively, the lifebelt may have been on the raft and had been dislodged near the time of the recovery. Nevertheless, a current and wind drift analysis for both objects is required to ascertain whether independent drift was possible and to determine if the objects were likely to have come from a common position of origin.

In comparison to a rubber raft and lifeboat, this type of raft construction produces greater water resistance on the structure and hence slower movement by the action of wind, current and waves. In this regard the free drifting and normally accepted wind factors of 5- 7% are of little relevance to the speed of the raft and a range of lesser values should be applied. Likewise, when compared to flotsam of a non- porous nature, the water absorbed by the kapok gradually reduces the profile and buoyancy of the lifebelt to the point where the action of the wind on the object would be negligible. It is therefore considered prudent to assess the drift of the lifebelt by current alone.

If 3% and 4% wind factors are applied to the liferaft, the drift distances for the 201 hours duration, including deviation, at the average wind speed for the period of 14.6 knots, vary from 106 to 142 nautical miles with respective velocities of 0.53 and 0.71 knots. The direct distances from the recovery position to the position of origin are 91 and 121 nautical miles on a central bearing of 155 degrees. Analytically and on this basis, the liferaft could only have reached the recovery point by current over deviated distances of 100 and 133 nautical miles in 201 hours, resulting in velocities of between 0.50 and 0.66 knots. Although the range of the drift rates for the liferaft and lifebelt are similar, the rates can be rationalized to reflect the independent drift speeds of the objects by wind and current. This can be achieved by assessing the drift rates equal to, or in excess of the average current.

When the rate of drift of the lifebelt equals the velocity of the current (0.58 knots), a similar velocity for the raft can be interpolated by using a nominated wind value of approximately 3.5%. This simply means, in order that the lifebelt maintains an average velocity of 0.58 knots by current, the raft should drift, albeit over a longer distance, to the same location and in the same timeframe at a slightly increased velocity of 0.62 knots (3.5% of wind). The relativities of wind and current can be further expanded to include velocities in excess of 0.6 knots, but this would produce results showing a surplus wind driven surface current component, an inconsistency which would compromise the accepted wind factor and ocean current estimates.

It is possible that the lifebelt could have drifted from the *Kormoran* to the recovery point at a lesser velocity than the prevailing current. The sprawling form of the object could easily have produced an erratic drift path accentuated by wave action and hence even drift at a slower rate in accordance with the equivalent wind value of the raft. From the scant information available on the shape and structure of the raft and floats, it is considered inappropriate to provide for a designated wind factor to determine the extent of drift by wind. Another explanation for lower than expected rates of drift for these and other objects relates to the actual position of origin. For example, if the objects were to have originated from a transition zone, an area of fluctuating weak currents influenced by the extremities of the Westralian and Leeuwin currents, then these abnormal conditions could effectively slow the initial drift and result in an overall reduction in velocity.

In summary, there are two possible means by which the drift of the objects can be finally measured. Firstly, that the lifebelt moved at approximately the speed and direction of the current and the raft moved by wind at a similar speed in a drift pattern consistent with the relevant applied wind factor (3.5%). In this instance, the central position of origin is at 25.46 S / 111.44 E on a bearing of 155 degrees, 106nm from the recovery position. Alternatively, the nature and shape of the drift material caused both objects to drift with an increased deviation within their respective drift paths, resulting in velocities of less than the average current equivalent. In this instance, at 3% wind drift and by current alone, a drift rate of about 0.5 knots (90% of current) could be expected from a central position of origin of 25.32 S / 111.37 E. A location within the drift area between the nominated positions is therefore the most likely point of origin for the raft and lifebelt.

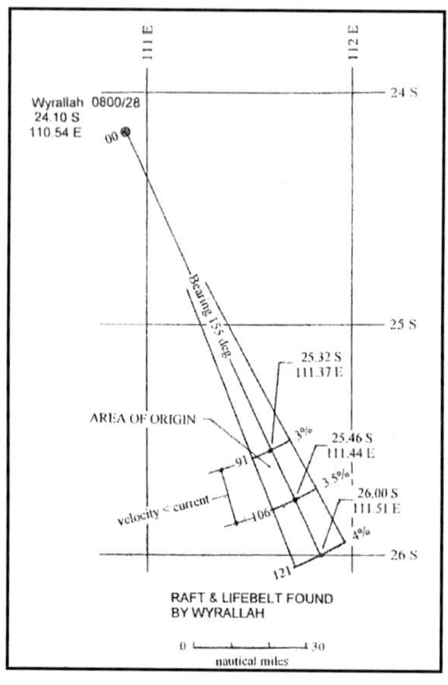

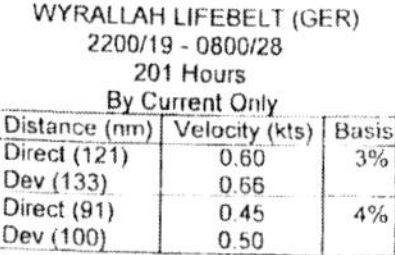

WYRALLAH LIFEBELT (GER)
2200/19 - 0800/28
201 Hours
By Current Only

Distance (nm)	Velocity (kts)	Basis
Direct (121)	0.60	3%
Dev (133)	0.66	
Direct (91)	0.45	4%
Dev (100)	0.50	

Deviation: 10%

WYRALLAH RAFT (GER)
2200/19 - 0800/28
201 Hours

	4% Wind	3% Wind
Distance (nm)	Velocity (kts)	
Direct (121)	0.60	
By Wind (135)	0.67	
Dev (142)	0.71	
Direct (91)		0.45
By Wind (101)		0.50
Dev (106)		0.53

Deviation: 5%

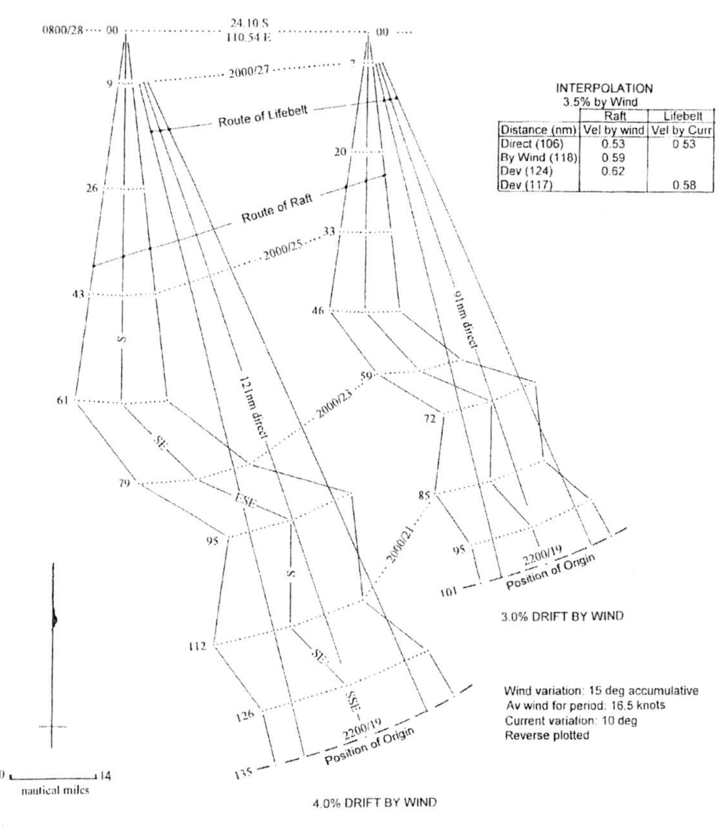

INTERPOLATION
3.5% by Wind

	Raft	Lifebelt
Distance (nm)	Vel by wind	Vel by Curr
Direct (106)	0.53	0.53
By Wind (118)	0.59	
Dev (124)	0.62	
Dev (117)		0.58

RAFT & LIFEBELT
FOUND BY WYRALLAH
EXTENT OF DRIFT BY WIND & CURRENT

RAN Carley Float (Raft) Found By Heros

The tug *Heros* – 380 tons, requisitioned by the RAN in 1939

On November 28 at 1100 hours, HMAS *Heros* recovered an RAN issue Carley raft in position 24.07 S / 110.58 E. The raft, which had been damaged by gunfire and containing an RAN lifebelt was found floating low in the water with the drogue flooring in the detached position. A wooden box, described as a dog kennel was found nearby. This type of raft, capable of supporting about 20 persons consisted of an oval- shaped copper tube about 450 mm in diameter with internal bulkheads dividing the tube into compartments to prevent total flooding, surrounded by cork and wrapped in canvas. That the raft was only just floating is indicative that most, if not all of the compartments had been holed and whatever buoyancy remained was due to the floatation properties of the cork. A raft in such condition should not be influenced by wind and would thus drift by current alone. The open dog box also should not have drifted by wind assistance alone because of the extent of its immersion below the water surface.

Considering that the objects were reportedly found in the same location, it would seem plausible to suggest that the raft and kennel originated from similar locations, but this is not necessarily the case. If the raft was relatively undamaged and retained normal buoyancy, it should have drifted by wind assistance at a velocity exceeding that of the kennel. In this instance it is obvious that later water intrusion of the internal compartments must have occurred, thus ultimately reducing the velocity of the raft to approximately the velocity of the kennel. If a maximum velocity for wind drift of 7% is employed in accordance with the established wind speed and direction, it is estimated that the raft (with drogue raised) originated about 26 nm south of *Kormoran's* position at 2300/19, the most southerly position possible for the origin of the raft. A lesser wind drift value would close the distance between *Kormoran* and *Sydney*. For example, a 5% value, which is probably considered a minimum for a raft of this type, would have *Sydney* located about 18 nm south of *Kormoran*. It should also be noted that if the drogue was already lowered when the raft began drifting, a slower rate of drift would occur due to the sea anchor effect, further reducing the southerly distance of *Sydney* from *Kormoran*. The probability that the raft originated from a position south of *Kormoran's* final location must therefore be weighed in the context of whether the raft later sustained further gunfire damage, which could only have resulted in the random actions of some of the *Kormoran* survivors.

The observed damage to the raft is supportive of the scenario that the raft was blown overboard during the initial engagement at 1830/19. This same raft, the only object in existence from *Sydney* and on display at the Australian War Memorial in Canberra shows some large holes in the floatation tube, undoubtedly caused by shrapnel, numerous bullet holes and a dislodged and fractured drogue. On entering the sea, water would have intruded into the floatation compartments very quickly through the large number of perforations, resulting in a sudden increase of the weight and drag resistance ratios and a dramatic decrease in buoyancy. Inevitably, the raft would drift unaffected by wind and at a rate of less than the prevailing current.

At 0130/20 when *Kormoran* was scuttled and the dog kennel began drifting, the relative position of the Carley float if drifting from 1830/19 is calculated at 2 nm south and 3nm east of *Kormoran*. This close proximity would suggest that both objects would have drifted at about the same velocity for the remaining 201.5 hours until retrieved at 1100/28 and therefore each object possessed similar buoyancy characteristics and were similarly influenced by the current. Such an analogy may be difficult to verify. However, the movement and buoyancy of the timber fabricated kennel should have been increasingly affected by the absorption of water until nearly all the object became immersed. The flat- sided shape could presumably also account for a degree of resistance or drag to further slow the object. Moreover, that these two objects may appear incompatible in regard to drift characteristics, it is evident that each could have moved at similar rates by current alone.

In consideration of the mass of each object and the affect of the current thereon, there is reason to suggest that the Carley float could have originated from a position north of the *Kormoran* sinking site. For this to have occurred, the raft moved at a lesser speed than the kennel. There is no doubt that compared to the kennel the weight of the raft had greater resistance to the current and wave action. That the raft moved slower is likely but impossible to measure. Of most relevance is the fact that the kennel, like most other flotsam, should remain largely unaffected by wave action and as a consequence maintain a more consistent velocity compared to the heavier flooded raft. For example, the comparative velocities for a position of origin of the raft nominally 10 nm north of *Kormoran* at 0130/20, demonstrates that the raft would drift 91nm at a rate of 0.45 knots (80% of current) and the kennel 101 nm at 0.50 knots (90% of current) to a common position of retrieval in 201.5 hours.

It has been shown that each object has different drift characteristics and although they both drift at less than the velocity of the current, the kennel has a drift rate in excess of the raft. The raft would also have a tendency to drift in a more direct path, whereas the smaller kennel would tend to cover additional distance (deviation), which would account for the overall increased velocity. The movement of these small and larger immersed objects further demonstrates the variation in the rate of drift by current. For instance, due to the extra weight of water within, a flooded or swamped lifeboat would be expected to drift at a lesser rate than the damaged Carley float.

The source of the apparent smaller holes in the raft is most perplexing and unlikely to have been caused by shell fragments or by any of *Kormoran's* armament. Even though the results of scientific examinations revealed these holes were not caused by small caliber bullets, there is prima- facie evidence from those aboard HMAS *Heros* who reportedly extracted some bullets as souvenirs. In the case of the raft receiving all of the damage whilst aboard *Sydney* and found 9 days later in a submerged state, it would indicate an extremely slow rate of drift in the order of from 0.2 to 0.3 knots, suggesting a position of origin about 45 nm north of *Kormoran*, a position which is considered incompatible with the established drift analysis of the other objects.

The results of this analysis indicate that the relative positions of origin of the objects are not too far apart. In consideration of the relative velocities, it has been demonstrated that *Sydney* could be conservatively located somewhere within the drift line extending 10 nm north or 10 to 15 nm south of *Kormoran*. More importantly, this exercise has identified that the objects were likely to have originated within a limited area of drift, extending centrally from 25.28 S / 111.31 E to 25.51 S / 111.40 E.

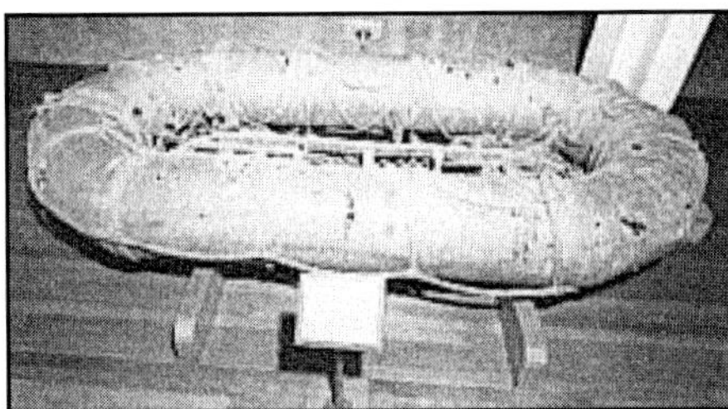

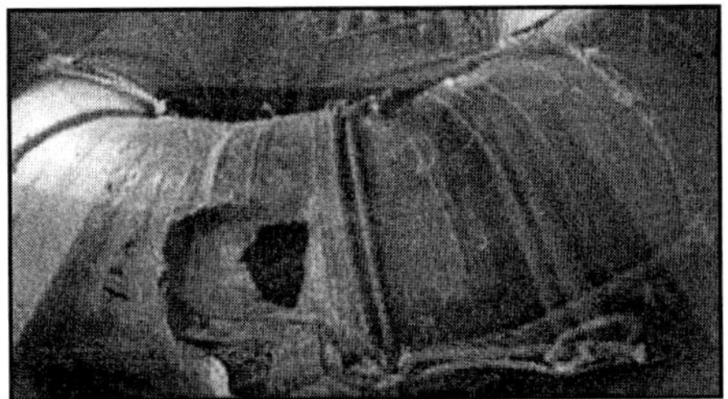

The Carley float (left) shows evidence of bullet holes and shrapnel damage (right)

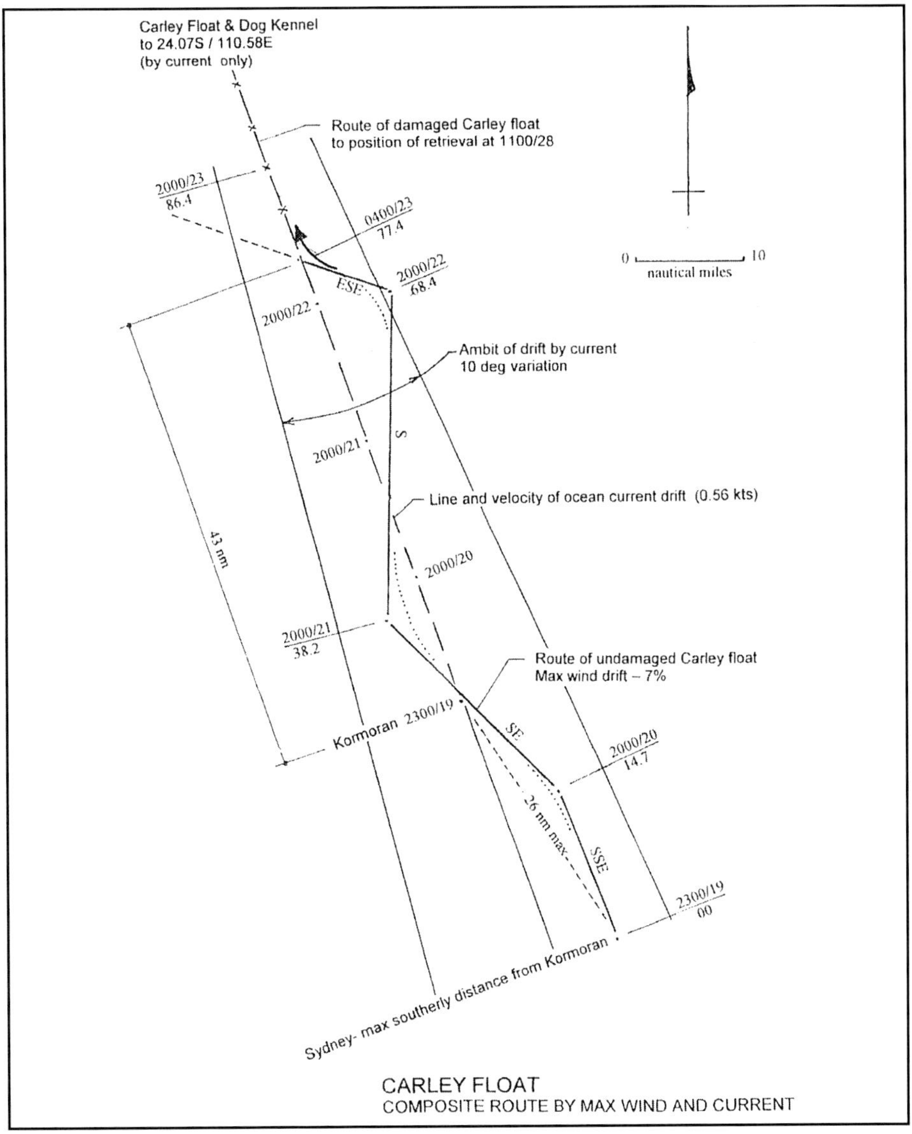

Carley Float & Dog Kennel
to 24.07S / 110.58E
(by current only)

Route of damaged Carley float
to position of retrieval at 1100/28

2000/23
86.4

0400/23
77.4

2000/22
68.4

ESE

2000/22

0 10
nautical miles

Ambit of drift by current
10 deg variation

2000/21

S

Line and velocity of ocean current drift (0.56 kts)

43 nm

2000/20

2000/21
38.2

Route of undamaged Carley float
Max wind drift – 7%

Kormoran 2300/19

SE

2000/20
14.7

26 nm max

SSE

2300/19
00

Sydney- max southerly distance from Kormoran

CARLEY FLOAT
COMPOSITE ROUTE BY MAX WIND AND CURRENT

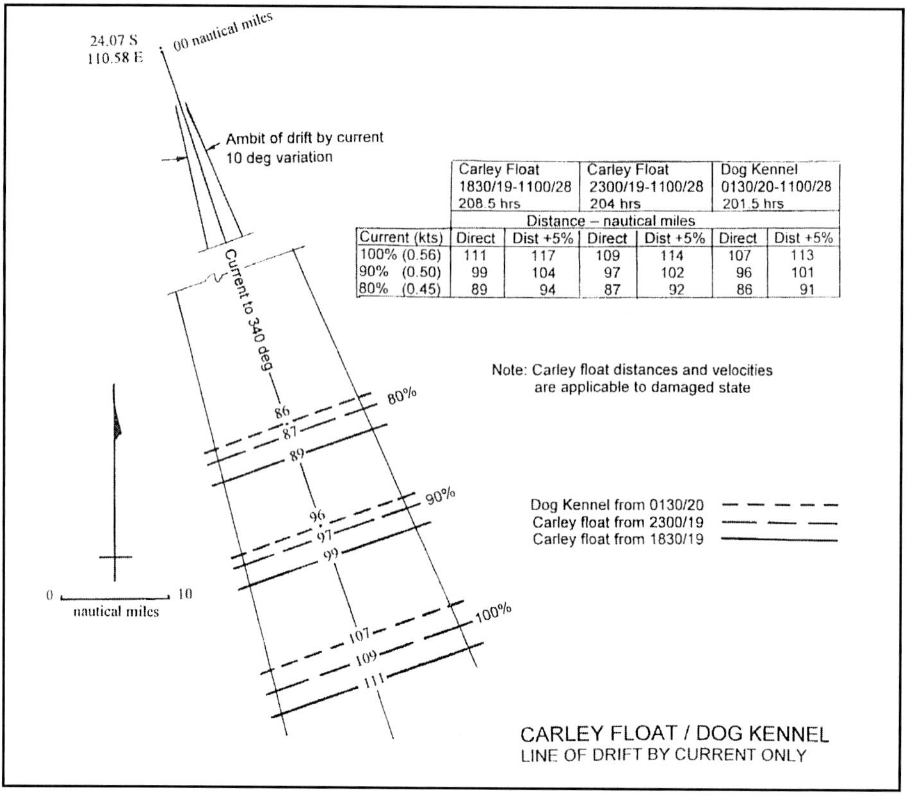

24.07 S
110.58 E
00 nautical miles

Ambit of drift by current
10 deg variation

Current (kts)	Carley Float 1830/19-1100/28 208.5 hrs		Carley Float 2300/19-1100/28 204 hrs		Dog Kennel 0130/20-1100/28 201.5 hrs	
	Distance – nautical miles					
	Direct	Dist +5%	Direct	Dist +5%	Direct	Dist +5%
100% (0.56)	111	117	109	114	107	113
90% (0.50)	99	104	97	102	96	101
80% (0.45)	89	94	87	92	86	91

Current to 340 deg

Note: Carley float distances and velocities are applicable to damaged state

86 87 89 80%

96 97 99 90%

107 109 111 100%

Dog Kennel from 0130/20
Carley float from 2300/19
Carley float from 1830/19

0 10
nautical miles

CARLEY FLOAT / DOG KENNEL
LINE OF DRIFT BY CURRENT ONLY

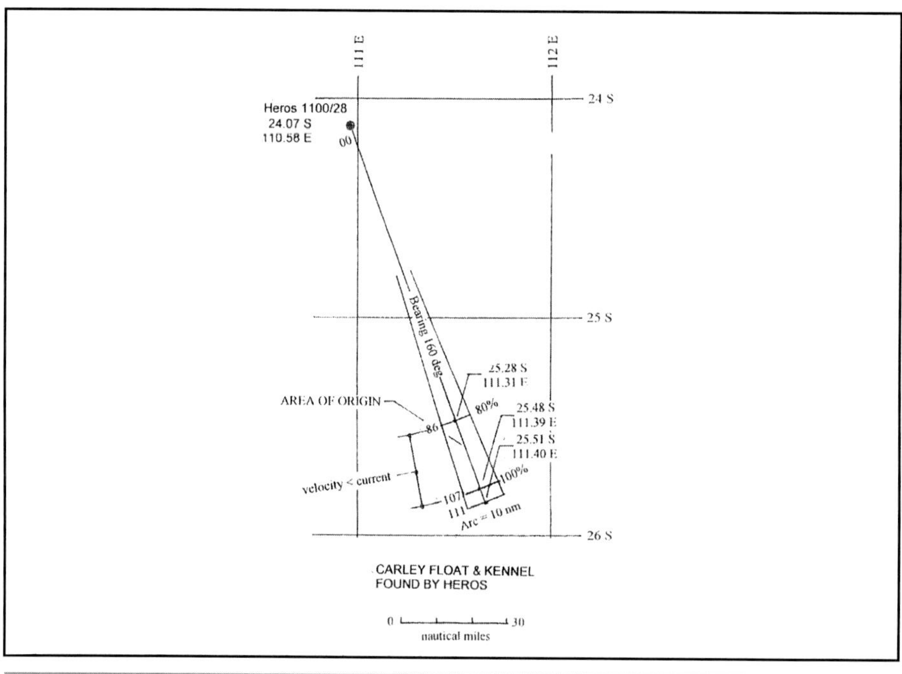

CARLEY FLOAT & KENNEL
FOUND BY HEROS

RAN Lifebelts Found By Evagoras & Wyrallah

On November 27 two lifebelts of the type issued to the crew of Australian warships and almost certainly from HMAS *Sydney* were recovered by search vessels in positions 26.06 S / 110.49 E at 1900 hours and at 24.22 S / 110.49E at 1815 hours. As both lifebelts were reported to be inflated, they had obviously drifted with wind assistance to their respective positions in about 188 hours. It is unusual that both objects had drifted for the same period, had similar drift characteristics and were found separated 16 nautical miles apart. It is possible that the lifebelt found by the British steamer *Evagoras* was lost overboard during the initial engagement and the other lifebelt began drifting from a southern location when *Sydney* was abandoned or capsized at about 2300/19. Alternatively, the *Wyrallah* lifebelt was the first to drift and the other lifebelt originated from a position to the north where *Sydney* had finally succumbed. However, in both instances it is difficult to conceive that the lifebelts could have been already inflated at the onset of the surprise attack, or that soon after, some of the crew had donned lifebelts and independently abandoned the ship. It is therefore considered that the drift of the lifebelts should be assessed on the basis that both had emanated from a common position.

That the *Wyrallah* lifebelt had apparently drifted slower and failed to match the approximate speed of the *Evagoras* lifebelt requires some explanation. Upon recovery, it was reported that the tie strap had been snapped and therefore very likely that the lifebelt had for a time supported a survivor from *Sydney*. In such a circumstance the lifebelt should have initially drifted at a significantly reduced speed, ostensibly at a lesser rate than the prevailing current until wave action had caused the strap to break and separate the deceased sailor. Given a common position of origin, the respective recovery positions and that both objects should have been subjected to the same wind conditions, the extent of initial drift of the *Wyrallah* lifebelt can be measured.

To ascertain drift consistent with the established wind speeds and directions, a range of appropriate wind factors for the lifebelts ought to be applied. If the normal wind value for a much larger buoyant liferaft is in the order of 5% to 7%, the inflated lifebelts should be conservatively assessed within the ambit of 3% to 5%, provided that the resulting velocities exceed the rate of current drift. A plot of these values shows an increasing and proportional range of drift distances and in each instance the initial drift line of the *Wyrallah* lifebelt (340 deg) intercepts within its projected drift path about 26 nm north of the position of origin at 2000/22 after 69 hours adrift at a velocity of 0.38 knots.

This velocity is representative of about 70% of the current and is considered consistent with the drift characteristics of a mainly submerged irregular-shaped object. It should be noted that if the light wind conditions of about 10 knots experienced for the 21 hours from 2300/19 to 2200/20 are used to measure the drift of the *Evagoras* lifebelt, the resultant velocities are less than the current and hence there is no applicable wind driven component. In order to correct the anomaly, a wind velocity of at least 14 knots is assumed for the purpose of identifying the actual origin, hereinafter referred to as the notional position of origin.

If the position of origin for both lifebelts is governed by the drift analysis of the *Evagoras* lifebelt, which remained inflated throughout the period of drift, an assigned wind value should therefore result in similar velocities for both items, a 16 nm difference in drift and also account for the initial drift distance of the *Wyrallah* lifebelt. An applied 3% wind factor value is found to result in low velocities of approximately equivalent to the current. However, in order to achieve the required separation distance, velocities of about 0.72 knots are achieved for both freely drifting inflated objects using a 4% wind factor, resulting in an initial velocity of 0.38 knots for the 'occupied' *Wyrallah* lifebelt for the required period of 69 hours. In this case the notional position of origin is calculated at 4 nm further south of the calculated origin, which is based on the actual wind velocity experienced at the time. Wind values used in excess of 4% show ever- increasing and incompatible velocities for the lifebelts and should therefore be discounted.

The drift analysis of these two identical objects recovered at the same time demonstrates a 0.72 knot correlation of wind drift, comprising 0.56 knots by current alone and 0.16 knots by wind driven current for a period of 118 hours by the *Wyrallah* lifebelt and 188 hours by the *Evagoras* lifebelt. That the liferafts emanated from a common position of origin and were found 16 nm apart is ascribed to the erstwhile laden *Wyrallah* lifebelt, which initially drifted slowly by current for 69 hours at 0.38 knots. The direct notional distance of drift of the *Evagoras* lifebelt from the recovery point is measured at 115 nm on a bearing of 158 degrees and the *Wyrallah* lifebelt 100 nm, bearing 155 degrees to the notional position of origin. The central coordinates of the notional arc, about 30 nm wide and hereinafter referred to as the actual position of origin, can therefore be identified as 25.53 S / 111.37 E.

WYRALLAH LIFEBELT
2300/19 – 1815/27
187.25hours
Forward Drift

Wind	Time (hours)	Distance (nm)	Velocity (kts)
3%	2300/19		
	2000/22(69)	26	0.38
	1815/27(118.25)	64	0.54
4%	2300/19		
	2000/22 (69)	26	0.38
	1815/27 (118.25)	86	0.72
4.5%	2300/19		
	2000/22 (69)	26	0.38
	1815/27 (118.25)	115	0.96

*All distances inclusive of deviation

EVAGORAS LIFEBELT
2300/19 – 1900/27
188 HOURS

Distance (nm)	Velocity (knots)
Drift 3% Wind	
direct (84)	0.45
by wind (94)	0.50
dev. (103)	0.55
Drift 4% Wind	
direct (112) 115*	0.60
by wind (125) 128*	0.66
dev. (138) 140*	0.73
Drift 4.5% Wind	
direct (125)	0.66
by wind (141)	0.75
dev. (155)	0.82

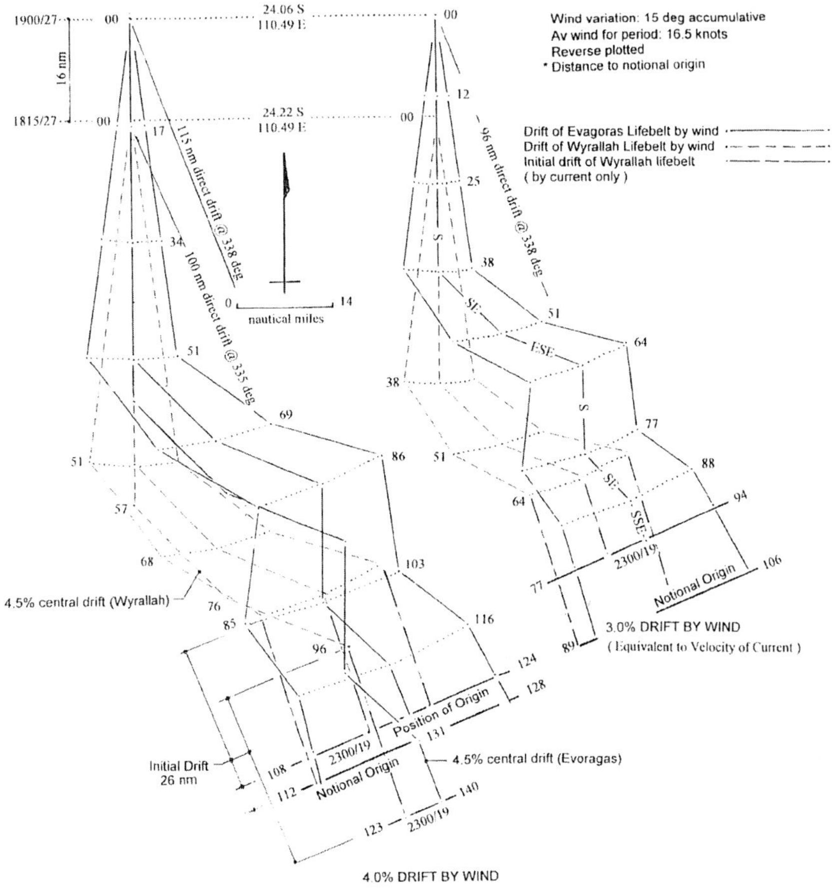

Wind variation: 15 deg accumulative
Av wind for period: 16.5 knots
Reverse plotted
* Distance to notional origin

Drift of Evagoras Lifebelt by wind
Drift of Wyrallah Lifebelt by wind
Initial drift of Wyrallah lifebelt
(by current only)

1900/27 00 24.06 S 110.49 E 00
16 nm
1815/27 00 24.22 S 110.49 E 00
115 nm direct drift @ 338 deg
100 nm direct drift @ 335 deg
96 nm direct drift @ 338 deg
0 nautical miles 14

4.5% central drift (Wyrallah)
Initial Drift 26 nm
Position of Origin
2300/19
Notional Origin
4.5% central drift (Evoragas)
4.0% DRIFT BY WIND
3.0% DRIFT BY WIND
(Equivalent to Velocity of Current)

RAN LIFEBELTS
EVAGORAS & WYRALLAH
EXTENT OF DRIFT BY WIND

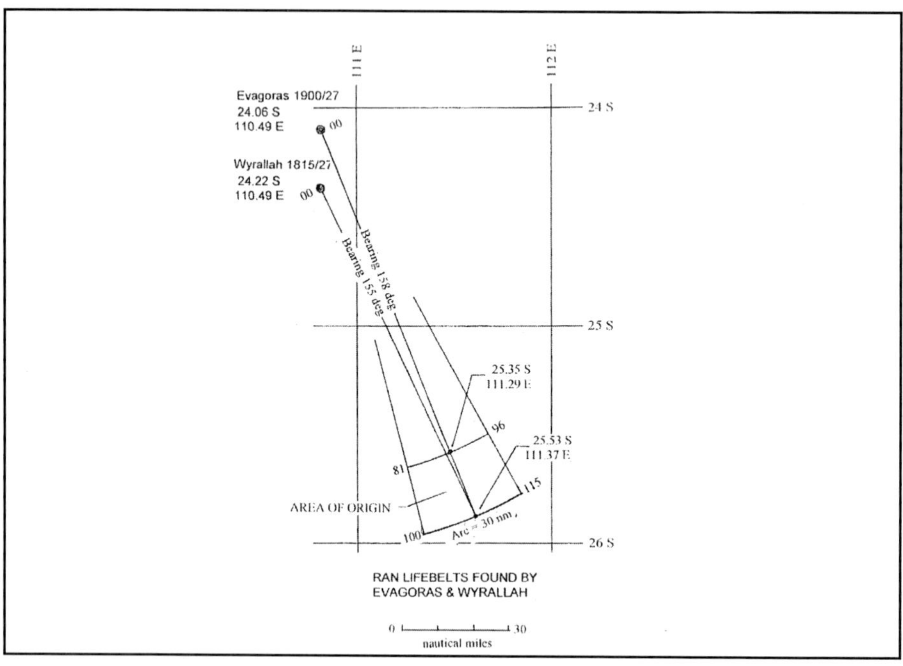
111 E
112 E
Evagoras 1900/27
24.06 S
110.49 E
00
Wyrallah 1815/27
24.22 S
110.49 E
00
24 S
Bearing 158 deg
Bearing 155 deg
25 S
25.35 S
111.29 E
96
25.53 S
111.37 E
81
115
AREA OF ORIGIN
100
Arc = 30 nm
26 S
RAN LIFEBELTS FOUND BY
EVAGORAS & WYRALLAH
0
30
nautical miles

LOCATING THE SITE

THE ORIGIN OF DRIFT shown in the diagrams for each object is representative of the minimum and maximum drift distances determined in accordance with the established daily wind and current conditions. In terms of assessing reliability of drift, it is considered that due to the unknown drift characteristics, the movement of the *Kormoran* metal raft and lifebelt is the most difficult to analyze. The objects found on November 27 and 28 and later influenced by southerly winds showed a similar pattern of drift to the north/north- west on an average direct bearing of 337 degrees. The other two objects, the rubber rafts from *Kormoran* containing survivors and found on November 23 and 24, drifted to 332 degrees due to the affect of the earlier and predominantly south-easterly winds. The combined areas of origin covers a drift distance of some 45 nautical miles, an area considered too large for an accurate assessment of the origin of drift and the final positions of *Sydney* and *Kormoran*. Interestingly however, if the diagrams of the areas of origin are superimposed a good indication of the relative positions of the sunken vessels can be obtained.

An overlay of the areas of origin displays distinct and common areas about 10 nautical miles wide from which the flotsam from *Sydney* and *Kormoran* could have originated. There is also an identified area from which all of the objects may have drifted, suggesting that *Sydney* and *Kormoran* were in close proximity at the point of sinking. However, in consideration of the *Sydney* lifebelts having originated further south, this area should be included within the *Kormoran* flotsam zone. The objects from *Kormoran* are thus shown to have originated north of the *Sydney* flotsam zone along a 12 nautical mile drift path from 25.40 S / 111.35 E to 25.28 S / 111.31 E on a central bearing of 338 degrees. The adjacent common area extending southerly 12 nautical miles to 25.51 S / 111.40 E is the most likely origin of the *Sydney* Carley float and lifebelts. Each 10 nautical mile wide area (to provide for wind and current variations) comprises 120 and 140 square nautical miles and demonstrably, these defined areas are very likely to contain the grave sites of *Sydney* and *Kormoran*.

It is significant that the drift analysis does not support the notion that *Sydney* could have been located to the north of *Kormoran*. The determining factor is of course the drift speed of the *Kormoran* liferafts. An over-estimated wind drift value in excess of 7% is required to be assigned in order for *Kormoran* to be sited south of *Sydney*. Alternatively, the average velocity of the reported light south- east winds on November 20 and 21 (10-14 kts) would have in fact been required to exceed 18 knots constancy until November 28. This however is completely at odds and inconsistent with the typical wind velocities recorded in any 8 day period in the vicinity of the flotsam area.

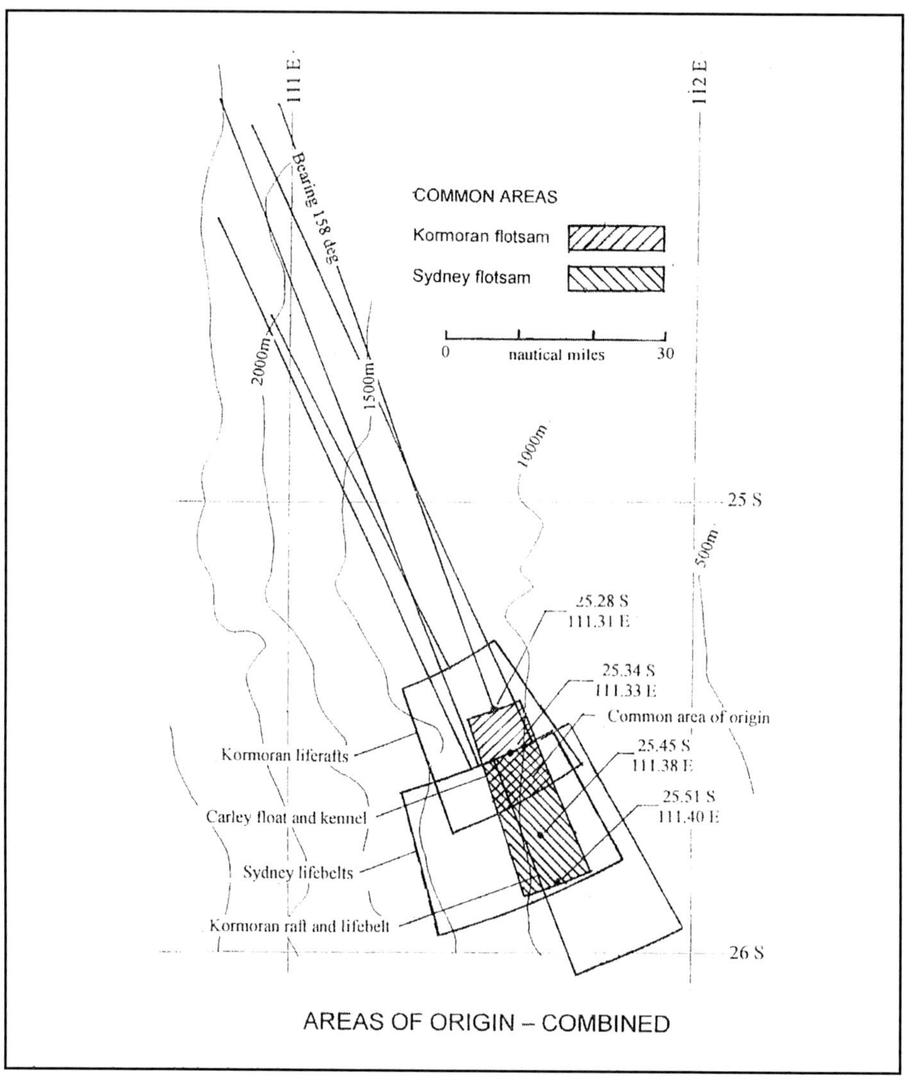

AREAS OF ORIGIN – COMBINED

Search Area Identified

The area location of *Kormoran* is confined within a central position between latitudes 25 S and 26 S and longitudes 111 E and 112 E, a distance of about 80 nautical miles north- east of the 'Official' *Kormoran* position of 26.40 S / 110.32 E, belatedly given by Detmers. It is inconceivable that any commander or navigator would be unaware of his approximate position at all times. After all, in this case there was plenty of time available to accurately confirm the position before *Kormoran* was abandoned and that Detmers subsequently gave a false position, only occurred after it was obvious there were no survivors from *Sydney*. However, the general position of 26 S / 111 E he most often referred to, generally satisfied his pretension.

Another more compelling argument concerns the deliberate misrepresentation of the position in order to negate the possibility of *Kormoran* ever being found. It is accepted that Detmers had no obligation to divulge specific details of the action, particularly those that may be considered unpalatable to the Australian authorities, or reveal information concerning the armament and equipment secreted on board *Kormoran*. Detmers appeared to adopt an opportunistic approach and only released sufficient information when required, including falsifying *Kormoran's* final position by reference to the diagonally adjacent and correlated coordinates. (Several *Kormoran* officers placed the engagement site north of his stated position).

The issue of whether Detmers selectively changed the position of the engagement site can be clarified in the context of the drift results. It becomes evident that the transposed position of 25.40 S / 111.32 E is located within the confines of the established *Kormoran* flotsam area. The position of 26.34 S / 111 E stated by Detmers when *Sydney* was first sighted at 1655/19 (transposed to 25.34 S / 112 E) also supports the relevance of the argument. Moreover, if the reconstructed path of *Kormoran* is reverse- tracked from the official position, the revised position of *Kormoran* at 1655/19 of 26.39 S / 110.56 E (transposed 25.39 S / 111.56 E) is within 6 nm of Detmers's stated position. Similarly, if the reconstructed path of *Kormoran* is tracked from Detmers's transposed position of 25.34 S / 112 E, *Kormoran's* final position of 25.35 S / 111.36 E is again located within the flotsam area. These transpositions in conjunction with the drift analysis results are largely considered to substantiate that the area location as previously determined for the *Kormoran* flotsam should be regarded as the most likely search area and in addition, confirmation that Detmers's 'Official' position is fictitious.

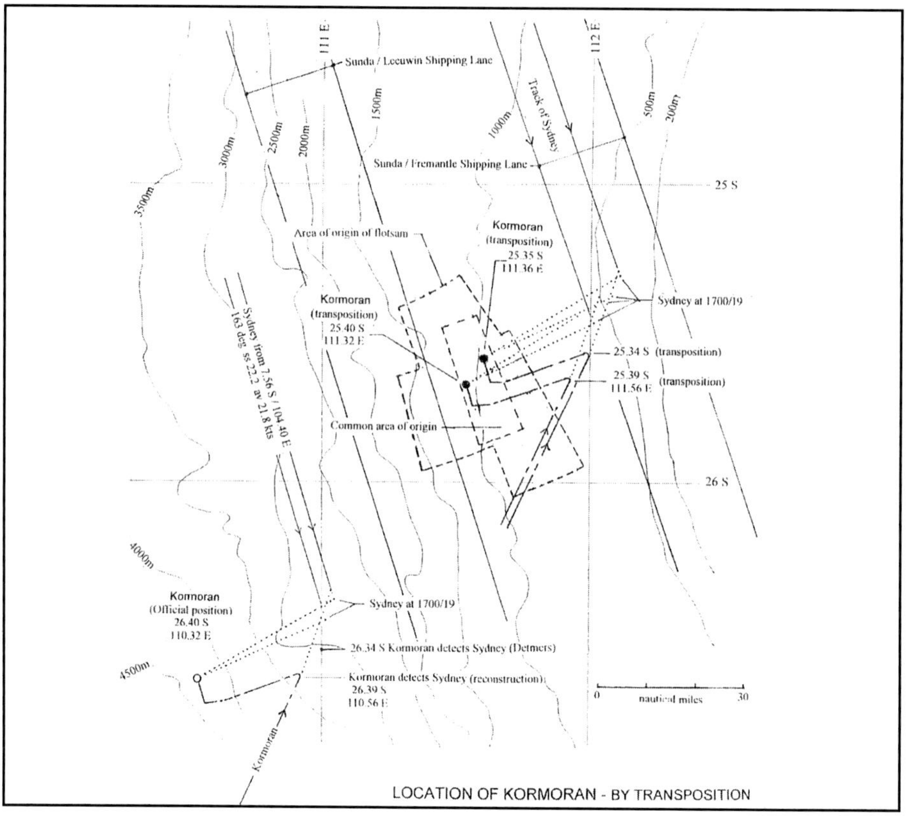

111 E
112 E
Sunda / Leeuwin Shipping Lane
Sunda / Fremantle Shipping Lane
Track of Sydney
3500m
3000m
2500m
2000m
1500m
1000m
500m
200m
4000m
4500m
25 S
26 S
Area of origin of flotsam
Kormoran
(transposition)
25.35 S
111.36 E
Kormoran
(transposition)
25.40 S
111.32 E
Sydney at 1700/19
25.34 S (transposition)
25.39 S
111.56 E
(transposition)
Common area of origin
Sydney from 7.56 S / 104 40 E
163 deg ss 22.2 av 21.8 kts
Kormoran
(Official position)
26.40 S
110.32 E
Sydney at 1700/19
26.34 S Kormoran detects Sydney (Detmers)
Kormoran detects Sydney (reconstruction)
26.39 S
110.56 E
Kormoran
0
nautical miles
30
LOCATION OF KORMORAN - BY TRANSPOSITION

111 E
112 E
25 S
26 S
25.28 S
111.31 E
by drift
25.34 S
111.33 E
by drift
AREA LOCATION OF KORMORAN
25.35 S
111.36 E
transposed
25.40 S
111.32 E
transposed
AREA LOCATION OF SYDNEY
25.45 S
111.38 E
by drift
25.51 S
111.40 E
by drift
32 nm
29 nm
Ambit of Sydney track
8 nm wide approx
Positions of Sydney at 1700/19
relative to Kormoran at 0130/20
Southern position of Sydney
limited by drift of RAN lifebelts
Search area 10 nm wide to allow
for wind / current variations
0
nautical miles
30
AREA LOCATION OF SYDNEY & KORMORAN

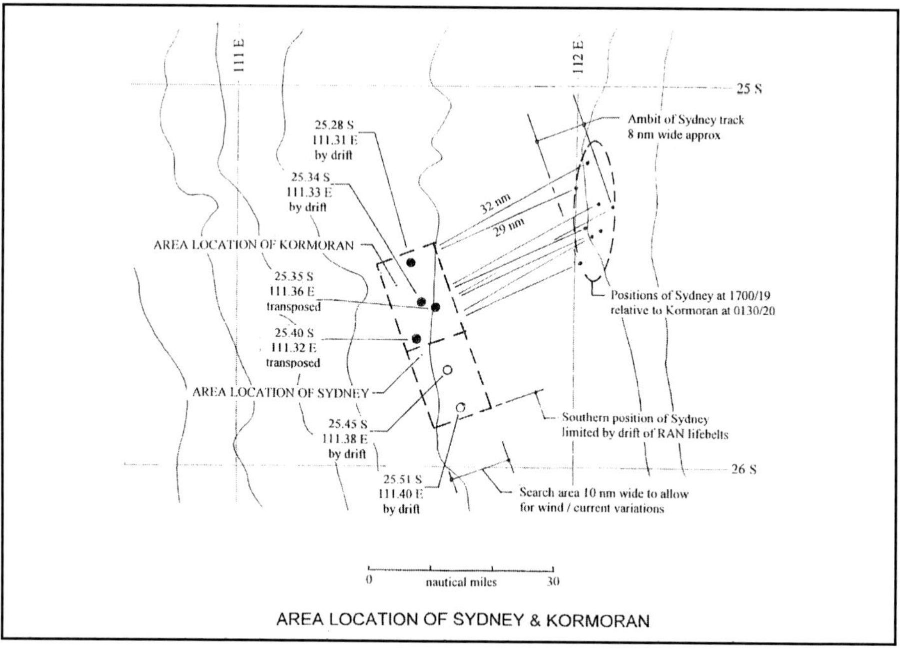

Contact Position

From the area location of *Kormoran* at 0135/20, it is possible to ascertain the position(s) of *Sydney* at 1700/19 in accordance with previously established relativities. As *Sydney* has already been shown to have been positioned 29 to 32 nm north- east, on bearings of 246 to 241 degrees respectively, a range of positions plotted from any point within the area location of *Kormoran* can be identified. The position of *Sydney* at 1700/19 from *Kormoran's* 0135/20 central location of 25.34 S / 111.33 E is calculated as 25.20 S / 112.03 E. Significantly, that this position is situated within the Sunda-Fremantle shipping lane is indicative of *Sydney's* movements on the return journey to Fremantle.

The range of available tracks that could have been employed by *Sydney* and the relevant positions at 1700/19 has previously been canvassed. In consideration of all of the available options, the coordinates of 25.21 S / 112 07 E is the most closely aligned to the above position of *Sydney* at 1700/19, thus revealing that *Sydney* had most likely sailed from 9.46 S / 105.59 E on a course of 160T at ss 22 knots after departing *Largs Bay* at 1900/17. In this case *Sydney* would have experienced a westerly drift of 9.2 nm compared to the previously calculated drift of 6.6 nm. It should be noted that because the allowable ambit of *Sydney's* track is about 8 nm wide to allow for the variation in sighting distances at 1655/19, a maximum westerly drift of up to 15 nm could have been experienced.

If it is accepted that Burnett decided to return via the most direct route to Fremantle on the standard course of 160T from the *Largs Bay* departure position, a simulation of the return track from the *Zealandia* handover position (7.56 S / 104.40 E) should also be investigated. In this instance the track of *Sydney*, inclusive of westerly drift is found to be located about 33 nm further west and remote from the flotsam and established areas of origin, and for this reason this return track should be discounted. However, if Burnett had chosen a course of 158Tfrom the handover position, *Sydney* at ss 21.5 knots would have been placed about 9 nm east of the 160T course from the *Largs Bay* departure position at 1700/19. Therefore, given the relatively close proximity to the established areas of origin, this appears to be the only alternative route that *Sydney* could have taken on the return passage to Fremantle.

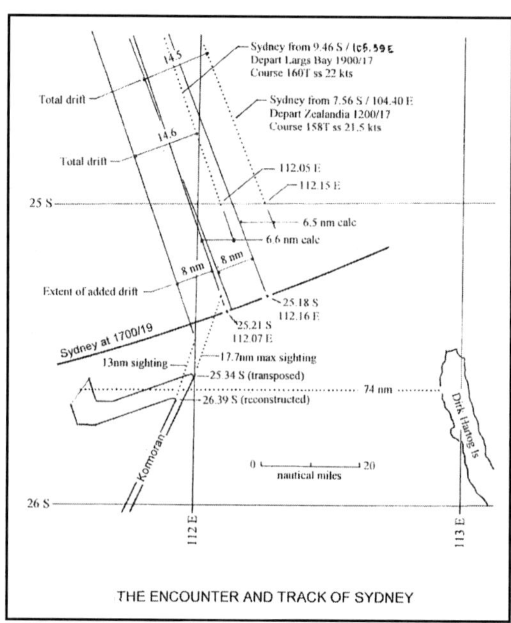

THE ENCOUNTER AND TRACK OF SYDNEY

Relative Locations

This analysis has established that the grave sites of *Sydney* and *Kormoran* lie somewhere within the confines of the defined areas of origin, herein referred to as flotsam / location areas. From the information previously gathered from the Action Report, the reconstructed search areas determined by hourly drift can be applied to the newly established location areas, providing that the relative locations of *Sydney* and *Kormoran* are found to remain within the respective location area boundaries. The final positions of *Sydney* and *Kormoran* are inextricably linked and assessed on the hitherto fact that *Sydney*, by necessity had stopped between 2000 and 2300 hours.

At 1925/19, the disabled and burning *Kormoran* was stopped and had ceased firing as *Sydney* continued toward the south-east at slow speed. It was only a matter of time before those in command of *Sydney* would have ordered the vessel to stop to control the fires and flooding. As previously canvassed, a vessel in such a severely damaged state would have predictably continued on course to extend the range to a safe distance before stopping. It has been inferred that the earliest opportunity arose at about 2000 hours with *Sydney* placed 8.5 nm south-east of *Kormoran*. It is also possible that *Sydney* continued on until 2300 hours (after which no further messages were received), or that *Sydney* had stopped during the intervening period.

The relative locations of *Kormoran* (adrift at 0.8 kts) and *Sydney* (south-east at 4.7 kts) from 2000 to 2300 hours should therefore be determined on an intermittent or hourly basis, noting that at any stage after *Sydney* had stopped (adrift at 0.8 kts) the distances between the vessels would have remained constant. The relative distances between the vessels assessed hourly from 2000 to 2300 hours vary from 8.5 to 24 nautical miles with an associated common drift of 0.8 knots after *Sydney* had stopped. Therefore, if these ambit distances are found to be situated at various positions within the respective location areas, the *Sydney* and *Kormoran* search areas can be more accurately defined.

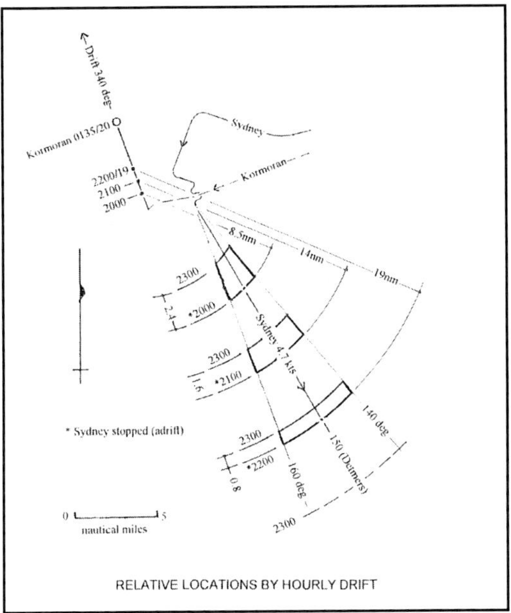

RELATIVE LOCATIONS BY HOURLY DRIFT

Location by Drift

In the case of *Sydney* adrift from 2000 to 2300 hours the separation distance of 8.5 nm is reduced to 6.1 nm (3 hours at 0.8 kts) by drift relative to *Kormoran's* position at 2000 hours and the final position of *Kormoran* at 0135/20 is located 4.4nm (5.5 hrs at 0.8 kts) further north along the drift line. If the above relative positions of *Kormoran* at 0135/20 and *Sydney* at 2300/19 are positioned within the respective location areas, the search areas become clearly delineated. In order to arrive at a consensual position, the central position within the search area should be used for the purpose of establishing a search datum and to allow for *Sydney* stopping between the hours of 2000 and 2100. In this instance, central positions of 25.36 S / 111.32 E (*Kormoran*) and 25.44 S / 111.39 E (*Sydney*) are easily identified.

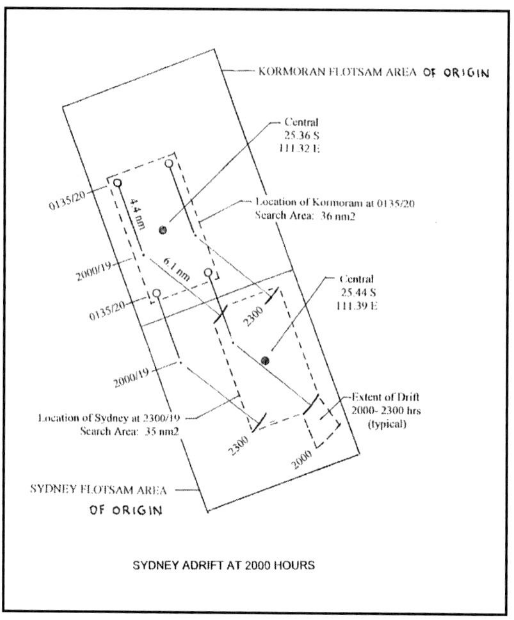

In the event that *Sydney* drifted between 2100 and 2300 hours the separation distance increases to 12.4 nm plus an additional drift of 3.6 nm by *Kormoran*. Although the resulting search areas extend toward the extremities of the location areas, the central positions of 21.33 S / 111.30 E (*Kormoran*) and 25.46 S / 111.40 E (*Sydney*) remain comfortably within the location parameters. Similarly, if *Sydney* drifted from 2200 to 2300 hours the total separation of 21 nm places *Kormoran* in a central position of 25.31 S / 111.29 E and *Sydney* at 25.48 S / 111.41 E.

In assuming that *Sydney* may have maintained the slow and constant speed of 4.7 knots until 2300 hours, the separation distance falls outside the boundaries of the location areas. This finding is significant because it supports the notion that *Sydney* would have, because of necessity, stopped before 2300 hours in order to stem the effects of the fires and flooding. It also supports the fact that *Sydney* had sunk before this time because no further messages were received in Geraldton after 2255/19. The expected message due at 2310 hours was never received.

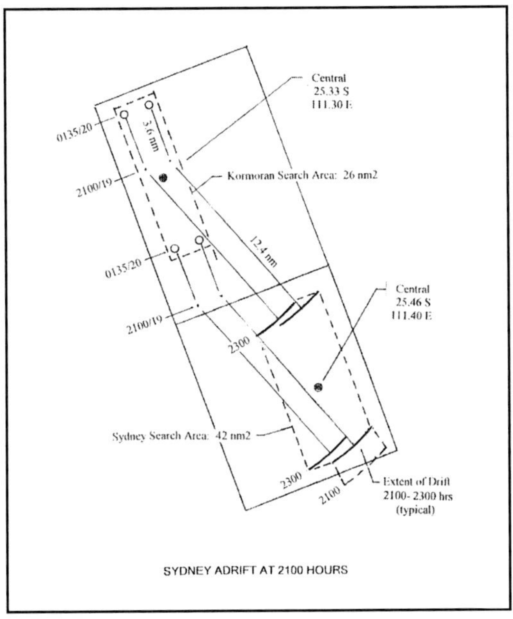

SYDNEY ADRIFT AT 2100 HOURS

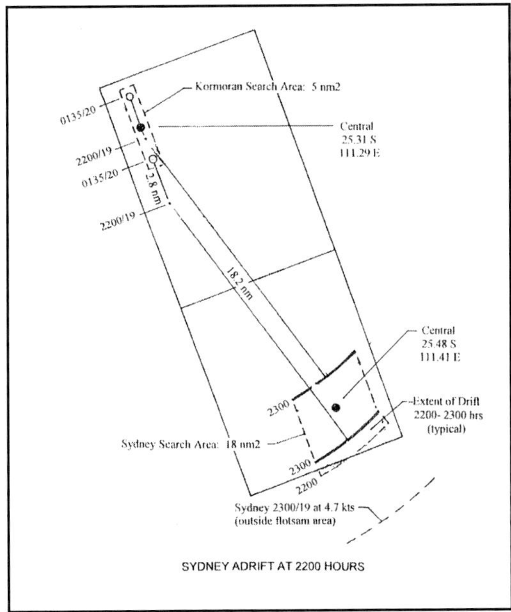

SYDNEY ADRIFT AT 2200 HOURS

Final Position

The datum positions described above form the basic coordinates of the search areas and are considered to be integral to finding the sunken vessels. The search areas are about 8 nm apart, each occupying an area of about 20 square nautical miles with central coordinates of 25.33 S / 111.30 E (*Kormoran*) and 25.46 S / 111.40 E (*Sydney*). *Sydney* should lie within 8 to 23 nm south-east of *Kormoran* on a bearing of 145 degrees. Located from the coast, the site is approximately 120 nm, bearing 243 degrees from Carnarvon and 130 nm, bearing 225 degrees (south- west) from Cape Cuvier. This compares with the 'Official' position which is situated 80 nm further south- west of Cape Cuvier. *Kormoran* can be expected to be discovered in depths ranging from 1100 to 1300 metres and *Sydney* in about 950 metres, approximately 30 nm west of the edge of the Continental Shelf.

It should also be noted that the location of the search area about 120 nm from the coast generally accords with the distance given by the survivors when *Sydney* was first sighted. However, it is now clear that the 'Official' position is based on the distance from the westerly protrusion of the coastline near Shark Bay. Similarly, this distance also applies to the search area from the northern coastal indentation near Carnarvon.

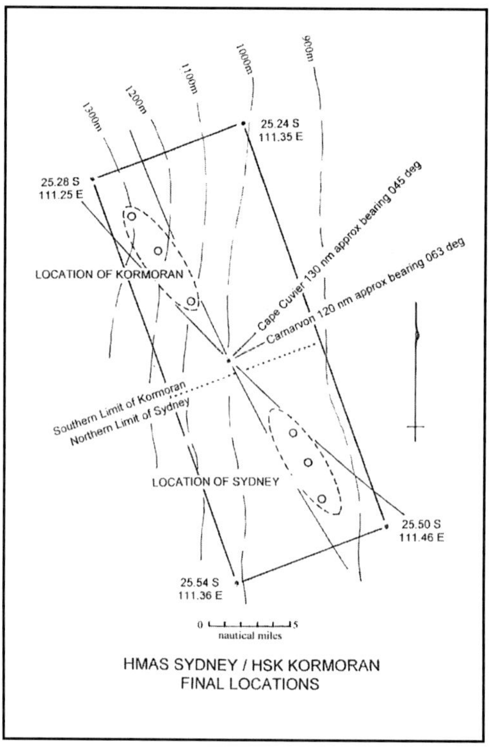

HMAS SYDNEY / HSK KORMORAN
FINAL LOCATIONS

It must be conceded that Detmers and in particular the officers involved in navigation and wireless telegraphy should certainly have been aware of the approximate position of *Kormoran*. Considering the array of positions given, it is indicative that Detmers succinctly ordered that the true location should never be revealed. Of all the stated positions, perhaps von Malapert unwittingly divulged the most accurate of them. Although he inadvertently suggested 24.32 S / 111.25 E, it is obvious that the latitudinal coordinate is demonstrably awry and could easily have been substituted in lieu of 25.32 S. However, in terms of general location, the most common reference to 26 S / 111E is representative of some 3,200 square nautical miles, a convenient location used to diffuse the issue of the wide range of positions previously stated by others. This same area could likewise be applied to any other specific coordinates.

SUSTAINING THE EVIDENCE

THERE ARE SEVERAL confirmatory avenues available to test whether the identified search area has been reasonably determined. This can be achieved by a detailed analysis of the hydrographic and oceanographic features of the area, by further redefining Detmers's motivations and bona- fides and a closer examination of von Malapert's Diary. The observations by those who purportedly witnessed an offshore battle and the discovery of debris ashore is also of relevance.

An indication of *Kormoran's* final location can be found in references contained in von Malapert's Diary. During the journey to the coast von Malapert made an attempt to estimate the daily distances sailed in the lifeboat commanded by Henri Meyer. The notes show that about 20 to 40 nautical miles per day were achieved, the rate of movement depending on the wind speed and direction. The final notation, estimating a total distance of approximately 153 nautical miles on November 25 is considered plausible and should therefore be examined in relation to the established search area.

Meyer's boat came ashore at Red Bluff about10 miles north of Cape Cuvier at 0800/25, a direct distance of 137 nm from the centre of the established search area on a bearing of 226 degrees. If in fact the boat originated from the search area, the actual distance sailed would have been greater due to the fluctuating wind directions during the 126.5 hour ordeal and the subsequent lateral drift (lifeboat bereft of keel) would have made the intended easterly heading impossible. The strong sea breezes causing a northerly drift within 15 nm of the coast and the maneuvering for a suitable landing place clear of the high cliffs would also contribute to the extra distance sailed.

In consideration of all these impediments, it should be concluded that Meyer's boat was affected enough by the natural elements to suggest it could easily have deviated an additional 16 nm to the landing point. An average speed of 1.2 knots (using a combination of sail and oars) was required to reach land within the timeframe. Petty Officer Paul Kohn's lifeboat completed a similar feat in 110.5 hours at 1.3 knots to land 16 hours earlier near Cape Cuvier at 1600/24. There is no way of confirming that the figure of 153 nm contained in the Diary refers to the total distance sailed. However, that this distance refers to November 25, it can be safely assumed that the notation was made at the end of the journey (0800 hours) and it is therefore conceivable that the Meyer and Kohn lifeboats originated from the established search area.

Flotsam Dispersal

One of the most contentious issues is the fact that only a small amount of flotsam was ever found. Apart from the liferafts, lifebelts and a dog kennel, no other debris was sighted by the numerous search ships and aircraft. It is accepted that sometimes there is little evidence of debris when ships are scuttled, explode or just lose buoyancy and this is often due to the peculiarities and vagaries of the seas, wind and current.

The general rules governing dispersal of flotsam are applied on the basis that the more buoyant objects are affected by wind and are therefore mainly wind assisted and the less buoyant are affected solely by current or a combination of both, depending on shape, size, and mass of the material. There is no doubt that the flotsam recovered from *Sydney* and *Kormoran* which drifted northwards were of buoyant material and thus more easily detected by the search vessels and aircraft, but what of the other objects which should have remained afloat throughout the search period?

The depth of the sea in the established search area varies from about 950 to 1300 metres, the area by definition, likely to be influenced by the Leeuwin Current. The sea bed, relatively flat from the coast to the 200 metre contour (Continental Shelf), develops a gentle slope to 1000 metres and then suddenly increases in depth. The 1000 metre contour defines the western limit of the Leeuwin Current in an area also likely to be influenced by the Westralian Current and termed, transition zone. In areas within the 100 to 1000 metre contours the weak Leeuwin Current tends to flow south- east towards the coast at an average velocity of 0.15 knots in November, although on occasions it has been recorded as flowing at more than twice the rate. This demonstrates that objects within the search area (and transition zone) could have drifted toward the coast from the effect of the Leeuwin Current, or alternatively northwards under the influence of the Westralian Current. That the search area was identified near the transition zone is regarded as fortuitous and should ultimately assist in resolving the dispersal of flotsam.

Southward Drift

During the quest to find survivors, the searching ships and aircraft combed an expansive sea area. The aircraft were ideally suited to finding large objects and evidence of patches of oil, which the search ships were directed to investigate. Of the few items found, it must be speculated that there was other wreckage which remained undetected due to the low buoyancy and an almost non existent profile above the water, making the prospects of finding such material very slim indeed. While most of the search ships were concentrated in the area where the survivors were found and to the north of those positions, the southern sector to latitude 28 S, searched mainly from the air was, apart from an unconfirmed sighting of an oil stain near the coast at latitude 27 S, found to be devoid of any wreckage. In this regard, the anecdotal evidence given by local coastal residents should be taken into consideration.

Although the claims of an action, reminiscent of a naval battle seaward of Port Gregory about 200 nm and remote from the established search area are difficult to substantiate, the evidence of wreckage and debris found ashore in the vicinity of Shoal Point and Bluff Point produces a more compelling argument. Some of the items recovered from the beaches shortly after *Sydney* disappeared are said to have included a rubber- tired wheel (*Sydney* and *Kormoran* both carried aircraft), a drum of cabbage, a large tank containing kapok and canvas covered lifejackets. Of most interest is the reported finding of a piece of timber marked 'HMAS *Sydney*' with a spent flare attached and a lifeboat of the type likely to have been stowed on board Sydney. That this debris came ashore on the few stretches of unprotected coastline is not surprising, and because most of the coastline to the north is protected by steep rocky cliffs it is obvious that other unseen and irretrievable debris could also have drifted to the coast.

The typical wind direction along the coastline varies from SW to SE with a strong southerly sea breeze extending 15 nm from the coast. As these conditions are not conducive to producing a southerly wind- assisted drift, the debris could only have drifted south by current alone and this could only occur with objects of low buoyancy (low profile). Except for the lifeboat and lifejackets, these characteristics can be ascribed to the other objects found on the shores.

The presence of the lifeboat is most perplexing and speculative to explain because it is not known whether it contained survivors. However if occupied, an undamaged boat would have predictably drifted to the north- west with the *Kormoran* lifeboats, or made headway toward the coast if there was some means of propulsion available. In this case the survivors should have been found. In contrast, an irreparably damaged boat whether occupied or not, that may have subsequently flooded or capsized while making for the coast, should have drifted unaffected by wind south- east in the current to landfall. The latter example is therefore demonstrative of the possible presence of the lifeboat north of Port Gregory. That the canvas lifejackets (probably filled with cork) came ashore independently is considered uncharacteristic because, as these items are generally subjected to wind drift, their presence can only be explained if they were somehow associated with the contents of the lifeboat.

That debris from the engagement was claimed to have been found north of Port Gregory about a week after *Sydney* disappeared, does not accord with the established drift criteria. In consideration of the drift distance (about 200 nm) from the search area and depending on the velocity of the Leeuwin Current at the time, (0.15 to 0.4 kts) the debris should have taken between 3 and 8 weeks to reach the coast near Port Gregory.

The Bodies

The claims of bodies seen floating near the coast is another issue which can be satisfactorily explained in terms of the location of the search area and the effect of the Leeuwin Current. The fact that a total of 725 sailors drowned (it is assumed that many were wearing lifebelts) as a result of the battle and only one body was recovered, indicates that the search vessels appear to have been inappropriately deployed.

Throughout the search process most vessels were searching too far north near where the flotsam and survivors were found and little attention was paid to searching the southern sector near the coast. Although the searching aircraft covered the coastal areas, altitudinal observations were not favorable to finding floating bodies. More importantly, by the time the search vessels arrived in the area on November 26, the bodies could have drifted, unaffected by wind, to the south- east from the identified search area at a rate of up to 9 nm per day, nearly 60 nm distant from the point of origin and only 30 nm from the coast. In the ensuing two- week period it is possible that some of the bodies, particularly those fitted with inflatable lifebelts, may have continued to retain some buoyancy. If so and due to the current, the trail of bodies could have spread over a distance of about 60 nm along the coast from latitudes 26.30 S to 27.30 S, confronting the Zuytorp Cliffs.

This raises the possibility of a link to the claims that the lighthouse tender, *Cape Otway* reported many bodies and debris in the water near the coast at an undisclosed location. The Shipping Plot indicates the vessel should have been close inshore in the vicinity of latitude 26.30 S on December 1 at approximately 1900 hours, a distance of about 105 nm (including allowance for deviation) from the search area. If in fact the bodies were observed in this area, they had drifted south easterly for 284 hours at a rate of 0.37 knots, a velocity consistent with that of the Leeuwin Current.

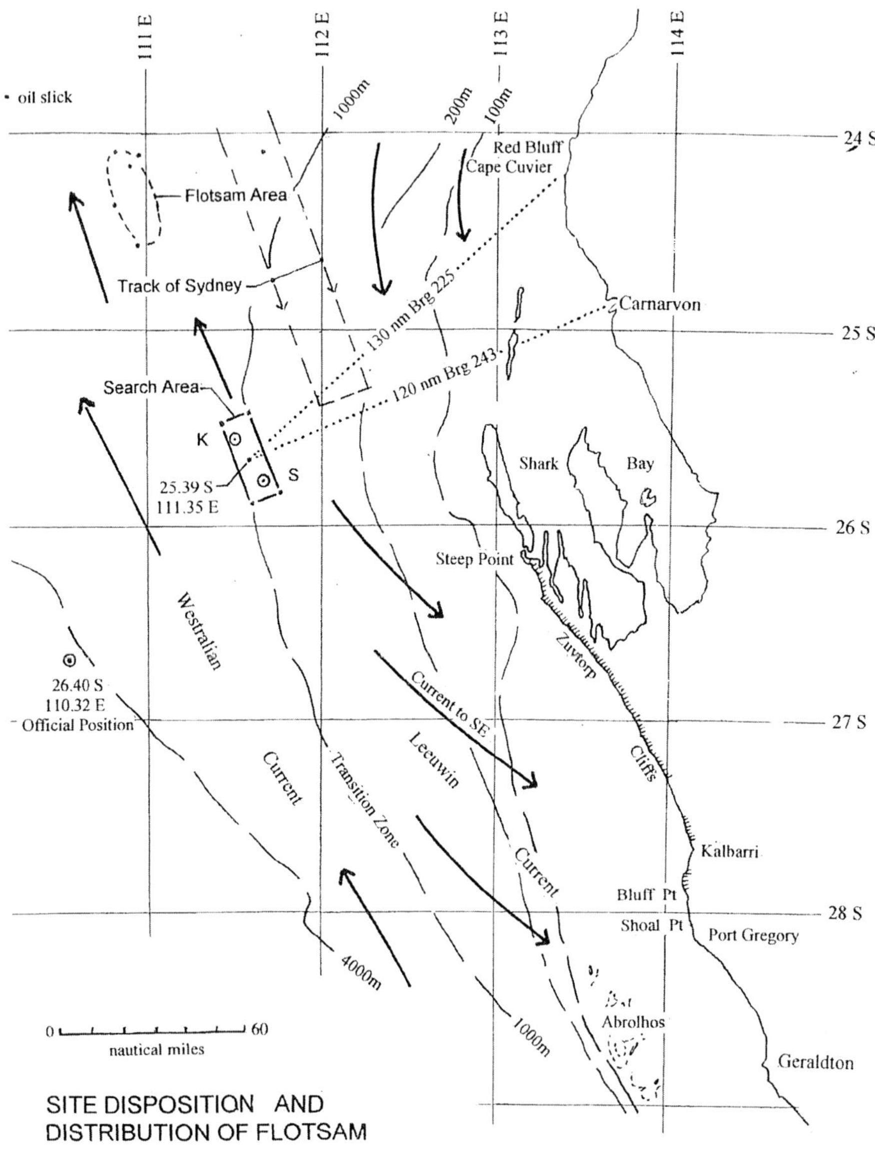

SITE DISPOSITION AND DISTRIBUTION OF FLOTSAM

Patches of Oil

Most of the objects found in the flotsam area had drifted there with wind assistance in the direction of the prevailing Westralian Current. The only objects found that could be argued were typical of the non wind assisted type were the dog kennel and possibly the kapok lifebelt, the drift rates of which would have been impeded by the gradual absorption of water. That these particular items originated from *Kormoran* and that the non wind assisted items from *Sydney* were not found in the flotsam area is not surprising and is due solely to *Kormoran's* location within the Westralian Current. This is further evidence that *Kormoran* should be located north- west of *Sydney* and that the non wind assisted debris from *Sydney* drifted in a different direction to the south- east. If this principle is consistently applied, it is possible to identify the source of the oil slick found by Catalina aircraft late afternoon on November 28.

Kormoran's diesel- powered engines consumed diesoline fuel, which would have been quickly dispersed by wind on the water surface and evaporated within a short period. In contrast, *Sydney* was equipped with steam turbine engines which used high viscosity fuel oil for firing the boilers. On contact with the sea, the thicker oil would also move rapidly with the wind due to the low coefficient of friction with the water, but take much longer to break down and spread over a wide area. In consideration of the respective properties of the fuels, the oil slick sighted in position 23.49 S / 110.10 E, about 40 nm beyond the flotsam area is regarded as most likely to have originated from the *Sydney*. The oil therefore drifted some 145 nm (direct) by wind from the established search area in about 210 hours at a velocity of 0.7 knots. However, in view of the increased susceptibility of the oil to wind variations, a velocity in the order of 1.0 knot over the deviated distance, is considered distinctly possible.

The origin of the linseed oil found in the flotsam area can be similarly determined. Both *Sydney* and *Kormoran* carried a supply of this oil, mostly used as a drying agent and additive for paint and on exposure to air, it thickens and becomes hard. The large quantity found by HMAS *Heros* floating in vicinity of where the vessel had retrieved the Carley float that same day on November 28 can be adequately explained. Those who observed the patch as circular, about 200 metres in diameter, very condensed and with the strong familiar aroma were describing accurately the appearance and properties of linseed oil in water. This signifies that a large container of the oil had obviously drifted by current to the area before leakage of the contents produced the unmistakable formation. It is considered that such an object, probably of made of steel and with low buoyancy could only have drifted by current without wind assistance and had therefore originated from *Kormoran*.

The Christmas Island Carley Float

The Carley float containing a body that came ashore on Christmas Island on February 6, 1942 and now accepted as having originated from *Sydney* is further evidence that the prevailing conditions and leeway values have been reasonably determined. The unidentified body was interned in an unmarked grave on the Island without autopsy and the float shipped to the naval authorities in Fremantle.

According to the Harbour Master, Reg Smith the float contained bullet holes (similar to the float found by *Heros*), but with no evidence of shrapnel damage. In both instances bullets were reportedly extracted from the floats, thus indicating they were of low velocity, probably the 9 mm ammunition used in automatic weapons such as the MP40 Schmeisser - the perforations certainly not as a result of the fusillade of *Kormoran's* smallest but much larger 20mm armament fired during the engagement. It therefore seems likely that some of the *Kormoran* survivors were responsible for this action and possibly for the death of the occupant(s) of the float. That the float had drifted for 79 days and had enough buoyancy to retain the deceased occupant suggests that most of the water-tight compartments remained intact.

As described earlier, the rate of drift of the buoyant float (by definition) can be assessed by the application of wind drift values or by a combination of wind assistance and current. If it is assumed that the drogue (flooring) was in the lowered position for most of the time adrift, the float was sure to have been significantly affected by the current. In this case the velocity of the wind would determine the additional rate of drift. However, if the drogue remained in the upper position, the speed of the float can be determined using an appropriate wind drift factor and without consideration of the prevailing current.

During November and December, the direction of the current and wind pattern from Carnarvon to Christmas Island show striking similarities. There is a north-west to north divergence of wind and current at about latitude 22 S, which would ultimately determine the initial direction of drift of the Carley float. However, that the float actually came ashore at Christmas Island can only be possible if it drifted northerly to about latitude 18 S and thence north westerly to its destination. It was unlikely to have otherwise drifted 953 nm at 0.51 knots (or 1000 nm including deviation) directly to the Island because the current and winds along this drift path tend westerly towards the South Equatorial Current. Therefore, the float most likely drifted along a north and north westerly route to Christmas Island, of which a detailed analysis can be made, according to the average wind and current conditions encountered from November to February.

As previously established, from about latitude 25 S the northerly- flowing ocean current (peak velocity in February) disperses over a wider area with a progressive reduction in velocity towards Christmas Island. The average northerly wind speed is also reduced, particularly north of latitude 18 S where an area of light (5 knots) variable winds, situated south-east of Christmas Island is evident for the months of January and February. In consideration of the location of these light winds and the timeframe of drift, it is likely that the Carley float deviated westerly and thence to a northerly direction in winds averaging 9.3 knots, in lieu of an easterly approach to its destination. As the current between latitudes 10.30 S and 18 S generally flows north-west at an average speed of 0.44 knots from mid December to early February (0.40 knots in November), the resultant wind/current vectors near latitude 12 S indicate that the Carley float most likely approached Christmas Island from the south.

Depending on the raised or lowered position of the drogue, two assessments of the speed of the float during the 1885 hours adrift can be made. In accordance with the average wind and current velocities between the respective latitudes, it is estimated that the float drifted a total distance of between 1105 and 1290 nautical miles at an average speed of from 0.58 to 0.70 knots in normal weather and sea conditions for the period. On average the float moved 60% by current and 40% by wind or local wind driven current. In summary, this float drifted slower than comparable rafts found much further south, no doubt due to the lighter winds of the region and the weed and barnacle growth reportedly attached during the 2 ½ months adrift.

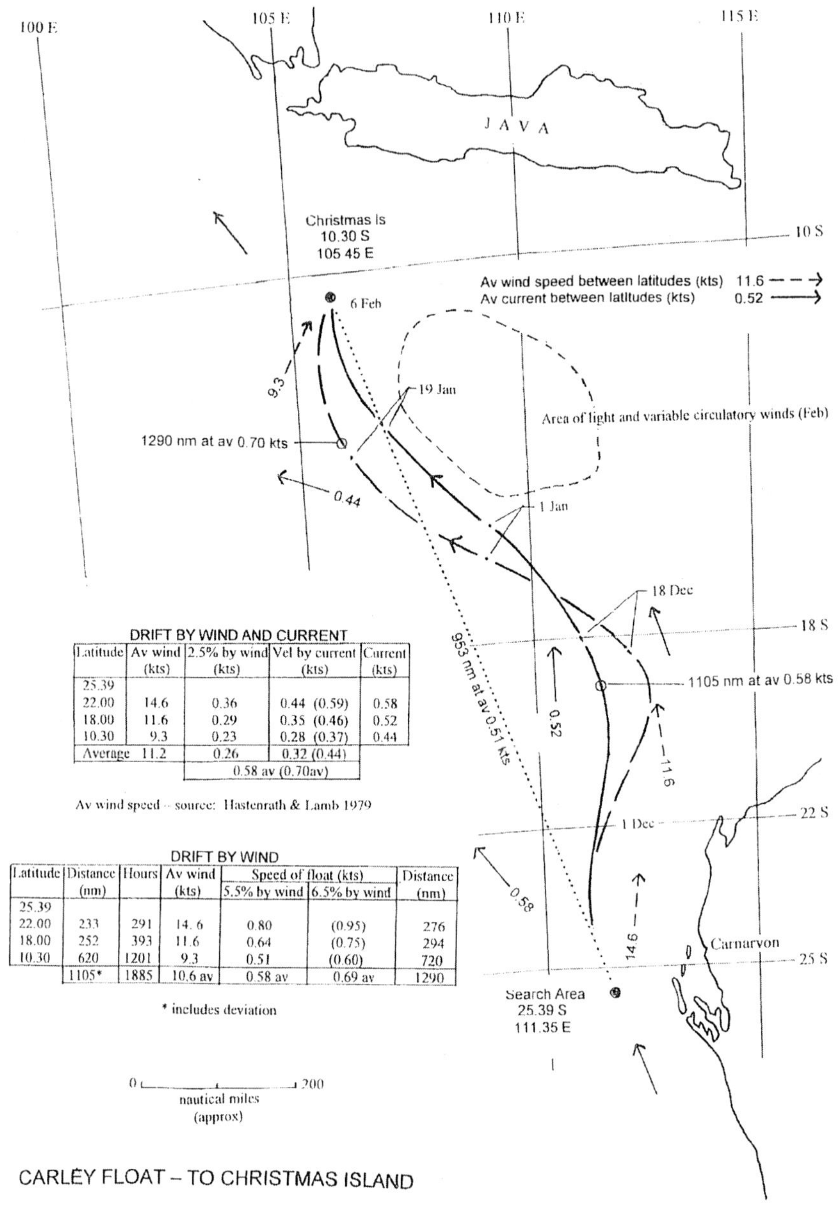

DRIFT BY WIND AND CURRENT

Latitude	Av wind (kts)	2.5% by wind (kts)	Vel by current (kts)	Current (kts)
25.39				
22.00	14.6	0.36	0.44 (0.59)	0.58
18.00	11.6	0.29	0.35 (0.46)	0.52
10.30	9.3	0.23	0.28 (0.37)	0.44
Average	11.2	0.26	0.32 (0.44)	
		0.58 av (0.70av)		

Av wind speed – source: Hastenrath & Lamb 1979

DRIFT BY WIND

Latitude	Distance (nm)	Hours	Av wind (kts)	Speed of float (kts)		Distance (nm)
				5.5% by wind	6.5% by wind	
25.39						
22.00	233	291	14.6	0.80	(0.95)	276
18.00	252	393	11.6	0.64	(0.75)	294
10.30	620	1201	9.3	0.51	(0.60)	720
	1105*	1885	10.6 av	0.58 av	0.69 av	1290

* includes deviation

CARLEY FLOAT – TO CHRISTMAS ISLAND

Concealing the Grave Sites

The initial reluctance by Detmers to provide a position for the engagement site is understandable because he was unaware of the actual fate and whereabouts of *Sydney* and whether there were any survivors. After all, the last observations that evening were only of the glow of the crippled *Sydney* at an indeterminate distance and after it had disappeared it was impossible to determine whether *Sydney* had already sunk, or had continued at slow speed out of sight, maybe even reaching the coast. On learning there were no survivors, he was at liberty to declare the false position in much deeper water in order to detract from any future search attempt in case *Sydney* had sunk in shallower depths. The false position also attests to Detmers's bona-fides regarding his description of the engagement.

It is unreasonable to suggest that Detmers's version of events should be accepted in totality. For example, his description of an unsuspecting *Sydney* drawing abeam of *Kormoran* before the surprise declaration is blatantly an illusion and an attempt to portray a careless Burnett as the reason for *Sydney's* demise. In spite of describing what are considered to be the plausible relative movements of the vessels after the engagement, he chose a believable story of deception to conceal the true circumstances of the initial encounter in order to allay any thoughts that he may have acted illegally such as firing while in surrender mode. In this regard and throughout the interrogation process, the survivors were solid in their support for Detmers, for they realized the consequences if the true circumstances were uncovered.

Furthermore, the subdued nature of the survivors is considered symptomatic of Detmers's actions. It is significant there were no obvious signs of euphoria at any time by the crew. Such a display would normally be expected following such a brilliant victory over a cruiser by an ordinary disguised merchantman, a feat which historically had never before been achieved. Instead, the rather somber and measured reactions evidenced were certainly not associated with the normal psyche, typical of the German style. One could imagine the celebratory mood if the tables were turned in favor of an Allied success, even regardless of the human cost.

Although the bulk of information given by Detmers may be truthful, that per se is of little consequence. The issue is not the relevance of what he has told us, the issue is clearly what he has omitted to tell us, and that is, an admission that he opened fire after surrender. Moreover, that his nomination of a fictitious position, which gained general acceptance but now proved false, was nothing more than a measure of his desperation to conceal forever the grave sites of *Sydney* and *Kormoran*.

Other Search Areas

Oceanography is not regarded as an exact science. That is why there has always been a wide variety of professional opinion on the whereabouts of the sunken vessels, the impact of current and wind being most contentious and often ill-defining. There has been a tendency to over-estimate both of these determining factors and this has invariably lead to the identification of search areas much further south than the location herein established. There are several reasons why this may have occurred.

An average velocity of the current near latitude 25 S for the month of November of up to 0.8 knots has been commonly specified, whereas the established figure, including wind-driven current (from the reconstructed schedules of shipping known to be in the area at the time) is in the order of 0.58 knots. This compares favorably with the Encyclopaedia Britannica reference of a minimum 0.39 knots in June increasing to 0.69 knots in January and setting at an average 340 degrees. Similarly, over-stated wind speeds of 19 to 25 knots have been often used to determine the extent of drift. Although winds of this strength intermittently occur in the area, they are regarded as maximum daily wind speeds. A 24 hour mean velocity of 13.8 knots (Hastenrath & Lamb) for November and von Malapert's assessment of 10 to 18 knots for the first five days adrift is considered most appropriate for the purpose of calculating drift. It should be noted that for the next three days during which 18 knot southerly winds prevailed, the mean wind speed from November 20 to 28 is assessed at 15.5 knots.

Of equal importance in finding the origin of drift, is the accurate assessment of wind direction. That the mean wind direction near latitudes 25 S to 26 S emanates from the south and is supported by most References, is probably an accurate assessment. However, although southerlies are most predominant, the offshore winds in fact vary to almost every direction during November (Refer to typical wind samples), and according to von Malapert during his time adrift the average wind was mainly from the south-east. This represents a reconstructed average wind direction of 319 degrees (SE) to November 25 and 342 degrees (SSE) to November 28 during which a southerly wind persisted (Refer diagram - wind direction options). This effectively rebuffs the erstwhile beliefs and assumptions that south winds prevailed throughout the rescue period and until the last of the flotsam was recovered. After all, von Malapert had little reason to mislead on the issue of wind direction.

The key to establishing the search area is totally dependent on back-tracking to the point of origin, the distance and direction of the objects retrieved by the search vessels. Undoubtedly, this same procedure (hind-casting) has previously been employed by most researchers. It is also possible that some may have been influenced in their determinations by the most common position given by the Germans of 26 S / 111E. If so, this may also help to explain why some of the identified search areas between latitudes 26 S and 27 S lie almost directly south of the area where the flotsam was found. Alternatively, the position given by the Germans may have prompted others to locate the search area south of where the flotsam was found because these coordinates give credence to the notion that a southerly wind predominated.

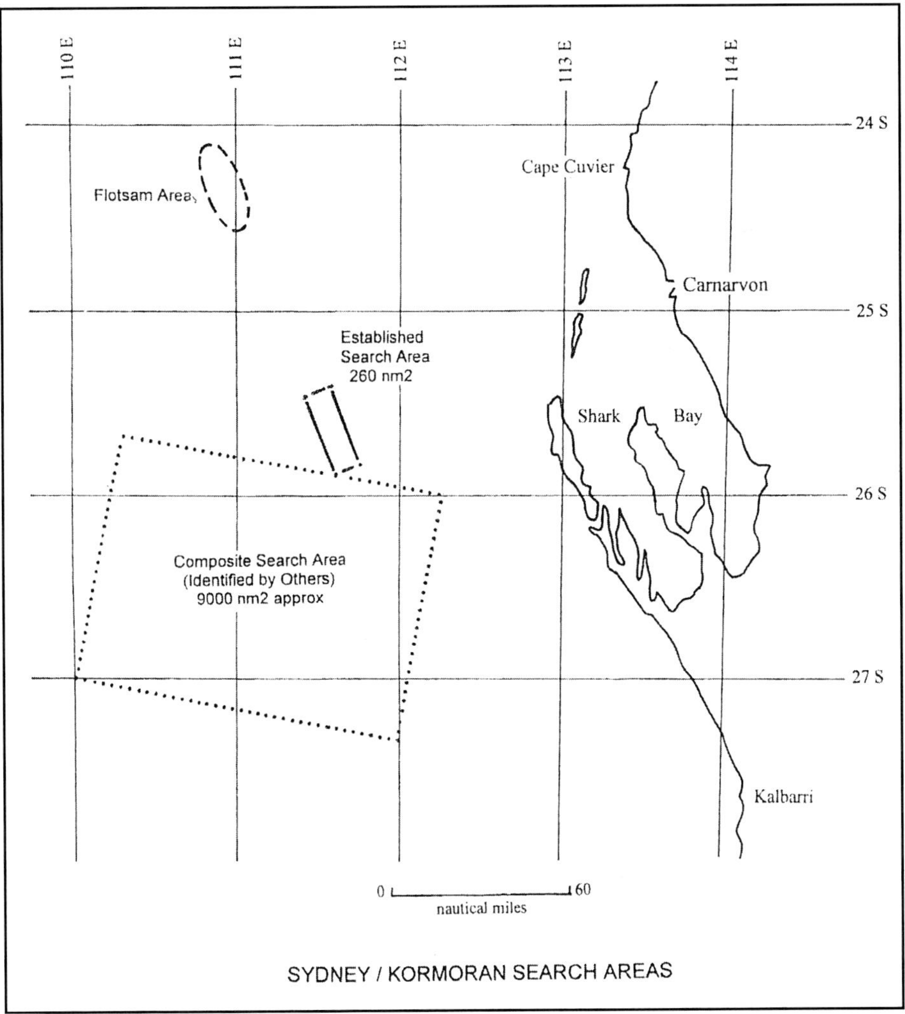

SPECULATION

THE LAST MESSAGE from HMAS *Sydney* recorded at the Esplanade Hostel in Geraldton was received at about 2200 hours on November 19. Although other messages were received until 2255 hours, these appear to have been an exchange of signals from D/F Darwin and unacknowledged by *Sydney*. The transmission of these signals is indicative that D/F Darwin or Singapore and *Sydney* were at least capable of some form of mutual contact until 2300 hours. In consideration of the unconfirmed signals from *Sydney* rumored to have been received by other overseas W/T stations, the plight and demise of *Sydney* can unfortunately only be assessed on the available evidence concerning the messages received at Geraldton.

The question of what actually caused the sudden disappearance of *Sydney* has understandably been the cause of much speculation. Due to the extensive damage sustained, was her demise about 4.5 hours after the engagement considered to be a fait accompli? How was it possible to have remained afloat for this period and then suddenly capitulate to the sea? Did something else happen to aggravate the already serious condition of the vessel? There are numerous imponderables. That the flooding resulted in loss of buoyancy or that she exploded are the obvious assumptions to be made, yet considering *Sydney* had stayed afloat for such a lengthy period during which there appears that some control over the flooding and fires was exercised, such beliefs may be seen to be illogically based. Therefore it is not so curious to ask: Could it have been that *Sydney* was deliberately or mistakenly sent to the bottom by outside intervention? After all, the glow of the burning and easily detectable *Sydney* at night would have presented a simple target.

Prelude to War

In November 1941, the shipping sea- lanes off the central western coast were not very busy. The merchant vessels loaded with raw materials and trading with South East Asia were few, with the sea traffic supplemented by the State Ships plying between the coastal ports. Occasionally, escorted troopships with Australian soldiers embarked and supply vessels made the voyage to Singapore to reinforce the British base. An assortment of small naval vessels, mainly engaged in protecting the harbor approaches were based in Fremantle. HMAS *Sydney* was the only Allied warship of significance along the coast of Western Australia.

The disposition and number of enemy vessels in the Indian Ocean was largely unknown to the Australian naval authorities and the Admiralty. However, there was an acute awareness of raider activity in the northern equatorial waters. After Raider F (*Pinguin*) was sunk in May by the Ceylon- based cruiser HMS *Cornwall* there were few Allied merchant ship losses. Thereafter, only three vessels, *Velebit* and *Mareeba* (sunk Bay of Bengal in June) and *Stamatios G. Embiricos* (near Seychelles in September) had been sunk by an unidentified raider, later believed to be Raider G, *Steiermark (Kormoran*). In addition, the Vichy French forces had a token presence in Madagascar, the Italian Navy in Somaliland was kept in check by the British Navy and German U Boats were not to enter the Indian Ocean until late 1942. The navies of the Axis Powers therefore had limited capabilities to attack Allied shipping in the Indian Ocean in November 1941. *Kormoran* was effectively the only enemy warship available to undertake such tasks.

During 1941, raider operations in the Pacific were conducted from Japan via the Naval Attache in Tokyo, Paul Wenneker. [Japan was a signatory to the Tripartite Agreement] By November, the raiders, *Orion*, *Komet* and *Atlantis*, the supply ship *Kulmerland* and the blockade- runner, *Spreewald* had been recalled to Germany when the Pacific war became inevitable. Wenneker and his radio operators, who remained in Tokyo, maintained wireless contact with the German vessels in the Indian Ocean and were purportedly in contact with *Kormoran* and *Kulmerland* after the action began. Wenneker's actions in handing over to the Japanese in December 1940 the captured secret documents taken from the British ship *Automedon,* (sunk by the raider, *Atlantis*) detailing the vulnerability of the Singapore base, was eventually to be a reassuring factor in Japan's decision to invade South- East Asia.

Japan's economy was dependent upon the availability of the essential raw materials (none of which it possessed) to provide for the escalating and ambitious military and naval construction programs. Japan gained access to iron ore after occupying Manchuria in 1905, but this was required to be supplemented with higher grade ore suitable for the new and advanced military hardware and warship construction. The other essentials, oil and rubber could be obtained in large quantities from the Dutch East Indies (later Indonesia) and Malaya. The quest for the supply of high grade iron ore began in 1934 and thereafter, a part of the Australian coastline would be host to Japanese naval interest.

Seeking Iron Ore

An exploratory visit to Koolan Island by a Japanese delegation lead by naval Captain Ohya in late 1934 saw the beginning of the challenge to secure reliable supplies of higher- grade iron ore. The party of five, comprising Okada, Fujimora, Omori and their spokesman, Umeda, were representative of the finest mining engineers, assayers and surveyors. After conducting their preliminary assessments, they were very impressed with the quality of the ore samples. Following talks with Nippon Steel, a contract for the development of Koolan Is, then held by the Yampi Sound Mining Company from leases held by Brassert & Company of London, was prepared in partnership with the Nippon Mining Company for an annual supply of one million tons of ore to Japan, worth half a million pounds.

Australia's fledgling iron and steel industry being prepared on nearby Cockatoo Island was also of interest and the leaseholders, Taffe & Buckley advised that no additional charges would apply to Nippon Mining for the superior grade of ore found there. However, the Australian media soon launched a sustained campaign to derail the venture after the arrival of seventy Japanese engineers. There was concern about the real bona- fides of Japanese interest: That they planned to build a naval base, that some of the workers were spies and a threat to our safety and that the cattle industry would become vulnerable to trade and marketing with Japan. Eventually and due to the ongoing military expansionism, the alliance contract, signed in October 1935 for mining to start in March 1936, lasted only until July 1938, when the Australian Government placed an embargo on the export of iron ore to Japan. No ore was ever exported. Nevertheless, Yampi Sound remained paramount to Japanese interests.

The Japanese were not dissuaded from further exploration, the embargo failing to deter their presence in the offshore islands of Yampi Sound until the advent of war. A specially equipped laboratory ship, employed for on- the-spot analysis of ore and always accompanied by a submarine, were regularly observed by coastal State Ships and they operated with relative impunity outside the then three mile territorial limit from the mainland. Intriguingly, the role of the submarine, which had probably sailed from the nearest submarine and seaplane base in the Caroline Islands, can be only surmised. However, it is believed that the submarine was an ideal vessel to assist in the extraction of ore samples close inshore or on the sea bed in areas which were known to be subjected to extreme tidal influences.

Although the extent of additional exploration carried out over two years is unknown, it is safe to assume that numerous offshore islands were investigated in the search for the high grade hematite, important for Japan's future economic and military aspirations. It could be argued these unbridled and secretive activities, sanctioned by the Japanese Navy and the Imperial regime, ultimately may have had some relevance to the proposed planned invasion of Australia and could even have be a factor in the disappearance of *Sydney*.

Source or Rumour

It has always been officially recognized that *Sydney's* demise was the result of the extensive damage received during the engagement. The implicit signals partly received in Geraldton and Detmers's own account leaves little doubt that after the engagement *Sydney* remained afloat for at least a few hours. On December 1, just twelve days after the battle, Bernard Hall, naval correspondent for the London Daily Express newspaper, published a conflicting report of the engagement. He declared unequivocally that after *Kormoran's* destruction by gunfire, *Sydney* was torpedoed by *Kormoran* or an attendant submarine when closing to pick up survivors.

The source of this statement was attributed to evidence given by the German survivors. However, as this description of events is clearly contrary to the evidence given by the bulk of the survivors and that reporters are invariably reluctant to reveal their sources, it is conceivable the information was sourced from a confidant within the Admiralty. If this was the case, the Far East Combined Bureau (FECB) in Singapore is likely to have been the original source. [The FECB monitored Japanese naval movements and direction finding in the Indian Ocean] More importantly, considering that distress signals were received hours after the engagement, any involvement of a submarine could only have occurred sometime after *Sydney's* escape to the south- east. Nevertheless, whether Hall's revelations were conceived or not, it would be remiss to preclude the involvement of a submarine without deliberation.

Submarine Deployment

In November 1941, the Japanese Navy possessed sixty-one operational submarines, comprising fourteen medium range (RO-class) and forty-seven long range (I-class) boats. A permanent force of nine boats of the RO-class were suitably assigned to the protected waters of the mandated Caroline Islands at bases in Ulithi, Palau and Truk and further east at Kwajalein in the Marshall Islands. In February 1939, when Japan seized Hainan Island, a base was established at Sanya to accommodate I-class submarines and in July 1941, the occupation of Indo-China provided additional access to bases at Haiphong and Camranh Bay. All of these bases were available to the submarine fleet well before the Pacific war began.

In contrast, the Allied submarine presence in the region consisted of about thirty American boats in Manila Bay and twelve Dutch boats in Java at Batavia and Surabaya. There were no British or Australian submarines in the region. The question of whether a Japanese submarine(s) could have been involved in the disappearance of *Sydney* on November 19, just three weeks before the opening of the Pacific conflict, can be firstly assessed in respect of the deployment of the Hainan Island force in support of the Malaya, Philippines and the Dutch East Indies operations.

Japan's inexorable move to ready for war required a divisional reorganization of the submarine fleet. The navy assigned a total of thirty I-class submarines to assist in the attack on Pearl Harbor and the South East Asia region (Southern Area Force) to assemble at Hainan Island was allocated eighteen boats comprising I-121 to I-124, I-53 to I-60, I-62, I-64 to I-66 and RO-33, 34. If the importance of the element of surprise to neutralize the US Pacific Fleet was essential to the Hawaii operation, the discreet deployment of the Southern Area Force was crucial to Japan's main objective, the capture of Singapore, the gateway to the control of South East Asia. However, the strategies employed for both operations were not guaranteed of success. If the pre-emptive strike on Pearl Harbor was discovered or failed to disable the Pacific Fleet, provision was made for a submarine cordon strategically placed to the west of Hawaii to protect the attack force and to engage any pursuing warships. In order to discourage further intervention by the British Navy from Ceylon, a similar insurance was required for the forces assigned to attack Malaya and Singapore.

By early November, plans for the invasion of the Philippines, Thailand, Burma, Borneo and Malaya had already been finalized. At Singapore, the naval base had been greatly fortified and there were nearly 300 aircraft and

90,000 soldiers available and with constant arrivals, the awareness of the rapid rate of troop build-up had not gone un-noticed by Japanese intelligence. [Ultimately, Singapore was defended by General Percival's 130,000 troops, compared to General Yamashita's victorious but vastly outnumbered force of 35,000] It would have therefore been imperative for the strategic planning to have included a containment strategy to prevent further influx of forces once the invasion began. The invading forces would also require protection from the possible intervention of the British Navy based in Ceylon. Accordingly, in order to forestall these possibilities and to avoid a prolonged action in Malaya and Singapore, it was necessary to position submarines and support vessels (similar to the Hawaii operation) in the approaches to the Sunda and Lombok Straits and specifically near the recognized shipping lanes.

The nearest submarines available for these tasks in the Indian Ocean were those of the Southern Area Force based at Hainan Island and they were required to be in position in early November, well in advance of the attack on Malaya. Discovery by British and Dutch air patrols in the shallow seas leading to the Sunda and Lombok Straits could place the Allied forces on premature alert and possibly jeopardize the timing of the Pearl Harbor attack and the forthcoming invasion. However, during October, Japan's Combined Fleet Headquarters ordered the display of 'friendly recognition markings' on all submarines to allay any British and Dutch concerns. At the same time, the vessels, Kokoku Maru and Arafura Maru, known to have been discreetly positioned off the Kimberley coast were available for supplies and refueling. Once in position, the role of the submarines and supply ships could only have been one of surveillance while awaiting operational orders. The efficacious plan to capture Singapore per se therefore signals a clear motive for the deployment of submarines stationed near the Sunda- Fremantle shipping lane on November 19.

The submarines based in Hainan could be used in a variety of roles, each with sufficient range (8000 to 10800nm) to effectively patrol the designated operational area. For mine-laying in the shallow waters around the Dutch East Indies, the KRS Type (I-121 to I-124) were specifically designed for the task. The other twelve I-class boats, the KD3 and KD4 type were faster (20 knots) and best suited to engaging enemy warships. The modern RO-33 and 34 (K5 type) were the first of the improved medium class and capable of 19 knots. Moreover, all of the boats could operate independently up to 4000 nm from base, inclusive of the southern approaches to the Dutch East Indies. Entrance to the Indian Ocean from Hainan could be gained via Sunda and Lombok Straits and although the boats were likely to be tracked by the British and

Dutch, there was little prospect of confrontation in the period before hostilities began. The return distance from the established engagement site via Sunda to Hainan of 2800 nm and 3100 nm via Lombok and the Celebes or Java Seas, would have taken 8 to 10 days at a sedate average speed of 14 knots.

An Irresistible Target

Given the specific purpose of the deployment, it is inconceivable that independent action could have been taken by a submarine commander to engage shipping within the operational area before the declaration of December 7. Crucial to the success of the forthcoming military and naval actions was the demand that any act of provocation be ignored and any act of aggression was to be avoided. However, the witness of an action between a German and British vessel may have required some contemplation and initiative on the part of the commander. If there was no enticement for initial intervention, then there could have been temptation a few hours later at the sight of a helpless and destructed *Sydney*. At night, drifting and on fire, *Sydney* would have made a simple target. In these circumstances, although the unseen submarine could deliver the coup de grace and its commander had exceeded orders, there was one redeeming factor - no trail of evidence.

It is also considered appropriate to canvass Burnett's likely reaction and available options in the event that *Sydney* was confronted by a submarine during the initial encounter with *Kormoran*. At a distance, the surfaced submarine could curiously observe the incident unfolding and in accordance with orders and in spite of the Tripartite Pact, no action could be taken. Similarly, if Burnett may have considered the presence a threat, there was little he could do - he was not permitted to engage, there was no war with Japan and he could not create an international incident. He was nonetheless likely to have been distracted while establishing *Kormoran's* bona-fides. It is therefore possible that the submarine could have remained in the area and later, without any formal decree, obtrusively dealt the final blow to *Sydney*.

The Suspects

The whereabouts of Japanese submarines on November 19 can be sourced from information provided by the National Institute for Defence Studies in Tokyo and augmented by historical publications. These documents convey the operational orders for the outbreak of war and the submarine squadron deployment and departure dates. Significantly, these records show that nearly all submarines, except for the nine RO-class boats based in the Carolines, departed from Japan to their respective bases at Kwajalein (Hawaii Force) and Sanya between November 11 and 24. Of the eight designated Hainan Island squadrons (18 boats), six squadrons (12 boats) reportedly departed Japan for Sanya from November 20 to 24. Another two transport submarines, the I-123 and I-124, based at Sanya, were ordered to leave on December 1 to blockade the entrance to Manila Harbour. Clearly, their prior operational whereabouts remains uncertain.

The operational orders signify that due to the distance from Japan to the engagement area (about 4200nm), it was impossible for any of the remaining twelve submarines to have been located there on November 19. The historical data therefore promotes the false impression that preparations had not been made to deploy the required submarines to the Indian Ocean in early November in advance of the invasion of South East Asia. It is also significant that no details are available on the whereabouts of squadrons 21and 28 of the Southern Area Force, comprising the boats, RO-33,34 and I-59,60. That they were not readied for deployment and supposedly undergoing repairs in Japan on December 5, only two days before the pre- planned invasions, requires examination.

The RO-33 and 34, launched in 1935and 1937, were the first of the modern series of medium class submarines similar in size and performance, but with a longer range than the contemporary American, British and Dutch boats. At only 1000 tons and considered unsuitable for the expansive Pacific operations for which the I-class was designed, they could comfortably patrol within 3000 nm from base and much further with supply vessel support. In comparison, the larger (2000 tons) I-59 and 60 of 1930's vintage had a maximum operating radius of 5000 nm and longer endurance without supply. That any of these boats may have been implicated in an opportunistic attack on *Sydney* can be assessed in terms of distance from the engagement area and projected return arrival to Japan.

There was little variation in the cruising speeds that could be attained by both classes of boats. If the boats were capable of their maximum statistical performance speeds of 19- 20 knots and long range cruising speeds of 10-12 knots over about 9000 nm, an optimum average speed of 15 knots could have easily been achieved over the distance of 4200 nm to the home ports of Sasebo, Kure and Yokosuka in Japan. In the event of an unauthorized attack on *Sydney* resulting in an immediate recall to Japan, each of the submarines could have returned from the engagement area in twelve days, arriving on December 2 and in time for the ensuing repairs.

It is difficult to accept that only days before the declaration, these submarines were under repair in Japan, 1400 nm from their assigned base. After all, the purpose-built Sanya base, 2800 nm from the engagement area was conveniently situated and after only 8 days sailing, an earlier arrival for 'repairs' on November 28 could be expected. These four boats were members of the 'Advance Expeditionary Force(s)' (AEF) and not the 'Striking Force' as referred to by Japan's Combined Fleet Headquarters in October 1941. Significantly, as early as September 9, all naval forces were ordered to be prepared for operations to commence in the first week of November. However, although the order defined the role and the operational areas of the Hawaii AEF, there are no specific details available of orders given to the Southern Area AEF. In retrospect, it is possible that a recall to Japan (if in fact it occurred) may have been an act of admonishment by the Japanese Navy that may have resulted in disciplinary action or even replacement of insubordinate submarine commanders. It should also be noted that a few weeks after the four boats purportedly returned to their Indian Ocean operational areas, I-60 was sunk near the Sunda Strait approaches. Of the other three boats, only I-59 survived the war.

Silhouette of RO-33

The Carolines Factor

In terms of the total submarine force requirements allocated to the invasion of South East Asia, the deployment of a small force of four boats to protect the southern East Indies approaches could be considered the optimum apportionment for the task. However, this does not preclude the possibility of other submarine involvement. This requires a determination of the movements of the nine submarines, designated RO-60 to 68, based permanently in the Carolines.

Although these older boats, built in the mid 1920's could not match the performance of the rest of the submarine fleet, they proved serviceable in the Island campaigns throughout the war. They had a reduced range of 5500 nm at 10 knots and a maximum speed of 16 knots. Palau was the closest base, 2600 nm from the engagement area, with Ulithi at 3000 nm and Truk at 3700 nm, the largest base. Construction of a major naval base at Kwajalein in the Marshall Islands, a further 900 nm east had begun and was soon to be a staging point for the Pearl Harbor submarine operations.

A submarine returning immediately to Palau at 12 knots from the engagement site should have taken nine days for the journey and arrive there on November 29 and at 14 knots, a day earlier. In order to be available for the planned support role for the assault on the American- held Wake Island, all three squadrons (9 boats) were scheduled to depart Kwajalein, 2000 nm further east from December 4 to 8, about seven days sailing from Palau. Requiring a minimum of seventeen days, including time for refueling, an RO-class submarine could therefore not have reached Kwajalein until December 7 to then have been readied for deployment to Wake Island the following day. This necessary discourse is important in its relevance to the Kwajalein departure schedule, showing that RO-63, attached to 33 squadron was conspicuously absent for the planned December 4 sailing and was assigned to depart later with the 26 squadron on December 8.

That the nominated departure dates for each boat were specified in the Navy Order of December 2, suggests that RO-63 was not expected to arrive in Kwajalein before December 7 and was therefore not available to sail with the squadron on December 4. Unless the obscurity of the movement of RO-63 can be clarified, the whereabouts of the submarine in early December, will remain suspicious. Of the nine boats comprising the South Seas Force, four survived the war, including RO-63.

The Fast Troopship

Generally, the operational areas allocated to the submarines of the South Seas Force did not include patrols of the Indian Ocean and any likely involvement in an attack on *Sydney* by these boats must surely be ascribed to circumstantial deployment. Therefore, consideration should be given to the contentious issue of the possible planned interception of *Aquitania*.

In the event that *Kormoran* and a submarine(s) had planned to act in concert to sink the troopship, an assignment from the closest available base in the Carolines (Palau) would have seemed a better proposition compared with deployment from Hainan. Even though Japanese naval history records show that in 1941 it was 'tactically impossible for a submerged submarine to carry out a torpedo attack with a surface ship', it was certainly feasible if the submarine was surfaced; and this could have been arranged jointly with the German naval attaché in Tokyo, Paul Wenneker and his Japanese counterparts. [It was Wenneker who directed German naval movements in the Indian Ocean, he could converse in fluent Japanese and it was he who admonishingly advised the Japanese Navy on improvements to their submarine tactics, which resulted in a Japanese submarine crew sent to Germany for tactical training]

Superficially, the planning for a joint attack on *Aquitania* would appear to be a difficult exercise and could only be carried out with short notice and tactically finalized after Japanese intelligence services reported the appearance of the troopship in Singapore on November 11. Although it could be safely assumed that *Aquitania* was due to depart soon after, bound for Australia to embark more troops, in view of the short notice there was no prospect of a rendezvous arrangement with *Kormoran* from submarines distantly based in the Carolines, or in Hainan. In terms of the immediate availability of a submarine near the area of engagement, clearly and if called upon, elements of the Hainan deployment of early November to thwart further reinforcement of Singapore were strategically located for a combined operation with *Kormoran*.

The failure of RO-63 to depart with the rest of the squadron (RO-64 and RO-68) as scheduled may have simply been due to mechanical problems while en route to Kwajalein from the distant bases in Truk or Palau. However, the Naval Orders of December 2 confirms that RO-63 remained operational and because it was not listed as undergoing repair, there was obviously some other reason for the belated arrival. In this regard, it is possible that the scheduled non arrival could have been associated with the continuing exploration for iron ore near Yampi Sound. Such an assignment would suggest that RO -63 could have been available for specific deployment to the Indian Ocean at short notice. A request from Tokyo for a combined effort to attack *Aquitania* (Wenneker's tactics) could therefore account for the whereabouts of the submarine.

Wenneker should have been immediately informed of *Aquitania's* arrival in Singapore on November 11 and in spite of the tactical difficulties, the temptation to arrange an attack on the troopship should have been irresistible. Although cooperation with German and Japanese naval authorities had always proved difficult, agreement could have been reached, providing that the tactics employed were designed to conceal Japanese involvement. The transfer of RO-

63 from Yampi to a pre-arranged rendezvous position for a combined attack on *Aquitania* could have been easily accomplished by November 15. That the attack never eventuated is irrelevant, nevertheless, it could have placed RO-63 in close proximity to *Sydney's* return path to Fremantle four days later.

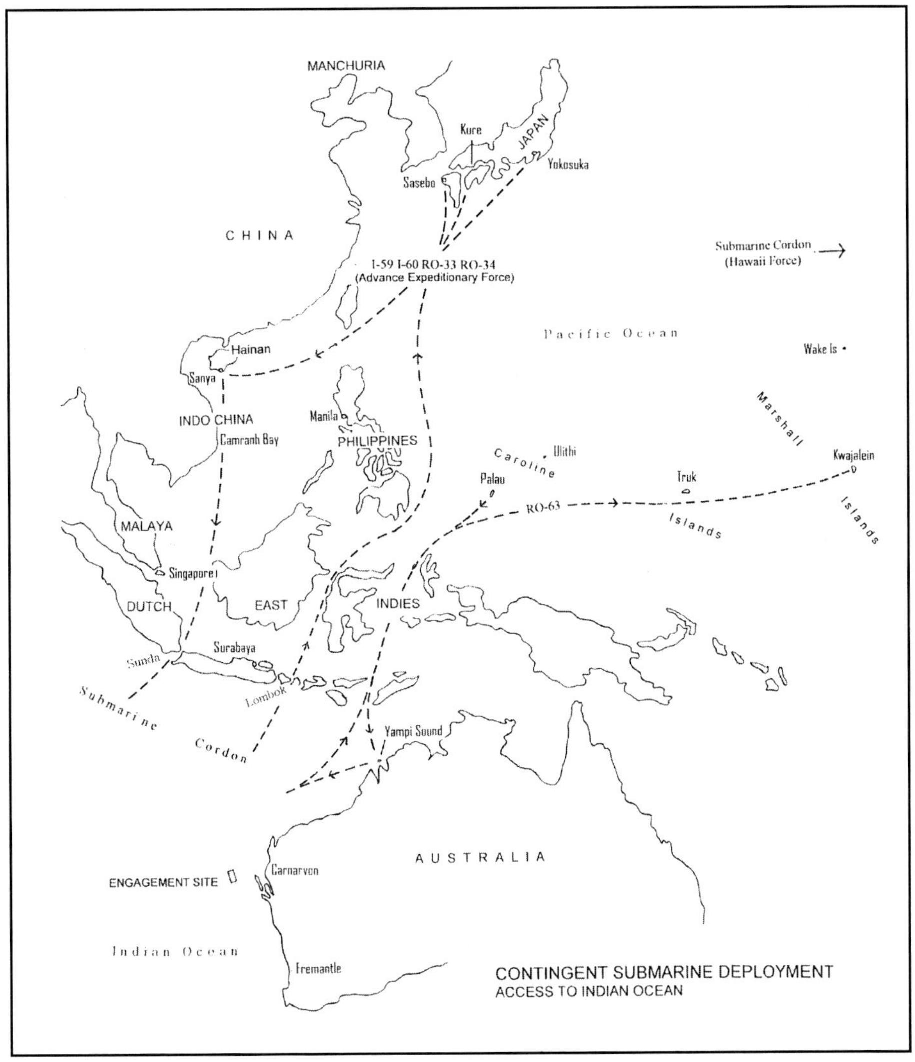

The Pastor and the Bosun

Perhaps one of the more intriguing and compelling arguments suggestive of Japanese submarine involvement concerns the evidence given by retired minister Ivan Wittwer to an Anzac Day service in Cleve, South Australia in 1997 and subsequently supported by statutory declaration. His evidence relates to a discussion with Heinz Grossman, a migrant worker on the Snowy Mountains Scheme in 1951and supposedly an ex crew member of *Kormoran*.

Grossman stated that a Japanese submarine, lying in wait, torpedoed *Sydney* from a distance and then set about destroying lifeboats and survivors. He detailed the statement, which was considered to be a plausible account in the company of Police and ASIO officers. He was later deported. According to Wittwer, these revelations were made possible because of his release from the Official Secrets Act which he signed in 1952 and of the relentless attacks made on Captain Burnett's reputation and his tactics in closing on *Kormoran*. Significantly, that ASIO has neither confirmed nor denied that the interview with Grossman took place is most typically taken as affirmative parlance. Moreover, if Grossman was in fact from *Kormoran* and considering that he freely volunteered his story, which is completely at odds with the German accounts, then his declaration was probably sincere. If not, there must have been a motive for making such a statement.

Sensitive information of this type is rarely left for contemplation for too long. If it is thought to contain an element of truth that conflicts with the acceptable version of events, steps are normally taken by the relevant authorities to silence the source of the information. In order to solve the problem, the simplest and most permanent method was to invoke deportation orders and in the case of Wittwer, a demand to sign the thirty-year Official Secrets Act. After this was achieved, the matter could be laid to rest. This action was also designed to prevent media intrusion and further speculation and as a result, it never became public knowledge until Wittwer's pronouncement.

In 1945, after an investigation into whether survivors from *Sydney* could have been taken to Japan proved negative, there were calls for public release and a full disclosure of the information held on HMAS *Sydney*. Strangely, the Director of Naval Intelligence, Commander Long who sheltered the information, declined to release it on the grounds that the public would still not accept the determination of the official findings. In consideration of the failure to divulge any details (which has naturally created the suspicions that have been evidenced ever since) and that ASIO had not made a unilateral decision on the Grossman matter without first consulting with Naval Intelligence, it is conceivable that Grossman's sensitive evidence was also acknowledged in naval intelligence files. Furthermore, Lt Cmdr G H Gill, a censorship officer, who had been recently commissioned to compile the official history of the Royal Australian Navy in World War II, would have been grateful of the non release of the information that could have produced ongoing controversy, distractions and a diversion from the officially accepted events which had always been in the public domain. In any case, to delve further into a new theory nine years after the event could sway public opinion to the extent that their long- held beliefs were influenced by a cover-up on the part of the Government and the Navy.

There is no evidence of further utterances from the mysterious Grossman after he returned to Germany. Regardless of whether their efforts were assisted by a third party, his famed 'companions' were destined to accept the kudos in a brilliant action for which some had been decorated. Nevertheless, the truth or otherwise of Grossman's attempt to expose Japanese involvement should become evident on inspection of the wreck when *Sydney* is ultimately found.

SUBTERFUGE

THIS ANALYSIS and investigation into the disappearance of HMAS *Sydney* cannot be finalized without reference to the wireless communications available at the time. It is presumptuous to conclude that because no official naval signals from *Sydney* revealing details of the disaster are found to exist in Australian or British archives, then for that reason, no distress signals were received because none were sent. After all, *Sydney* was equipped with a high powered transmitter and two reserve sets, each of which were located in different and relatively safe positions below the main deck and along the centre of the ship. If damage was caused to aerials as a result of the action, temporary repair should not have proved insurmountable. At the time, a number of stations were capable of receiving transmissions and for direction finding (D/F) purposes stations were located around the Indian Ocean rim and in eastern Australia. This demonstrates that the potential for communication with *Sydney* should not have been underestimated and that other associated factors may account for the non receipt of distress signals and a dearth of archival information.

Ever since Samuel Morse invented his namesake code in 1838 there has been a propensity for countries to adopt their own secret cryptographic versions during times of war. In the late 1890's wireless telegraphy (W/T or radio) made its appearance and its rapid development saw it used by nearly all the armies and navies in the world. However, it lacked secrecy and the messages could be heard by the enemy as well. This resulted in the development of complicated codes and ciphers, which in turn required the expertise of cryptographers and cryptanalysts for encoding and decoding messages. As more emphasis was placed on the development of naval and diplomatic codes as a means of communication in far away places, clandestine intelligence networks were formed to decode signals in order to gain nationalistic and military advantage. Signals were normally transmitted in encoded morse or variations thereof on a selected wavelength (radio wave or carrier) and for voice messages, modulation was required to enable regular change of frequency and amplitude.

Intelligence Services

The British code breakers generally had more success than others and in 1920 the first diplomatic signal was decoded. Thereafter during the inter war years, sophisticated and rapid advancements were made. By 1930, British and United States intelligence services had successfully decoded Japanese naval messages. These successes were accomplished by the cryptanalysts at the secret Government Code and Cipher School (GCCS) in London, headed by Alistair Deniston and by United States Naval Intelligence, known as OP- 20G. The US Army's Signals Intelligence Service (SIS) set up by William Friedman amid inter-service rivalry worked independent of its naval counterpart.

These agencies employed expert linguists to decode signals, which in the case of Japanese codes, usually contained kana, the phonetic symbols of the written Japanese. The German Navy used the prescribed coded Enigma settings for all warships stationed in the Atlantic. However, this same Enigma code, broken by GCCS in early 1941, used different settings for German raiders in the Indian Ocean, which British Intelligence was never able to read. When transmissions occurred, it was possible to locate these vessels only by D/F methods if suitable cross bearings were obtained by a least two of the D/F stations.

In addition to the D/F stations, the British Navy in the 1930's had created a world-wide signals intelligence network so that all warships could communicate with the Admiralty in London. For coverage of the Indian and Pacific Ocean regions, high- frequency (H/F) stations were built at Singapore, Hong Kong, Melbourne, Wellington, Colombo, Aden and Simonstown, with all transmissions and intercepts coordinated by the GCCS.

In November 1941, during HMAS *Sydney's* fateful voyage, the Far East Combined Bureau (FECB) at Singapore (China Station) and HMAS Harman in Canberra (via Melbourne) were the principal mediums of communication, while simultaneously the FECB were making intercepts of Japanese naval wireless traffic. Stations capable of intercepting Japanese signals in Australia were located at the RAN's Coonawarra base near Darwin, in Melbourne by the Naval Intelligence Division and in Watsonia by the Defence Signals Division. The closest US Intelligence base at Cavite in the Philippines could also monitor Japanese naval signals. Intriguingly, elements of the Kamer 14 Dutch secret wireless intercept station in Batavia had been recently dispersed to Darwin and Carnarvon.

The Known Secret Code

As early as 1927 the GCCS were able to read Japanese naval messages, including ship to shore signals. The SIS soon developed a replica encoder for the new cipher (code-named Purple) used by Japanese diplomatic staff and were able to receive, in advance, secret diplomatic messages. In 1939, the Japanese introduced a new naval code, referred to as JN- 25 by the Americans and thereafter until early December 1941 it was used for all naval communication to warships. The code was decrypted by the GCCS later that year.

Responsibility for the monitoring of the code intercepts was passed to the FECB in Hong Kong and Singapore. The signals decoded by the GCCS were sent to the Admiralty and were then made available to Prime Minister Churchill for perusal. The knowledge of Japanese naval movements was therefore confined to a select few. The general operational tasks of the FECB in Singapore were known to the Americans and the Dutch, but the intrinsic nature and volume of the JN-25 intercepts was never divulged to Britain's closest allies. In the period leading up to *Sydney's* disappearance, the secrecy of the British intelligence network was in all respects, at its zenith.

Although British Intelligence was aware that OP-20G was also decrypting some JN-25 messages, they went to great lengths to secret the vast array of information they held. The intercepts by FECB, immediately decoded by the GCCS were provided to the US on a needs-to-know basis, but only with the approval of Churchill, who even confided with President Roosevelt to acquire a Purple machine from SIS in exchange for an Enigma decoder. However, the deal soured Anglo- US relationships when the British refused to supply the Enigma after having received two Purple machines, thus enabling the long sought-after surveillance by the FECB of Japanese diplomatic messages, that even the Dutch in Batavia were successfully intercepting. That the mistrust between Britain and the US could not be contained is symptomatic of Australia's relationship with Churchill and with British Intelligence in November 1941.

Australia too, was extremely concerned about Japanese expansionism and their intentions in the South East Asian region. Naval Intelligence in Melbourne, a part of the British network, had stations capable of intercepting JN-25 messages, but was not privy to information gathered by the FECB or the GCCS. The Government of John Curtin were totally reliant upon Churchill's assurances that Singapore could be defended and were totally unaware of the true state of the weaknesses as outlined in the secret documents taken from the *Automedon* and now in Japanese hands. Churchill knew that his promised 70-day plan of defence, allowing sufficient time for a battle fleet to arrive was undeliverable and while failing to notify Australia and New Zealand of the vulnerability of Malaya and Singapore, the Dominions continued to send reinforcements.

Churchill's display of annoyance when Curtin recalled Australian troops serving in the Middle East, eventually resulted in the token presence of two capital ships (HMS *Repulse* and HMS *Prince of Wales*) in Keppel Harbour. This small deployment, reluctantly agreed to by Churchill, was typical of his lack of concern for Australia's welfare and exposure to attack and Curtin, like Roosevelt, had every reason to question the real motives of Britain's leadership. Moreover, the events leading up to Pearl Harbor are further damming of the motives of British Intelligence and of Churchill.

A Betrayal of Trust

In September 1941, the Japanese invasions plans and the Pearl Harbor operation were unveiled to Emperor Hirohito, whose objections resulted in a deferment to await the outcome of negotiations on the trade embargo (modus vivendi) with the United States. As the talks proceeded over the next months, it led Churchill to believe that the US was trying to avoid the impending conflict and that the crucial sought- after alliance with Britain would be dashed. He reasoned that if the US avoided an all- out war with Japan, the British and Dutch would be at the mercy of an onslaught which they could not alone contain. The important intercepts subsequently made by the FECB were thus destined to be withheld from the US intelligence services.

From November 7, when Admiral Yamamoto issued the 'ultra-secret' Order No 2 for the first preparations for war, the FECB made regular intercepts of JN-25 and finally established the whereabouts of the Japanese carrier task force and the preliminary date (December 7) for the attack. With the expected invasion of British and Dutch possessions aside, the FECB and GCCS deduced that the location of the Japanese Fleet in the Kurile Islands meant in all probability, an attack on Pearl Harbor. Although Churchill was somewhat indulged by the possibility, he saw no reason to alert Roosevelt because, as OP-20G was also reading JN-25, he considered that the Americans had been sufficiently warned. Thus, the role played by the FECB in the Pearl Harbor debacle without doubt, demonstrates both the efficiency and the uncooperative nature of the British Intelligence network towards the US, prior to the Pacific War. That information from the FECB, when HMAS *Sydney* signaled for help has not been released, is not surprising.

Britain's concerted effort to secret information from the Americans is further evident at the time of the Japanese advance on Malaya. That British

Intelligence was cognizant of Japan's intentions at Pearl Harbor is also compounded by their advanced knowledge of the whereabouts of the initial invasion force.

The first signs of an impending invasion became evident on Saturday morning on December 6, 1941 (Singapore time) when a fleet consisting of twenty five troop-transports was sighted off the Vietnam coast heading south from Camranh Bay by a RAAF Hudson (Flt Lt Ramshaw). The next morning, a Catalina carrying out reconnaissance is shot down, the Pacific War's first battle casualty. Later that day, another Hudson identifies the invasion fleet only 60 nm from the Malayan coast and shortly after midnight on December 8, Japanese forces landed at Kota Bahru and engaged the British defenders, thus officially marking the beginning of the Pacific War. Two hours later, the Pearl Harbor assault began.

This brief chronology of events demonstrates the extent of British awareness of the impending Japanese attacks in South East Asia and the misconception that the Pacific War started with the attack on Pearl Harbor. If the British possessed knowledge of the Pearl Harbor operation and failed to notify Roosevelt, and they had accurate information on the Malaya invasion force, they also failed to warn of an imminent attack on the American forces stationed in the Philippines. Consequently, on December 8, the Japanese unleashed heavy air strikes on Manila and by the time they had made landings in the north of Luzon on December 10, US air power and communications had been crippled.

That British Intelligence failed to warn the US Intelligences services at Cavite, is unconscionable. Although the Pearl Harbor destination of the Japanese carrier force was a prediction based on the interception of the JN-25 naval code, on this occasion and due to the confirmed sightings, there was no question of uncertainty, or of imminence.

Chronology of Events

Singapore Time GMT + 7hrs	Tokyo Time GMT + 9hrs	Hawaii Time GMT - 11hrs	Event	Hours before PH attack
am Sat Dec 6		am Fri Dec 5	RAAF Hudson sights invasion fleet	48
am Sun Dec 7		am Sat Dec 6	Patrolling Catalina shot down	24
0600h Dec 7		1200h Dec 6	Hudson sights invaders at 60 nm	20
0015h Dec 8	0215h Dec 8	0615h Dec 7	Invasion of Malaya at Kota Bahru	2
	0325h Dec 8	0725h Dec 7	Planes launched for PH attack	0.5
	0400h Dec 8	0800h Dec 7	Attack on Pearl Harbor begins	-

Note: Manila Time : GMT + 10hrs
Washington Time : GMT – 4hrs

Source: The Fall Of Malaya – Ward & Modder, 1991

Transmissions by Sydney

After detaching from *Zealandia* near the Sunda Strait, *Sydney* was to remain under the control of C-in-C China Station in Singapore and in contact with the high frequency receiving station at FECB until reaching latitude 15 South, whereupon she was to revert to Australia Station and resume W/T contact with HMAS Harman in Canberra. Apart from the signals received by radio at the Geraldton Hostel, there is no recorded evidence available to suggest that the FECB and, or Harman made any interceptions. This is most unusual because the mode of transmission by *Sydney* was consistent with the interception frequencies monitored by both receiving stations.

If the detection of high frequency signals by the FECB requires short wave transmissions (wave length of less than 100 metres), then the distress signals received in Geraldton on the short wave length of 24.5 metres (frequency = 12 mega-cycles) should have been detected by the high- powered FECB receiving station in Singapore. Furthermore, that the distress signals were transmitted for over an hour, it should have enabled adequate time for detection.

The closest high- powered receiving station, FECB in Singapore, situated 1670 nm direct from the established search area should theoretically have been first to detect distress signals. However, the atmospheric conditions at the time and the amount of applied transmission power may have also determined the quality of the message received. If *Sydney's* engines were stopped, some form of emergency or battery power was required to effect transmissions. Even low- powered transmissions were capable of detection, provided that suitable weather conditions prevailed. Therefore, and cognizant of the (unreleased) signals received at Kilindini near Mombassa, 4040 nm away, it is possible that several of the intelligence network stations received distress signals from *Sydney*.

That signals may have been received 1750 nm distant in Melbourne by the RAN's Naval Intellingence Division (NID) cannot be ruled out. The NID, essentially linked to the global intelligence network and the GCCS as an entity under Commander Long and engaged in monitoring H/F signals such as the JN-25 naval code, was capable of intercepting short wave signals from *Sydney*.

Commander Eric Nave of the NID, renowned and expert JN-25 cryptanalyst and author, revealed in his book (Betrayal at Pearl Harbor) that Japan commenced hostilities against Australia on November 19, 1941, when an I-class submarine torpedoed *Sydney* after closing *Kormoran* to pick up survivors.

He states the Admiralty was immediately informed. This revelation, made 45 years after journalist Bernard Hall's similar article could have been instigated by the expiry of the Official Secrets Act. Nevertheless, if true, Australia and Britain were never in a position to take action against Japan at the time. If action were to be taken, it would have invited Japanese aggression against the British Empire alone and dealt a severe blow to an American alliance. Indeed, to prevent public awareness and to circumvent possible knowledge by Japan of such an occurrence, would have required Commander Long, the GCCS, Admiralty, et al to suppress (or destroy) the content of the intercepts in keeping with Churchill's often declared ambition to ally with the United States.

There is no doubt that the signals transmitted by *Sydney* and received at Geraldton on the short wave radio receiver were indicative of the desperation and plight of the crew and of the serious state of the ship and the message, conveyed on the short wave length of 24.5 metres was initially designed to be specifically picked up by any of the global H/F receiving stations.

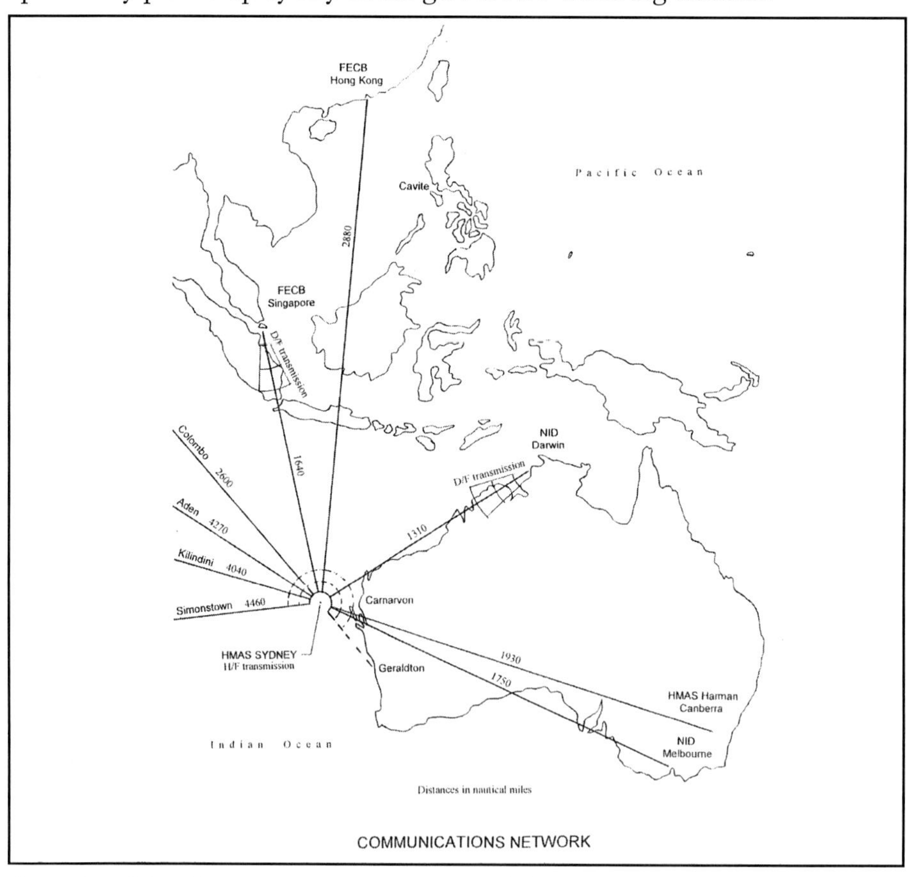

COMMUNICATIONS NETWORK

After failing to receive response from the H/F stations, the wireless operators on *Sydney* would have surely sought the attention of the closest receiving station at Darwin, requesting a D/F transmission (low frequency) so that *Sydney's* H/F signals could be intercepted and a bearing obtained. However, because the text of the message included a request for 'Singapore to contact Darwin', it is indicative that *Sydney* may have been previously in H/F contact with the FECB in Singapore. This is more likely to have occurred because it was essential that simultaneous D/F transmissions from both Singapore and Darwin were required to obtain a fix on the H/F signals emanating from *Sydney*.

Considering that D/F transmissions are of low frequency (500 to 2000 K/cs), corresponding to wave lengths of 600 to 150 metres, it is unlikely *Sydney* would have detected them to confirm that a positional fix had been made. Therefore, the only real prospect of rescue was dependent on the interception of the H/F signals containing the vital coordinates, and although they were not contained in the Geraldton messages, which were received intermittently for over an hour, it must be assumed that these details had previously been transmitted and not detected. The question of whether the H/F signals from *Sydney* were received by the FECB or by other network stations is likely to be associated with, or pertinent to the non release of British Intelligence records of the Far East.

A Secret Affair

The reasons for with-holding the British Intelligence files dealing with the events prior to the Pacific War, particularly in relation to the role of the FECB, GCCS and the Admiralty, has never been properly explained. If much of Churchill's own records and memoirs of the period remain unavailable and unpublished, it can be argued that the British were cognizant of Japanese military and naval intentions before the Pacific War began. Obviously, this information has been retained because it is so secretive that even after nearly seventy years, full disclosure could do irreparable damage to British relationships with the US and Japan. That most of the intelligence gathered during the conflict with Germany is now publicly available, is a measure of its sensitivity.

Details of the decrypts held by the British regarding Japanese diplomatic and naval intercepts remains top secret and Britain's secret agency MI6 and its operatives who worked closely with the GCCS, are protected by the Official Secrets Act. In 1942, the FECB, after relocation to Ceylon, destroyed all of its intercepts from the Hong Kong and Singapore operations, although fortunately duplicate GCCS records exist but still remain locked away. The few JN-25 decrypts that have been released by the US contain little intelligence information in relation to the period before Pearl Harbor and the question of whether any intercepts were made by OP-20G or the SIS and decrypted in time to reveal Japan's intended plans of attack, remains conjectural. Australia's role in the secret intelligence business could not be deemed effective without access to the information secreted by the FECB.

The nexus between Australian and British intelligence was a requirement of necessity, by reason of common regional interests and the security threat posed by Japan, for in that era, it would have been inconceivable for Britain to have deserted Australia's British forefathers. The close cooperation that existed was reinforced by Naval Intelligence Director, Commander Long, MI6 operative in Australia and head of the Combined Operational Intelligence Centre covering all armed services. The Naval Intelligence Division, an integral part of British Intelligence and preoccupied with gathering intelligence from only within Australia were reliant on the FECB for information outside Australia Station. Generally, the NID functions and structures were consistent with and inseparable from British Intelligence.

No signals of any importance relating to *Sydney's* loss have been forthcoming from the NID and the Defence Signals Directorate and the Government continue to maintain that all available records have been released. As to the truth or otherwise of the engagement, the full extent of the German account, which the Government has accepted almost in totality, remains the official version of events within the public domain. This is clearly evident from GH Gill's description of the *Sydney/Kormoran* engagement contained in the official history, wherein he presents the information supplied by the German survivors, there being no doubt about the authenticity of the German evidence.

Although the findings of the Parliamentary Inquiry in 1999 maintained the status quo, the promising recommendation that the Public Records Office in London be searched for any records of a Board of Inquiry report into the loss of HMAS *Sydney*, did not go far enough. After all, except for the brief Geraldton messages, the fact that no archival records of signals from *Sydney* are available in Australia, an approach to the British Government ought to have been made requesting the search for specific *Sydney*- related signals, suspected to be embargoed along with other secret FECB and GCCS intelligence reports.

CONCLUSION

An exhaustive assessment of the ocean currents and wind direction for the month of November has been paramount to establishing and limiting the parameters of the search area. This has been achieved even though oceanographic estimates of the velocity of the current in the proximity of the search area vary markedly. The larger estimated values appear to be distorted by the inclusion of an evaluated surface wind driven current component applicable to the wind driven objects such as the liferaft. As this component has only a minimal drift affect on the flotsam, the results of which have effectively identified the search area, it is concluded that an additional and excess wind driven current should not apply to the prevailing average net current velocity estimate of 0.58 knots in the vicinity of the search area. This investigation has likewise confirmed the inappropriateness for the application of similar rates of drift of the quite dissimilar floating objects retrieved by the search vessels.

The drift analysis results also confirms that the drifting objects could not have originated from the 'official' position elucidated by Detmers, 150 nm south of the main flotsam area and 80 nm south-west of the established search area. Velocities in excess of the current are not considered achievable for those objects assessed by net current drift alone. Similarly, the wind assisted objects would have been required to move at a rate of 1.6 knots, which attributes to a wind speed that far exceeds the average velocity and constancy for wind recorded in the area. Furthermore, that a constancy of wind prevailed for the period of drift from a southerly direction, is not supported by Weather Bureau statistics.

The location of the search area, established prima facie by the action of the prevailing sea conditions on the individual drifting objects also explains the distribution of the debris after the engagement. That only a small amount of flotsam was recovered, is attributed to the divergent affect of the current on the objects within the transition zone. As a result, most of the immersed objects drifted south-east to the coast and, except for possibly some objects claimed to have been found ashore, were trapped against the high cliffs, never to be recovered. Due to their individual drift characteristics, the drift analysis for those few objects retrieved by the search and rescue vessels has been separately assessed.

Contrary to speculation that Burnett may have been searching for a raider on the return voyage, the established location of the search area suggests otherwise. It is evident that after leaving *Zealandia,* Burnett chose a course of 160T directly to Fremantle and should *Sydney* have been briefly escorting *Largs Bay*, a course of 162T would have placed *Sydney* in similar positions at 1700/19. In assessing the validity of the search area, this investigation has been mindful of the coordinates (26.34 S / 111 E) given by Detmers when *Sydney* was first sighted. That this position is some 80 nautical miles south-west of the actual position has been most deceiving and very likely transposed from 25.34 S / 112 E.

The notion that *Sydney* circled *Kormoran* from abaft to the starboard quarter 900 metres distant can not be substantiated within the Action Report timeframe. Moreover, such a maneuver, in contravention of standard identification procedures, would have seriously exposed *Sydney* to more risk of attack from the unidentified '*Straat Malakka*'. It has also been often argued that due to a mistranslation, *Sydney* did not go out to 9000 metres. However, in accepting Hans Linke's claim that *Sydney* approached *Kormoran* from a westerly direction after conducting a less hazardous semi circular sweep as shown by timeline diagram, *Sydney* is found to be positioned on *Kormoran's* starboard quarter about 970 metres away with the port side exposed to the angled underwater torpedo.

Detmers's Action Report is adjudged to be inaccurate on two counts. Firstly, that *Kormoran* unleashed the guns and torpedoes whilst sailing at 14 knots, was obviously designed to conceal the fact that he was not ordered to stop and *Sydney* was completely unsuspecting and that his vessel was not possessed with underwater torpedo tubes. This notion has been effectively discounted not only by reconstructed timeline diagram, but also more recently by ex *Kormoran* mines officer, Heinz Messerschmidt. Secondly, of most importance is the fact that Detmers's Report carefully avoids any suggestion that he surrendered. That he surrendered and was nearly stopped was fortuitous, for it enabled him to deliver the element of surprise when *Sydney* was distracted while preparations were being made to board. However, although the bulk of the Report is regarded as a credible version and easily discernable, it was later evident that contravention of the international rules of engagement, lest it was exposed, haunted Detmers until he died in 1976, aged 74.

Based on the stated separation distances between *Sydney* and *Kormoran* and the given timeframes, there are important conclusions that can be drawn from the mode and aftermath of the engagement. Firstly, *Sydney* was found to have initially departed the scene of the battle at a faster rate than previously thought, actually incurring a speed of 12 knots prior to launching her torpedoes. Also, that *Sydney* was observed from *Kormoran* to have subsequently escaped to the south-east instead of a north- west direction at about 5 knots, has been confirmed by the analysis. To suggest otherwise, *Sydney* would have required an unattainable constant speed of about 15 knots for nearly half an hour to maintain separation, while being even more perilously exposed to *Kormoran's* guns. *Sydney* should therefore lie south-east of *Kormoran.*

This analysis also finds that *Kormoran* is the most likely vessel to be found first because it is possible that the simple transposition of the coordinates from the official position could reveal the location of the wreck.

It is a logical argument that *Sydney* stopped soon after *Kormoran* ceased fire (1925 hours) to control the fires and flooding and considering that the last message was received at 2255 hours on November 19, it is indicative that *Sydney* suddenly lost buoyancy and succumbed at about 2300 hours. Accordingly and by drift analysis, it is concluded that *Sydney* lies 6 to 18 nautical miles south-east of *Kormoran*, within the established search area with central coordinates of 25.39 S / 111.35 E. In the event that *Sydney* remained afloat for a longer period, the relative distance between the sunken vessels is unchanged.

The issue of possible submarine intervention has always been contentious and in some respects, divisive. Nevertheless, an investigation into the fate of *Sydney* cannot be deemed complete unless full consideration is given to the matter. From the limited information available on Japanese submarine activity in the pre war period, the investigation specifically focuses on the whereabouts of submarines known to have been involved in the planned invasion of South East Asia. Whenever similar assertions of Japanese involvement have been made in the past, it has invariably attracted adverse and sometimes hysterical comment and this investigation may be no exception. However, unless the exact whereabouts and operations of those nominated submarines can be further clarified, then they will continue to be of considerable interest.

The expose of the intelligence services leads to the conclusion that the FECB in Singapore and the GCCS were most likely conscious of *Sydney's* plight.

For the period prior to Japanese aggression, virtually no signals information has ever been released and the few items that have become available from the Defence Signals Directorate in Australia are not directly related to the Sydney / Kormoran affair. Accordingly, the role played by the secretive British intelligence network and of Churchill's inflamed desire to secure an alliance with the United States, will ultimately be revealed when the relevant embargoed Japanese decrypts are finally released.

The competency of the Captain of a warship is often judged by his success or otherwise in an engagement with the enemy. This is why their reputations are inclined to be classified anywhere from the 'glorious to the ignominious'. The category imposed on Captain Joseph Burnett varies considerably, depending on individual belief on whether he took the appropriate action during the engagement with *Kormoran*. He has many detractors, but in reality they are mistaken, for they mainly base their opinions on the German account of the action. If we disregard the erstwhile belief that *Sydney* sailed at 14 knots close to and parallel with *Kormoran* before the surprise attack, and if cognizant of the fact that Detmers had surrendered when *Sydney* closed quickly to capture in accordance with orders, then under these circumstances the action taken by Burnett must have been considered appropriate. It maybe too late to rewrite the history, but it is not too late to pay recognition to a man who was doing his utmost for his country at war.

Before her execution, Edith Cavel retorted: 'Patriotism is not enough'. Burnett possessed more than enough and his epitaph has been often unfairly immortalized.

APPENDIX

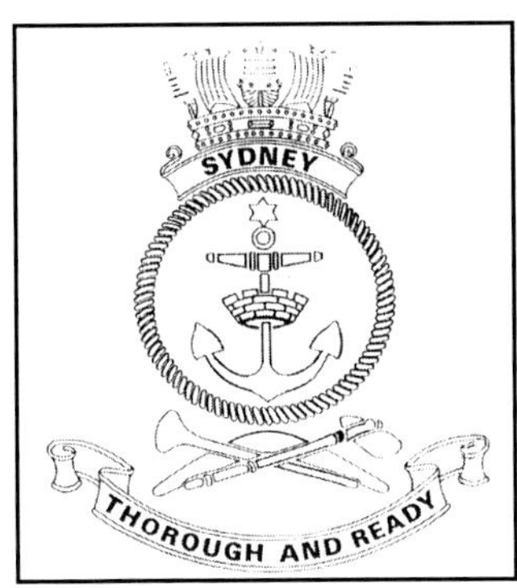

Officers and Crew of HMAS Sydney

Finally, after 66 years their graves should soon be commemorated. Lest they will always be remembered

Captain, Joseph BURNETT, RAN (VIC)

Commander, Edmund Wybergh THRUSTON, DSC, RN (UK)

Commander, (Engineer) Lionel Sydney DALTON, DSO, RAN (NSW)

Commander, Thomas Francis MAYNARD, RAN (VIC)

Commander, (Surgeon) John Reid HASKER, RAN (VIC)

Lieutenant Commander, Clive Alexandra Craig MONTGOMERY, RN (UK)

Lieutenant Commander, Michael Morgan SINGER, RN (UK)

Lieutenant Commander, Alexander MacKay WILKINSON, RAN (NSW)

Lieutenant Commander, Jack Cawston BACON, RN (UK)

Lieutenant Commander, (Engineer) Richard Daniel HANDCOCK, RAN (NSW)

Lieutenant Commander, (Surgeon) Francis Harrison GENGE, RAN (NSW)

Lieutenant, Thomas Garton BROWN, RAN (VIC)

Lieutenant, John Allan COLE, RANR (NSW)

Lieutenant, Thomas Edgar DAVIS, RAN (NSW)

Lieutenant, Andrew Ian KEITH, RANR (NSW)
Lieutenant, Eric Elton MAYO, RAN (SA)
Lieutenant, Ian Thomas Roy TRELOAR, RAN (VIC)
Lieutenant, (Engineer) William Thomas ANDERSON, RANR (NSW)
Lieutenant, (Engineer) Allan Wallace WILSON, RANR (NSW)
Lieutenant, Robert Ernest RIDOUT, RANR (VIC)
Lieutenant, (Surgeon) Mervyn Clive TOWNSEND, RAN (VIC)
Sub-Lieutenant, Albert Edwin BYRNE, RANR (QLD)
Sub-Lieutenant, Alexander Vinrace EAGAR, RANR (QLD)
Sub-Lieutenant, Edwin Ross EDDY, RAN (VIC)
Sub-Lieutenant, Bruce Alfred ELDER, RAN (NSW)
Sub-Lieutenant, Allen James KING, RANVR (SA)
Sub-Lieutenant, Frederick Harold SCHOCH, RANVR (WA)
Sub-Lieutenant, James Irvine CLIFTON, RANR (WA)
Sub-Lieutenant, Charles McGregor MITCHELL, RANR (VIC)
Sub-Lieutenant, Donald Wolsey McCABE, RAN (TAS)
Flying Officer, Raymond Barker BARREY, RAAF (SA)
Gunner, Frank Leslie MACDONALD, RN (UK)
Gunner, James Edward PETERSON, RAN (VIC)
Gunner, John Kerr HOUSTON, RAN (SA)
Warrant Engineer, William George BATCHELOR, RAN (VIC)
Warrant Engineer, Alexander Baillie BIGGS, RAN (NSW)
Warrant Engineer, Frederick William REVILLE, RAN (NSW)
Warrant Engineer, Robert Wesley NICHOLSON, RAN (NSW)
Warrant, John Albert Ernest FULLER, RAN (NSW)
Warrant, William Albert OWEN, RAN (NSW)
Chaplain, George STUBBS, RAN (NSW)
Schoolmaster, Percy Francis SKEWES, RAN (QLD)

ABERNETHY, Roderick Bell, Petty Officer Telegraphist (NSW)
ABSOLOM, John Francis, Leading Stoker (TAS)
ADDISON, Roy Hilton, Leading Seaman (NSW)
AGAR, Lavington Henry, Chief Mechanic (VIC)
ALLISON, John Albert Curtis, Able Seaman (NSW)
ANDERSON, Cecil John, Ordinary Seaman (SA)
ANDERSON, Ronald Harry, Able Seaman (WA)
ANDREWS, Arthur John, Able Seaman (WA)
ARCHBELL, Allen Walter, Leading Seaman (VIC)
ARMSTRONG, Harold James, Ordinary Seaman (VIC)

AUMANN, Cyril, Leading Stoker (VIC)
AVERY, George William, Able Seaman (NSW)
AYLOTT, William Lewis, Petty Officer (NSW)
AYTON, Leslie George, Ordnance Artificer (VIC)

BAIN, William John, Able Seaman (TAS)
BAKER, Victor Leslie, Ordinary Seaman (QLD)
BAKER, William Alfred, Stoker (NSW)
BALDING, Harold Ross, Able Seaman (WA)
BARCLAY, Victor Nathaniel, Supply Assistant (VIC)
BARHAM, Eric Ralph, Petty Officer, (VIC)
BARKER, Benjamin Joseph Herbert, Able Seaman (WA)
BARTLETT, Maxwell Edwin, Able Seaman (NSW)
BATH, Walter James, Ordinary Seaman (NSW)
BATTEN, Keith Carrington, Stoker (NSW)
BAVERSTOCK, Ernest George, Able Seaman (WA)
BEATTIE, Alexander, Leading Stoker (NSW)
BEATTIE, Eric Peter, Stoker (NSW)
BECKETT, Richard James, Stoker (TAS)
BELCHER, Edgar Raymond, Wireman (VIC)
BENNIE, Graham Russell, Able Seaman (NSW)
BERWICK, George Ross, Wireman (VIC)
BETTANY, John Henry, Able Seaman (WA)
BETTERMAN, Donald Richard, Able Seaman (SA)
BETTINSON, Walter Edward, Leading Seaman (NSW)
BEVAN, Hanbury Victor, Able Seaman (WA)
BEVERTON, John Troy, Stoker (QLD)
BIBBY, Ivo Ignatius, Engine Room Artificer (NSW)
BIRAM, Bernard Frank, Petty Officer Cook (NSW)
BIRCH, James William, Leading Stoker (VIC)
BLACKWOOD, James, Stoker (NSW)
BLAKE, John Shaldis, Leading Stoker (SA)
BLOM, Leslie Michael, Stoker (WA)
BODMAN, Anthony Athur, Able Seaman (WA)
BONE, Gordon Frederick, Able Seaman (NSW)
BONHAM, Henry George, Engine Room Artificer (NSW)
BONNER, Reginald, Mechanic (NSW)
BOOL, James, Ordinary Seaman (VIC)
BOOTH, Ernest Albert, Able Seaman (VIC)

BOWDEN, Lawrence, Stoker (VIC)
BOWES, Keith Andrew Joseph, Stoker (NSW)
BOX, Robert Aubrey, Stoker (TAS)
BOYD, David William, Leading Sick Berth Attendant (VIC)
BRADLEY, Ross, Ordinary Seaman (WA)
BRENNAN, Ernest Norman, Able Seaman (NSW)
BRIND, Max, Able Seaman (NSW)
BRODIE, Raymond Roy, Leading Seaman (TAS)
BROOKS, Donald Leslie, Ordinary Seaman (SA)
BUCHANAN, Alan Ridley Morton, Petty Officer Stoker (VIC)
BUCK, Clifton Charles, Able Seaman (SA)
BUCKINGHAM, Clarence Frederick Parett, Able Seaman (WA)
BUCKLEY, Daniel Stanley, Ordinary Seaman (VIC)
BUDDEN, Keith Eric, Yeoman of Signals (NSW)
BUNDY, Frederick Philip Keith, Petty Officer (NSW)
BUNTING, James, Able Seaman (QLD)
BURGESS, William Robert, Signalman (NSW)
BURGOYNE, Maxwell Aubrey, Leading Steward (NSW)
BURKE, Kenneth Thomas, Telegraphist (VIC)
BURKE, Leslie, Leading Cook (VIC)
BURKE, William, Chief Engine Room Artificer (NSW)
BURNS, John Roardon, PO Stoker (NSW)
BURNSYDE, William Edmund, Stoker (WA)
BURROWES, Douglas James, Able Seaman (SA)
BURT, Alwyne Stewart, Wireman (VIC)
BUTLER, Kenneth Norman Hilton, Supply Assistant (WA)
BUTLER, Stanley Wilfred, Able Seaman (NSW)

CABBAN, Victor Roy, Stoker (NSW)
CANNON, Lionel James, Telegraphist, (WA)
CAREY, Henry Robert Joseph, Able Seaman (VIC)
CAREY, Thomas Leslie, Chief Petty Officer Cook (VIC)
CARR, John William Aaron, Able Seaman (NSW)
CARTHY, George Thomas, Able Seaman (VIC)
CARTWRIGHT, Alexander Mitchell, Able Seaman (NSW)
CATLEY, Raymond Rex, Able Seaman (NSW)
CAUDLE, Douglas William, Ordinary Seaman (SA)
CHALLENGER, Charles William, Chief Stoker (VIC)
CHAPMAN, Neville Owen, Ordinary Seaman (WA)

CHAPMAN, William Roy, Stoker (NSW)
CHARLTON, Claude Leyshon, Cook (TAS)
CHRISTIE, Albert Thomas Norton, Stoker (TAS)
CHRISTISON, John Maxwell, Ordinary Seaman (QLD)
CLARK, Donald Murchie, Leading Stoker, (NSW)
CLARK, Thomas Welby, Able Seaman, (QLD)
CLARKE, Arthur, Leading Aircraftsman, RAAF (VIC)
CLARKE, Harry, Leading Stoker (WA)
CLAYTON, Alfred, Stoker (WA)
CLEMENT, William, Ordinary Seaman (VIC)
CLIVE, Alfred Walter, Stoker (WA)
COLBEY, Robert Sabey, Ordinary Seaman (SA)
COLE, John Vincent, Ordinary Seaman (NSW)
COLE, Sydney Arthur William, Able Seaman (QLD)
COLEMAN, George Edward, Wireman (NSW)
COLHOUN, Robert Alan, Stoker (VIC)
COLLIE, Cyril Brian, Stoker (QLD)
COLLIER, Richard Thomas, Leading Seaman (VIC)
COLLINS, Charles Ernest, Able Seaman (NSW)
COLLINS, William Henry, Able Seaman (NSW)
CONQUIT, William Clarence, Able Seaman (VIC)
COOKESLEY, Clifford William, Stoker (WA)
COONAN, Bevis Royal, Leading Seaman (WA)
COOPER, Alfred Langley, Leading Stoker (VIC)
COOPER, Arthur Donald Wilfred, Stoker (VIC)
COOPER, Bertie, Able Seaman (VIC)
COOPER, Reginald, Stoker (WA)
COOPER, Rex Albert, Able Seaman (NSW)
COPPIN, George William, Steward (SA)
CORK, William James Morris, Ordinary Seaman (SA)
CORMICK, Thomas George, Engine Room Artificer (VIC)
COURTIS, Roy John, Stoker (WA)
COX, Harold William, Leading Stoker (NSW)
COX, John Lionel, Signalman (TAS)
CRAGG, George Lewis, Stoker (NSW)
CRAIKE, Brian Wesley, Able Seaman (TAS)
CRANWELL, Henry Alfred Geoffrey, Stoker (TAS)
CRASKE, Benjamin Jack, Ordinary Seaman (VIC)
CRAWFORD, Thomas Alfred, Able Seaman (VIC)

CROCKER, Leslie Joseph, Petty Officer Cook (VIC)
CROWLE, Jack Alfred Francis, Stoker (VIC)
CUMMINGS, James, Able Seaman (NSW)
CUNNINGTON, Alan Leonard Fyffe, Ordnance Artificer (VIC)
CURTIS, Clifford Leslie James, Wireman (VIC)
CURTIS, Richard, Petty Officer (VIC)
CURWOOD, Walter Leslie, Wireman (VIC)

DANIEL, Kevin Henry, Ordnance Artificer (VIC)
DARBY, Stanley Maurice, Able Seaman (WA)
DAUNT, Arthur Robert, Stoker (NSW)
DAVEY, John Stanley, Petty Officer Cook (VIC)
DAVIES, Sidney John, Electrical Artificer (WA)
DAVIS, Stanley Roy, Leading Seaman (NSW)
DEACON, William Frank, Able Seaman (VIC)
DEANE, Wallace Bertram, Ordinary Seaman (NSW)
DEE, Thomas, Leading Steward (NSW)
DeFOREST, McAdam Carruthers, Stoker (VIC)
DeGRACIE, John Philip, Ordinary Seaman (WA)
DEMPSTER, Herbert James, Stoker (VIC)
DEVEREUX, Eric Gordon, Able Seaman (WA)
DHU, Lionel Edward, Able Seaman (NSW)
DIEWS, Bernard Albert, Able Seaman (NSW)
DIMMOCK, Donald Charles, Able Seaman (NSW)
DIX, Gordon Kenneth, Leading Stoker (WA)
DIXON, Thomas Charles, Leading Stoker (WA)
DOBSON, Herbert Hartfield, Able Seaman (WA)
DODDS, Richard, Leading Aircraftsman, RAAF (NSW)
DOXEY, Alexander Harold, Able Seaman (WA)
DOYLE, Edward Francis, Able Seaman (SA)
DRAKE, Albert Reginald, Able Seaman (VIC)
DRAKE, John Richardson, Stoker (VIC)
DUNCAN, Emanuel Robert Thomas, Supply Assistant (VIC)
DUNDON, Stephen, Able Seaman (NSW)
DUNIN, Thomas, Steward (VIC)

EDENBOROUGH, Alan Grosvenor, Ordinary Seaman (NSW)
EDGOOSE, John Franklin, Ordinary Seaman (VIC)
EDWARDS, Ernest John, Able Seaman (QLD)

EDWARDS, Frederick, Petty Officer Stoker (NSW)
EVANS, Francis Richard, Petty Officer (NSW)
EWENS, Robert Underdown, Able Seaman (SA)

FAHEY, William Richard, Able Seaman (NSW)
FARRAND, Leonard Charles, Ordinary Seaman (NSW)
FAULKNER, Arthur John, Able Seaman (QLD)
FERGUSON, David Wallace, Able Seaman (NSW)
FERGUSON, Kenneth Charles, Ordinary Seaman (QLD)
FIBBENS, William Sidney, Telegraphist (NSW)
FINDLAY, Gordon Lindsay, Ordnance Artificer (VIC)
FINLAYSON, Harry, Mechanic (NSW)
FISHER, John William, Leading Cook (NSW)
FITZGERALD, Augustine Francis, Blacksmith (VIC)
FITZGERALD, Lloyd Gerald, Supply Petty Officer (NSW)
FLEMING, Wilfred Stafford, Able Seaman (NSW)
FOOTE, Reginald Eric, Cook (SA)
FORBES, Robert Gordon Staunton, Ordinary Seaman (NSW)
FORSYTH, Glenbervie Edwin, Electrical Artificer (VIC)
FORTH, Herbert, Able Seaman (VIC)
FOSTER, Norman Douglas, Engine Room Artificer (NSW)
FOSTER, Roy, Leading Aircraftsman, RAAF (QLD)
FOULKES, Robert Eugene, Telegraphist (NSW)
FRANKLIN, Edward William, Leading Seaman (NSW)
FRASER, Noel James, Ordinary Seaman (NSW)
FREER, Walter Edward Albert, Able Seaman (SA)
FRIAR, Jack Allan, Engine Room Artificer (NSW)
FRISCH, Ernest Dudley, Able Seaman (QLD)
FRITH, William Railton Oliver, Petty Officer, RN (UK)
FRY, Robert Aubrey, Stoker (VIC)
FRYER, Kenneth James, Ordinary Telegraphist (NSW)

GAMBLE, Frank Harold, Petty Officer Telegraphist (VIC)
GAMBLE, Ronald Frederick, Petty Officer Telegraphist (NSW)
GARDINER, Heathcote Diggery, Ordinary Seaman (WA)
GARNETT, William Henry, Leading Stoker (NSW)
GARRETT, Basil Farmer, Able Seaman (WA)
GALE, Raymond, Leading Supply Assistant (NSW)
GENTLES, Harry Spencer, Chief Stoker (NSW)

GILSENAN, Dudley John, Steward (VIC)
GLACKIN, Thomas Nevin, Stoker (QLD)
GLASBY, Harold, Able Seaman (NSW)
GOODWIN, Neil Francis, Able Seaman (NSW)
GOODWIN, Wilfred James, Able Seaman (VIC)
GOTHARD, Edwin, Petty Officer Telegraphist (VIC)
GRACO, Henry Mathias, Able Seaman (WA)
GRAHAM, George Albert, Ordinary Seaman (NSW)
GREAVES, Sidney, Able Seaman (QLD)
GREEN, Arthur Eric, Stoker Petty Officer (QLD)
GREEN, John Rex, Ordinary Seaman (TAS)
GREEN, Theo Lawrence, Cook (NSW)
GREENWOOD, James Herbert, Ordinary Seaman (QLD)
GREGSON, Michael Oswald, Ordinary Seaman (SING)
GRINTER, Norman Francis, Leading Stoker (VIC)
GRONBERG, Ernest Edward, Stoker (WA)
GWYNNE, David Andrew, Able Seaman (SA)

HAAG, Francis Vincent, Stoker (VIC)
HAGAN, Allan, Steward (NSW)
HAMMOND, Lawson, Able Seaman (NSW)
HARE, Richard William, Able Seaman (QLD)
HARRICKS, Sydney William, Able Seaman (NSW)
HARRINGTON, Albert Frederick, Leading Seaman (WA)
HARRIS, Ronald Charles, Able Seaman (VIC)
HARRISON, Leslie Alexander, Petty Officer Steward (NSW)
HARTMANN, Frederick Holland, Regulating Petty Officer (VIC)
HASLAM, Aubrey Cecil, Leading Seaman (NSW)
HASS, Mervan Loui Wallace, Able Seaman (QLD)
HATTERSLEY, Jack Osberg, Able Seaman (NSW)
HAWKER, George Clarence, Steward (WA)
HAWKES, Sydney William, Able Seaman (WA)
HAYNES, Frank James, Stoker (NSW)
HAYWOOD, George James, Ordinary Seaman (TAS)
HEATON, Edmund, Electrical Artificer (NSW)
HENDERSON, William Laurence Douglas, Stoker (WA)
HENRICKSON, John Olaf, Stoker (NSW)
HERINGTON, Henry Foster, Stoker (NSW)

HERITAGE, Roy George, Able Seaman (SA)
HERROD, Herbert Frederick, Leading Stoker (NSW)
HEWETT, Edmund Herbert, Able Seaman (VIC)
HICKEY, Robert Arthur, Able Seaman (NSW)
HILL, Douglas Hugh, Stoker (SA)
HILL, Peter, Able Seaman (WA)
HILL, Robert Henry, Engine Room Artificer (SA)
HOBBS, George James, Able Seaman (VIC)
HOGAN, Michael Henry, Ordinary Telegraphist (SA)
HOLDER, Edward Harrison, Telegraphist (NSW)
HOLM, Clarence Kenneth Asby, Able Seaman (VIC)
HOMARD, Keith, Leading Aircraftsman, RAAF (NSW)
HOMER, Arthur Wilfred, Chief Stoker (NSW)
HONOR, Charles Leslie, Telegraphist (SA)
HOOPER, Edgar Norman, Ordinary Seaman (QLD)
HOPCRAFT, Robert Beauchamp, Shipwright (NSW)
HORE, Keith Beresford, Able Seaman (NSW)
HORRIGAN, Cornelius, Able Seaman (VIC)
HOWARD, Leonard John, Able Seaman (WA)
HUDSON, James Lloyd, Signalman (QLD)
HUTCHINSON, Richard, Able Seaman (VIC)
HUTCHINSON, Roy Harold, Able Seaman (NSW)
HUTCHISON, James Robertson, Stoker (NSW)

INGHAM, John Wakelin, Leading Stoker (WA)

JAMES, Martin Curtis, Able Seaman (NSW)
JARVIS, William John, Stoker (VIC)
JEFFS, Francis William, Ordinary Seaman (VIC)
JENNINGS, David Mathias, Able Seaman (NSW)
JESNOEWSKI, Leslie Albert, Ordinary Seaman (WA)
JOHNSON, Percy Albert, Stoker (TAS)
JOHNSTON, Douglas Erskine, Able Seaman (QLD)
JOHNSTON, Edgar William, Able Seaman (NSW)
JOHNSTON, George, Writer (VIC)
JOHNSTONE, Trevor James Armistice, Able Seaman (VIC)
JONES, David James, Stoker Petty Officer (NSW)
JONES, Donald Edgar, Able Seaman (NSW)
JONES, Ivan David, Engine Room Artificer (WA)

JONES, John Banks, Engine Room Artificer (NSW)
JONES, Philip Trevor, Chief Petty Officer (VIC)
JONES, Wilfred George, Chief Shipwright (NSW)
JORDAN, Ernest John, Able Seaman (NSW)
JORDAN, Horace David, Able Seaman (NSW)
JOYCE, William Robert John, Able Seaman (NSW)

KEANE, Walter John, Chief Ordnance Artificer (VIC)
KEARNON, Rex Allan, Ordinary Seaman (NSW)
KEENAN, Francis Bernard, Stoker (WA)
KELLY, James Vincent, Able Seaman (VIC)
KELLY, Neville Andrew, Stoker (NSW)
KENNEDY, Robert John, Stoker (NSW)
KENNEY, Arthur Henry Lawrence, Chief Petty Officer (SA)
KENT, Lloyd Shackleton, Signalman (VIC)
KETTLE, Edward James, Able Seaman (NSW)
KETTYLE, James Thomas, Leading Stoker (VIC)
KEYS, Rodger Francis, Able Seaman (VIC)
KIRKHAM, Eric James, Able Seaman (WA)
KITCHIN, Clayton Peter, Stoker (SA)
KLEINIG, Arthur Albert, Telegraphist (SA)
KNAPMAN, Wesley Bowden, Engine Room Artificer (SA)
KNAPP, Douglas John, Stoker (VIC)
KNIGHT, Neil Kenneth, Steward (WA)
KREIG, Archibald Douglas, Assistant Steward (SA)

LAFFER, Peter Morton, Ordinary Seaman (SA)
LANG, John, Able Seaman (QLD)
LANG, William Hugh, Stoker (NSW)
LAWLER, Neil Charles, Ordinary Seaman (TAS)
LAWSON, James Neil, Supply Assistant (VIC)
LAXTON, Stewart Thomas, Sick Berth Attendant (VIC)
LAYCOCK, Royce Stanley, Stoker (VIC)
LEWIS, Ambrose Henry, Stoker Petty Officer (NSW)
LEWIS, Desmond Henry, Bandsman (NSW)
LEWIS, Leslie Raymond, Leading Seaman (NSW)
LILLYWHITE, Harry Edgar, Shipwright (NSW)
LOCKARD, Terrence Godfrey, Signalman (TAS)
LOVE, Snowden Edward, Stoker (WA)

LOWENSTEIN, William, Stoker (TAS)
LOWRY, Frederick William, Able Seaman (QLD)
LYNCH, Stephen Maxwell, Able Seaman (TAS)
LYNE, Raymond Vivian, Ordinary Seaman (VIC)

MACKINNON, Murdoch, Petty Officer (WA)
MALES, Trevor, Shipwright (TAS)
MANN, Keith Arthur, Ordinary Seaman (VIC)
MANNING, Maurice, Leading Cook (NSW)
MARLEY, Sidney, Flight Sergeant, RAAF (NSW)
MARSON, Albert Richard, Mechanic (VIC)
MARTIN, Alan Douglas, Ordinary Seaman (SA)
MARTIN, James Hearle, Able Seaman (VIC)
MARTIN, Leslie Frank, Steward (VIC)
MARTIN, Leslie James Frederick, Ordinary Seaman (NSW)
MATHESON, Edward Austin John, Ordinary Seaman (NSW)
MATHEWS, John William, Able Seaman (VIC)
MAXWELL, Ian Maxwell, Ordinary Signalman (TAS)
MEDLEN, Lindsay James, Sick Berth Attendant (SA)
MELANDRI, Percy Ernest Vincent, Bandsman (NSW)
MENZIES, William, Able Seaman (NSW)
MILLER, George James, Cook (VIC)
MILLER, James Douglas Haig, Able Seaman (VIC)
MILLER, Kenneth Roscoe, Ordinary Seaman (VIC)
MILLER, Martin Patrick, Steward (VIC)
MILLER, Robert Alfred, Stoker (WA)
MILVERTON, Peter Frederick, Able Seaman (QLD)
MINNS, Leslie Charles, Sick Berth Attendant (VIC)
MITCHELL, Francis Joseph, Supply Assistant (VIC)
MOGLER, Richard Charles, Stoker (NSW)
MORDAUNT, Francis Xavier, Petty Officer Writer (NSW)
MORISEY, Ronald, Able Seaman (WA)
MORPHETT, Merton James, Cook (NSW)
MORRIS, Edgar Percy, Petty Officer (NSW)
MORRIS, Raymond Keith, Able Seaman (SA)
MOULE, Albert, Stoker (NSW)
MUDFORD, Leslie Francis, Able Seaman (VIC)
MULHALL, John Dillon, Bandsman (NSW)
MURDOCH, Raymond Charles, Able Seaman (SA)

MURRAY, Malcolm, Able Seaman (WA)
MUTCH, Hector MacDonald, Able Seaman, RN (UK)
MYERS, Henry William, Stoker (VIC)
McAULAY, Angus Campbell, Bandsman (NSW)
McAUSLAN, Arthur Robert, Chief Engine Room Artificer (VIC)
McBAIN, Joseph Henry, Chief Engine Room Artificer (NSW)
McCABE, Ernest Victor, Able Seaman (NSW)
McCALLEM, Duncan, Canteen Assistant (UK)
McCLAREN, Alfred Allan, Petty Officer (NSW)
McCONNELL, Robert Nicol, Stoker (NSW)
McCULLOCK, Sydney, Able Seaman (NSW)
McCULLOUGH, Samuel James, Wireman (QLD)
McDONALD, John Denis, Able Seaman (NSW)
McDOUGALL, Wallace, Able Seaman (NSW)
McGREGOR, Donald Alexander, Cook (NSW)
McGOWAN, Thomas Henry, Able Seaman (VIC)
McHAFFIE, Edward Hunter, Painter (VIC)
McKAY, Allan Murdoch, Leading Supply Assistant (NSW)
McKECHNIE, Glen Morton, Ordinary Seaman (SA)
McKENZIE, Donald James, Able Seaman (VIC)
McKEOWN, Malachi James, Able Seaman (NSW)
McLEAN, William Ernest, Stoker Petty Officer (NSW)
McLEOD, Herbert Charles, Leading Stoker (VIC)
McLEOD-SMITH, Albert Fraser, Petty Officer 9WA)

NESBITT, Jackson, Able Seaman (VIC)
NEWMAN, Charles Albert, Able Seaman (VIC)
NICHOLLS, Malcolm Godfrey, Able Seaman (WA)
NICHOLS, Francis Roy, Ordinary Seaman (TAS)
NICOL, Thomas Enright, Wireman (NSW)
NOBLE, Charles Taylor, Regulating Petty Officer (NSW)
NOELL, Alfred John, Stoker (WA)
NORBERY, Stephen William, Able Seaman (QLD)
NORMAN, Charles George James, Able Seaman (SA)
NORMAN, Frederick William, Leading Seaman (WA)
NORTON, John Thomas Henry, Leading Stoker (NSW)
NORTON, Montague Alfred Huxley, Engine Room Artificer (NSW)
NORTON William Frederick Cecil, Able Seaman (NSW)
NUGENT, Cyril James, Stoker (VIC)

NYAL, Leslie John, Stoker (WA)

OAKFORD, Phillip James, Ordinary Seaman (TAS)
O'BRIEN, Edward Bedford, Shipwright (NSW)
OGILVIE, Luarence, Able Seaman (VIC)
OLIVER, Alan Henry, Ordinary Seaman (TAS)
OPAS, Maurice, Canteen Manager (NSW)
OWENS, Edward Harold, Able Seaman (NSW)

PALING, Dennis Ross, Able Seaman (NSW)
PARKES, Douglas Leon, Able Seaman (NSW)
PARR, George Frederick, Chief Electrical Artificer (VIC)
PARTINGTON, Leslie Warburton, Bandsman (NSW)
PASCOE, Percival Holman, Stoker (WA)
PASTOORS, William Cecil, Stoker (NSW)
PATRICK, Charles William, Ordinary Seaman (QLD)
PAUL, Stanley Robert, Stoker (QLD)
PAYNE, John Robert, Sick Berth Attendant (VIC)
PEAK, John McGhie, Stoker (WA)
PEARCE, Eric Victor, Engine Room Artificer (NSW)
PELHAM, Frederick Charles, Bandsman (TAS)
PERGER, Frederick James, Able Seaman (TAS)
PERRYMAN, Richard Severn, Able Seaman (WA)
PETERS, Maxwell Wesley, Telegraphist (SA)
PETERSON, Peter William, Stoker (VIC)
PHILLIPS, Frederick Ernest, Able Seaman (NSW)
PIKE, J OHN William, Able Seaman (NSW)
PITT, William Harold, Able Seaman (NSW)
PLATT, Robert, Stoker (VIC)
POPLE, Alfred, Bandsman (NSW)
POTTER, Alfred William, Ordinary Seaman (VIC)
POTTER, Clyde Ashby, Supply Petty Officer (WA)
POWELL Lyal Llewellyn, Able Seaman (NSW)
PRIKE, Joseph John, Able Seaman (WA)
PRIMMER, John Foster Royal, Able Seaman (QLD)
PRITCHARD, Herbert Lloyd, Ordnance Artificer (VIC)
PSAILA, Samuel, Canteen Assistant (NSW)
PULHAM, Edward George Montague, Leading Stoker (WA)
PURDON, Eric Thomas, Leading Seaman (NSW)

PURKISS, Cecil Edward, Wireman (NSW)
PUTMAN, Albert Edward, Ordinary Seaman (VIC)

QUILTY, John Edward, Leading Seaman (VIC)
QUINN, George Frederick, Petty Officer Cook (NSW)

RAMSAY, Ernest Wilson, Able Seaman (WA)
RANFORD, John Irvine, Ordinary Telegraphist (SA)
RAY, Harold George, Able Seaman (QLD)
REDFEARNE, Charles Hugh, Stoker (WA)
REDMOND, Eric Neville, Ordinary Signalman (WA)
REED, George Percival, Writer (VIC)
REES, Robert John, Ordinary Seaman (TAS)
REEVES, Ellis Leslie, Able Seaman (NSW)
REEVES, Raymond Henry, Ordinary Seaman (NSW)
REID, Graham Roy, Signalman (NSW)
REILLY, James Brian, Engine Room Artificer (VIC)
REMFRY, Ernest John, Able Seaman (NSW)
RICARDO, John Layton, Chief Petty Officer (NSW)
RICE, Desmond Maxwell, Stoker (VIC)
RICHARDS, Harold Nelson, Engine Room Artificer (SA)
RICHTER, Arthur John, Supply Petty Officer (NSW)
RILEY, Edwin Martin, Ordinary Seaman (QLD)
RIPPEN, Adolph Heinrich Gerhard, Telegraphist (WA)
RITERS, Edward, Able Seaman (NSW)
ROBERTS, Lyndon Irvine, Stoker (WA)
ROBERTS, Ronald Charles, Cook (VIC)
ROBERTSON, Michael John, Leading Seaman (NSW)
ROBERTSON, Thomas Noel, Stoker Petty Officer (NSW)
ROGERS, Charles Allan, Able Seaman (NSW)
ROGERS, Ralph Carey, Signalman (TAS)
ROLFE, Edmund Sturgeon, Able Seaman (NSW)
ROLLEY, Ernest David, Steward (QLD)
ROSEVEAR, Geoffrey, Able Seaman (NSW)
ROSEVEAR, Lance, Able Seaman (TAS)
ROSS, Donald, Petty Officer Steward (NSW)
ROSS, James Thompson, Supply Petty Officer (NSW)
ROTHBAUM, Lionel, Steward (WA)
ROWE, Allan Lawrence, Able Seaman (WA)

ROWE, James Ronald, Telegraphist (WA)
ROWE, Lindsay Thomas, Stoker (VIC)
ROWLANDS, Harold Edward, Supply Chief Petty Officer (NSW)
RUDALL, Peter Sutherland, Ordinary Seaman (SA)

SALMON, John, Able Seaman (NSW)
SAMPSON, Louis Nicholas, Supply Chief Petty Officer (NSW)
SANDS, William Archibald Martin, Chief Petty Officer (NSW)
SAVAGE, Leonard Roydon, Stoker (VIC)
SAWBRIDGE, George William, Bandsman (NSW)
SCHACHE, Walter Herbert, Chief Petty Officer Cook (VIC)
SCHMIDT, Alan Harley, Ordinary Seaman (SA)
SCHULZ, Raymond Arthur, Stoker (NSW)
SCOTT, George Gillick, Petty Officer (NSW)
SHADLOW, Eric Henry, Stoker (NSW0
SHEPHERD, Alfred Horwood, Engine Room Artificer (WA)
SHEPHERD, David John, Chief Petty Officer Telegraphist (NSW)
SHIERS, Arthur Ernest, Able Seaman (SA)
SHIPSTONE, Henry Buccleuch, Petty Officer (QLD)
SHORT, Harry Kenneth, Able Seaman (WA)
SIEVEY, Richard Thomas, Ordinary Seaman (NSW)
SILK, Stanley George, Chief Petty Officer, RN (UK)
SIMPSON, Benjamin, Petty Officer Telegraphist (NSW)
SIMPSON, Charles Henry, Able Seaman (VIC)
SIMPSON, Reginald Austin, Ordinary Telegraphist (SA)
SLATER, Alec George Hamilton, Cook (VIC)
SMITH, Allen Leslie, Chief Electrical Artificer (NSW)
SMITH, Alfred James, Stoker (TAS)
SMITH, Cornelius Francis, Able Seaman (WA)
SMITH, Douglas William Charles, Engine Room Artificer (SA)
SMITH, Ernest Edward Frederick, Able Seaman (WA)
SMITH, George William, Stoker (VIC)
SMITH, Ronald George Singleton, Engine Room Artificer (VIC)
SMITH, Roy Clarence, Supply Assistant (NSW)
SMITH, Roy Somerville, Stoker (QLD)
SMITH, William Frederick Albert, Able Seaman (VIC)
SMITH, William Harrison Randall, Engine Room Artificer (VIC)
SMITH, William Reginald Devine, Petty Officer (NSW)
SOUTAR, William Nicoll, Supply Assistant (NSW)

SPILLER, Harold James, Able Seaman (VIC)
STAFF, Robert Frank, Steward (VIC)
STAMMERS, Robert, Cook (WA)
STANDISH, George Frederick, Able Seaman (SA)
STEAR, Ernest Victor Lloyd, Bandmaster (VIC)
STEED, Philip William, Ordinary Seaman (NSW)
STEELE, Roy McLellan Morgan, Able Seaman (NSW)
STENTON, Stanley Peter William, Stoker (VIC)
STEPHENS, George, Yeoman of Signals (NSW)
STEPHENSON, Walter Thomas William, Stoker (TAS)
STERLING, Leslie, Able Seaman (NSW)
STEVENS, Horace John, Bandsman (TAS)
STEVENSON, Robert, Stoker (NSW)
STRIDE, Cecil Meadus, Stoker (NSW)
STRIETHORST, Raymond Conrad, Able Seaman (NSW)
STRIPE, Alexander Edward, Able Seaman (SA)
STRUGNELL, John William, Petty Officer (NSW)
STUART, James Richard Keith, Stoker (NSW)
STUART, William Fancourt, Writer (VIC)
STUBBS, Kimberley, Stoker (WA)
STURLA, James Robert, Chief Stoker (NSW)
SUTTON, Denis O'Reilly, Able Seaman (WA)
SUTTON, Kingsley, Stoker Petty Officer (VIC)

TABOR, Frederick Arthur, Leading Seaman (SA)
TASSEL, Harry Woodrow, Petty Officer (WA)
TATTERS, George Nelson, Able Seaman (QLD)
TAYLOR, John, Telegraphist (WA)
TAYLOR, John Ernest, Able Seaman (QLD)
TAYLOR, John McLean, Able Seaman (VIC)
TAYLOR, Keith, Ordinary Seaman (VIC)
TAYLOR, Kenneth George, Able Seaman (WA)
TAYLOR, Rupert Allenby, Leading Stoker (TAS)
TENNANT, Ronald George, Engine Room Artificer (NSW)
THOMPSON, Harry Edward, Wireman (VIC)
THOMPSON, William Raymond, Stoker (VIC)
THOMSON, Archibald James, Stoker (WA)
TRENBATH, Jack Stephen, Stoker (NSW)
TRENWITH, Harry George, Stoker Petty Officer (NSW)

TRIGGS, Robert, Master-at Arms (QLD)
TUFFIN, Edwin Daniel, Able Seaman (WA)
TURK, Herbert, Able Seaman (NSW)
TURNER, George Alfred, Ordinary Seaman, (VIC)
TURNER, Harold, Signalman (NSW)
TURNER, Kenneth James, Ordinary Seaman (VIC)
TURNER, William Ross, Able Seaman (WA)
TYLDSLEY, James, Chief Yeoman of Signals (NSW)
TYLER, Charles Desmond, Bandsman (VIC)

UNWIN, John Edward, Able Seaman (VIC)
UREN, Thomas William James, Leading Steward (VIC)

VASSETT, Alexander William, Electrical Artificer (VIC)
VOGT, Ronald Mathew, Able Seaman (SA)

WAIT, Howard Thomas Charles, Supply Petty Officer (NSW)
WALDRON, Thomas Arthur, Stoker (VIC)
WALKER, Arthur Joseph, Cook (NSW)
WALKER, Edward John, Yeoman of Signals (NSW)
WALKER, Kenneth James, Able Seaman (VIC)
WALKER, William Albert Gordon, Leading Signalman (WA)
WALLACE, William Raymond, Stoker (NSW)
WALSH, Gordon Stuart, Supply Assistant (SA)
WALSH, Michael Henry Joseph, Able Seaman (VIC)
WARD, Frederick Ernest Charles, Able Seaman (WA)
WARD, James Joseph Richard, Leading Stoker (NSW)
WARE, Leonard Frank, Joiner (NSW)
WARREN, Vincent, Bandsman (VIC)
WAYE, Leonard William, Leading Stoker (SA)
WEBB, Arthur Charles, Able Seaman (VIC)
WEBB, Oliver Ernest Raymond, Petty Officer (NSW)
WELLER, Royce Henry, Shipwright (TAS)
WHITE, Hans James Leo, Signalman (VIC)
WHITE, Robert George, Able Seaman (NSW)
WHITFIELD, Leonard William, Chief Petty Officer Writer (NSW)
WHITHEAR, Alan George, Stoker (NSW)
WILLIAMS, Alfred David, Able Seaman (NSW)
WILLIAMS, David Leslie, Petty Officer (NSW)

WILLIAMS, John Bruce, Stoker (VIC)
WILLIAMS, John Harris, Stoker (WA)
WILLIAMSON, Maurice Douglas, Leading Stoker (TAS)
WILLIIAMSON, Sydney Thomas Lawrence, Petty Officer (VIC)
WILLIS, George Boyd, Able Seaman (NSW)
WILLIS, Percy John Christian, Plumber (NSW)
WILLIS, Lloyd Martin, Cook (NSW)
WILLIS, Ronald Verdun, Steward (QLD)
WILSON, Clifford, Telegraphist (NSW)
WILSON, Jack Stanley, Able Seaman (SA)
WILSON, Roderick Richard, Sick Berth Attendant (SA)
WILSON, Roy Weedon Dawes, Ordinary Seaman (NSW)
WINDHAM, Russell Bertram, Ordinary Telegraphist (SA)
WITTON, Bertram Lindsay, Leading Telegraphist (WA)
WIXTED, Ronald James, Stoker (NSW)
WOOD, Arthur Thomas, Able Seaman (WA)
WOODCROFT, William George, Leading Steward (VIC)
WOODHAMS, Reginald Bernard Craig, Stoker (WA)
WOODS, William Raymond, Engine Room Artificer (WA)
WOODSFORD, Alfred Charles, Leading Seaman (SA)
WOOLMORE, Laurence Thomas, Chief Petty Officer (VIC)
WORSLEY, William Cornelius, Electrical Artificer (NSW)
WRIGHT, Charles Alan, Able Seaman (TAS)
WRIGHT, Charles Patrick, Signalman (TAS)
WRIGHT, Harold Douglas, Steward (NSW)
WYATT, Eric William, Telegraphist (SA)

YEOMAN, Walter Clifford, Stoker (NSW)
YORK, Leonard Dennis, Able Seaman (NSW)
YOUNG, John Robinson, Able Seaman (QLD)

ZAMMITT, Salvatore, Canteen Manager (NSW)

Representative Country or State

United Kingdom	9
Singapore	1
New South Wales	246
Victoria	164
Western Australia	92
South Australia	55
Queensland	42
Tasmania	36
Total Complement (Loss)	**645**

INDEX

C

D

S

T

ABOUT THE AUTHOR

Greg Bathgate's lifelong interest in maritime history has not surprisingly led to the challenge to help solve Australia's most famous wartime mystery. Undeterred by the many stories and often conflicting information, he has meticulously calculated a limited area where HMAS Sydney and HSK Kormoran are likely to be found. This research has occupied his spare time for nearly ten years.

Born in Kalgoorlie in 1946, Greg's previous occupation for nearly forty years as a draftsman and civil designer for the Water Corporation in Perth has been invaluable in the formulation and presentation of the many maps and diagrams contained in the book.

Greg's interest in all kinds of ships has also resulted in the possession of a vast collection of photographs taken over the past forty years. He has many varied interests but these are often set aside when preoccupied with fishing and travel. More importantly, since retirement, he has more opportunity to be involved in an array of maritime pursuits.